In Pursuit of the *Seikatsusha*

JAPANESE SOCIETY SERIES
General Editor: Yoshio Sugimoto

Lives of Young Koreans in Japan
Yasunori Fukuoka

Globalization and Social Change in Contemporary Japan
J.S. Eades, Tom Gill and Harumi Befu

Coming Out in Japan: The Story of Satoru and Ryuta
Satoru Ito and Ryuta Yanase

Japan and Its Others:
Globalization, Difference and the Critique of Modernity
John Clammer

Hegemony of Homogeneity: An Anthropological Analysis of Nihonjinron
Harumi Befu

Foreign Migrants in Contemporary Japan
Hiroshi Komai

A Social History of Science and Technology in Contempory Japan, Volume 1
Shigeru Nakayama

Farewell to Nippon: Japanese Lifestyle Migrants in Australia
Machiko Sato

The Peripheral Centre:
Essays on Japanese History and Civilization
Johann P. Arnason

A Genealogy of 'Japanese' Self-images
Eiji Oguma

Class Structure in Contemporary Japan
Kenji Hashimoto

An Ecological View of History
Tadao Umesao

Nationalism and Gender
Chizuko Ueno

Native Anthropology: The Japanese Challenge to Western Academic Hegemony
Takami Kuwayama

Youth Deviance in Japan: Class Reproduction of Non-Conformity
Robert Stuart Yoder

Japanese Companies: Theories and Realities
Masami Nomura and Yoshihiko Kamii

From Salvation to Spirituality: Popular Religious Movements in Modern Japan
Susumu Shimazono

The 'Big Bang' in Japanese Higher Education:
The 2004 Reforms and the Dynamics of Change
J.S. Eades, Roger Goodman and Yumiko Hada

Japanese Politics: An Introduction
Takashi Inoguchi

A Social History of Science and Technology in Contempory Japan, Volume 2
Shigeru Nakayama

Gender and Japanese Management
Kimiko Kimoto

Philosophy of Agricultural Science: A Japanese Perspective
Osamu Soda

A Social History of Science and Technology in Contempory Japan, Volume 3
Shigeru Nakayama and Kunio Goto
Japan's Underclass: Day Laborers and the Homeless
Hideo Aoki
A Social History of Science and Technology in Contemporary Japan, Volume 4
Shigeru Nakayama and Hitoshi Yoshioka
Scams and Sweeteners: A Sociology of Fraud
Masahiro Ogino
Toyota's Assembly Line: A View from the Factory Floor
Ryoji Ihara
Village Life in Modern Japan: An Environmental Perspective
Akira Furukawa
Social Welfare in Japan: Principles and Applications
Kojun Furukawa
Escape from Work: Freelancing Youth and the Challenge to Corporate Japan
Reiko Kosugi
Japan's Whaling: The Politics of Culture in Historical Perspective
Hiroyuki Watanabe
Gender Gymnastics: Performing and Consuming Japan's Takarazuka Revue
Leonie R. Stickland
Poverty and Social Welfare in Japan
Masami Iwata and Akihiko Nishizawa
The Modern Japanese Family: Its Rise and Fall
Chizuko Ueno
Widows of Japan: An Anthropological Perspective
Deborah McDowell Aoki
In Pursuit of the Seikatsusha:
A Genealogy of the Autonomous Citizen in Japan
Masako Amano

Social Stratification and Inequality Series

Inequality amid Affluence: Social Stratification in Japan
Junsuke Hara and Kazuo Seiyama
Intentional Social Change: A Rational Choice Theory
Yoshimichi Sato
Constructing Civil Society in Japan: Voices of Environmental Movements
Koichi Hasegawa
Deciphering Stratification and Inequality: Japan and beyond
Yoshimichi Sato
Social Justice in Japan: Concepts, Theories and Paradigms
Ken-ichi Ohbuchi
Gender and Career in Japan
Atsuko Suzuki
Status and Stratification: Cultural Forms in East and Southeast Asia
Mutsuhiko Shima
Globalization, Minorities and Civil Society:
Perspectives from Asian and Western Cities
Koichi Hasegawa and Naoki Yoshihara
Fluidity of Place: Globalization and the Transformation of Urban Space
Naoki Yoshihara

Advanced Social Research Series
A Sociology of Happiness
Kenji Kosaka
Frontiers of Social Research: Japan and beyond
Akira Furukawa
A Quest for Alternative Sociology
Kenji Kosaka and Masahiro Ogino

MODERNITY AND IDENTITY IN ASIA SERIES
Globalization, Culture and Inequality in Asia
Timothy S. Scrase, Todd Miles, Joseph Holden and Scott Baum
Looking for Money:
Capitalism and Modernity in an Orang Asli Village
Alberto Gomes
Governance and Democracy in Asia
Takashi Inoguchi and Matthew Carlson
Liberalism: Its Achievements and Failures
Kazuo Seiyama
Health Inequalities in Japan: An Empirical Study of Older People
Katsunori Kondo

In Pursuit of the *Seikatsusha*

A Genealogy of the Autonomous Citizen in Japan

Masako Amano

Translated by
Leonie R. Stickland

Trans Pacific Press
Melbourne

First published in Japanese in 1996 by Chūō kōronsha as *'Seikatsusha' to wa dareka: jiritsuteki shiminzō no keifu*.

First published in English in 2011 by
Trans Pacific Press, PO Box 164, Balwyn North, Victoria 3104, Australia
Telephone: +61 (0)3 9859 1112 Fax: +61 (0)3 8611 7989
Email: tpp.mail@gmail.com
Web: http://www.transpacificpress.com
Copyright © Trans Pacific Press 2011
Designed and set by Digital Environs, Melbourne, Australia. www.digitalenvirons.com
Printed by BPA Print Group, Burwood, Victoria, Australia

Distributors

Australia and New Zealand
DA Information Services/Central Book Services
648 Whitehorse Road
Mitcham, Victoria 3132
Australia
Telephone: +61-(0)3-9210-7777
Fax: +61-(0)3-9210-7788
Email: books@dadirect.com
Web: www.dadirect.com

USA and Canada
International Specialized Book Services (ISBS)
920 NE 58th Avenue, Suite 300
Portland, Oregon 97213-3786
USA
Telephone: 1-800-944-6190
Fax: 1-503-280-8832
Email: orders@isbs.com
Web: http://www.isbs.com

Asia and the Pacific
Kinokuniya Company Ltd.

Head office:
3-7-10 Shimomeguro
Meguro-ku
Tokyo 153-8504
Japan
Telephone: +81-(0)3-6910-0531
Fax: +81-(0)3-6420-1362
Email: bkimp@kinokuniya.co.jp
Web: www.kinokuniya.co.jp

Asia-Pacific office:
Kinokuniya Book Stores of Singapore Pte., Ltd.
391B Orchard Road #13-06/07/08
Ngee Ann City Tower B
Singapore 238874
Telephone: +65-6276-5558
Fax: +65-6276-5570
Email: SSO@kinokuniya.co.jp

All rights reserved. No production of any part of this book may take place without the written permission of Trans Pacific Press.

ISSN   1443–9670 (Japanese Society Series)

ISBN   978–1–920901–21–9 (Hardcover)
        978–1–920901–27–1 (Paperback)

Cover illustration: An intersection with diagonal crosswalks in Shibuya, Tokyo, where many types of *seikatsusha* come and go amidst the drizzling rain. Courtesy of PIXTA.

Contents

Tables   viii
Preface   ix

Prologue: in search of the *seikatsusha*   1
  1 Under a fascist regime   12
  2 Towards a post-war departure   40
  3 Negotiating consumer society   89
  4 From 'theory' to the 'activism' stage   122
  5 In lieu of an epilogue: an overview of the *seikatsusha*
    discourse and its prospects   166
Afterword   198

Bibliography   200
Index   210

Tables

3.1: Comparison of consumer and *seikatsusha* (1)   93
3.2: Comparison of consumer and *seikatsusha* (2)   118
5.1: Genealogy of the '*seikatsusha*' concept   196

About the author
Masako Amano is currently President of Tokyo Kasei-Gakuin University and Professor Emeritus at Ochanomizu University, as well as a member of The Japan Sociological Society and The Japan Society of Educational Sociology.

Her field of specialisation is sociology—particularly social networking theory, sociology of gender, and educational sociology.

Her recent publications include *Kyōiku to jendā* (Education and gender) (2009), Iwanami shoten; *Oi e no manazashi: Nihon kindai wa nani o miushinatta ka* (An eye towards ageing: what has the Japanese modern age lost sight of?) (2006), Heibonsha; and *'Tsukiai' no sengo shi: sākuru nettowāku no hiraku chihei* (The post-war history of 'socialising': the horizons opened up by circle networks) (2005), Yoshikawa kōbundō.

About the translator
Leonie Rae Stickland researches issues of gender, sexuality and ageing in the Japanese context and teaches Japanese language at the University of Western Australia. Her publications include *Gender Gymnastics: Performing and Consuming Japan's Takarazuka Revue* (2008), Trans Pacific Press.

Preface

Dr. Wolfgang Seifert
Emeritus Professor
Institute of Japanese Studies, Centre for East Asian Studies
University of Heidelberg
Germany

The significance of the book

The translation of Masako Amano's work into English is a remarkable contribution to our understanding of Japanese society for many reasons. First, this publication offers to the broader professional audience—people interested in Japan, but who do not read Japanese—insight into the intellectual foundation of important new social movements in post-war Japan. Secondly, in this sense, this translation familiarises the reader with the significance of the *ordinary citizen* (*seikatsusha*) as a category beyond 'class,' 'stratum' and 'estate,' and further illustrates the sociological and ethnographical theories surrounding this term in Japanese research, as well. Finally—and this is where the subject of this book leaves the field of Japanese Studies to awaken a more general scholarly interest—Amano's insistence on giving a substantial definition of *seikatsusha* means that we should take the social reality which the term describes seriously. Opening a discussion on the meaning of *seikatsusha*, a term which defies a translation into Western languages, Amano stimulates reflection on how members of a society could be grasped sociologically, as individuals within *all* their spheres of activity and their voluntary social relations: in other words, according to their real existence. Since the term *seikatsusha* encompasses all the spheres of activity of an individual, yet does not lend itself to a clear definition, its use could lead to new reflections in sociology and ethnography. Social structure and stratification are central research objects of sociology, and are also taken up by political theory. Yet, which are the dominant terms in this field?

In the now-classical, early analysis of modern European civil society (*bürgerliche Gesellschaft*, as the whole of society, not only as that part of it which is critical to state intervention), male adult individuals were primarily defined as 'citizens' (*shimin/ Bürger*). The 'citizen' was henceforth designated to play the main role in that modern society. His action, in theory and analysis, was divided mainly into two spheres of action: the sphere of independent 'economic activity,' independent of the state, through which he became the *bourgeois*, and the sphere of 'political participation in public affairs,' through which he became the *citoyen* as a member of a political association. Being a member of a society, which had built a modern nation-state, he became a 'citizen of the state' (*kokumin/ Staatsbürger*). In political liberalism, citizens (*shimin*) are ascribed with the right to defend themselves against repressive acts of the state, whereas republicanism stresses the participation of citizens in public affairs.

With the progress of industrialisation, a new class of 'free wage-earners' emerged, besides the large social groupings of peasants and artisans, and this class became the focus of scientific and political interest. The quickly-growing class of 'wage-dependent workers' (*chingin rōdōsha*) soon encompassed two main groups made up of both genders: workers and employees. Most obviously, the wage-dependent employees have scant resources at their disposal, given their economic activities; and on the basis of their low incomes, they are not able to build capital or to become investors. For a long time, the thesis of the increasing polarisation of society into the two classes of '*bourgeoisie*' ('the capitalists') and the 'proletariat' claimed the prerogative of interpretation within social structure analysis. Yet, it is such social groupings as the self-employed (craftsmen, artisans, small shop-keepers and other occupational groups) and members of the civil service that are revealed to be equally relevant to the analysis of modern societies' social structures.

In addition to the domains of production and administration, consumption increasingly came to be of interest to sociological research: members of a society came to be analysed in their capacity as consumers. Thus, three main terms in sociology and political analysis came to the forefront, in order to grasp the political and social characteristics of the individual in modern society: the individual (1) as a national or member of a nation (*kokumin*); (2) as a worker (*rōdōsha*); and (3) as a consumer (*shōhisha*). Most adult individuals in modern society combine those three sides described with these terms within their existence; they are involved in the three according spheres of activity, albeit to varying degrees. In addition, further aspects of the individual's existence were investigated, such as his or her role as a father or mother within the sociology of the family.

However, from this rough sketch of fields important to the scientific sociological analysis of the individual in modern societies, other spheres of activity of the adult individual have been omitted. Indeed, spheres such as 'recreation,' 'entertainment' and 'education' are equally as important as 'production,' 'work' and consumption,' and thus should not be neglected. Furthermore, 'education' is not limited to 'instruction.' One of the intellectuals who articulated the concept of *ordinary citizen*, the architect and ethnologist Wajirō Kon (1881–1973), understood 'education' to mean primarily 'cultivation' (*kyōyō*) of an individual person. By the same token, recreation, entertainment and education cannot simply be subsumed under the sphere of 'consumption.' In order to view the individual no longer as a 'partial individual' in sociological analysis, a term would have to be found through which *all* the spheres of activity of an individual in society could be included in the observation. A person whose unfolding of life takes place in all spheres, and who earns the means of livelihood as a precondition for that, is called a *seikatsusha* in Japanese. It is surprising that there is no adequate word for such an encompassing and integrating term for the various areas of life in Western languages, at least as far as I know.

Amano informs us that the word *seikatsusha*, coined for the first time in 1917, is today an omnipresent 'verbal talisman' in Japan, used by political parties, associations and companies in their respective strategies of advertising. On the other hand, in Japan *seikatsusha* is also a concept used by new social movements in an emphatic sense. Whereas *seikatsusha* is a commonplace term for some, it is for others strongly connected to a specific kind of thought: it describes someone who shapes his or her life independently and actively. Such a person is not predominantly a consumer (*shōhisha*). This integrating view of the individual, characterised as 'active,' was developed in philosophy and later had an effect on the sciences, as well.

'Life' and 'Life Culture'

While the common term for 'life' in modern Japanese philosophy is *sei* (and is used as a fundamental term in biology and medicine), the philosopher Kiyoshi Miki (1897–1945) understood 'life' rather in the sense of livelihood, which had to be created every day. *Seikatsu* apparently follows that meaning in Japanese. Accompanying the wave of Europeanisation in the Meiji period (1868–1912), Japanese elites propagated *cultural life (bunka seikatsu)* as a means of appropriating Western culture. Miki contrasted this with *life culture (seikatsu bunka)*. As Miki said: 'Up until now, mention of 'culture' always immediately brought to mind literature, fine arts and the like, and something such as life culture hardly ever became an issue. By contrast, 'life culture' could be found in life itself, such as language, cooking, socialising, customs—these completely ordinary things, so to speak, [constituted] an important and fundamental part of the culture that humans create, and was something in the base layer of "our old traditions"'(Miki 1941, quoted in Amano 2011). Here, it has to be pointed out that Miki understood 'life culture' not as the traditional arts of Japanese elites, such as the tea ceremony which was reserved for only a small part of the population. Amano highlights that, beginning with Miki's thought, Japanese intellectuals could, for the first time, appreciate the everyday culture of a wider population without prejudice. In doing so, the bearer of this everyday culture came into focus: the *ordinary citizen*.

The current of thought which was developed by Miki and others before 1945 was continued after the end of war, but was simultaneously modified. New currents of thought and research areas were developed, when, under the influence of American pragmatism, philosophers such as Osamu Kuno or Shunsuke Tsurumi felt compelled to study the 'philosophy of ordinary people.' In 1959, the journal *Shisō no kagaku* pointed out the importance of 'nameless *seikatsusha*' for society. Such ideas later were integrated into the objectives of consumer co-operatives. The discourse on the consumer society evolved at times of rapid economic growth, and was started by Nobuyuki Ōkuma (1893–1977). An economist, Ōkuma enhanced the appreciation of the term *seikatsusha* as early as in 1940. According to him, economics attributed all activities for preserving human life to the two sectors of production and consumption, while mainly focusing on matters of production. Consequently, the existence of human beings was also subsumed under these two categories. Thus we lost sight of our own 'life activity' (*seikatsu*). Ōkuma's criticism of economics was based on a new definition of *seikatsu* and *seikat-*

susha. Seikatsusha was not used as a synonym, but as a *counterpart* of consumer (*shōhisha*). As skepticism towards industrialism, mass production and consumption emerged in the 1960s and 1970s, scholars again picked up Ōkuma's concept of *seikatsu*.

In the 1960s and 1970s, political and social movements of a new type used the word *seikatsusha* in a positive sense, and caused sociology and political science to partly broaden their analytical approach to society. The 'Citizens' Federation for Peace in Vietnam' (*Beheiren*), active since 1965, was based on a loose union of individuals, neither affiliated to parties nor any other political organisations. Its participants considered themselves to be citizens (*shimin*) *and* 'ordinary people,' living in their personal circumstances (*seikatsu*), and claiming a sphere of decision-making which was autonomous from government and state. On the other hand, the new consumers' movements emerging from 1965 onwards tried to distance themselves from the previous consumers' co-operatives that had had a large membership in Japan. They named themselves Seikatsu kurabu seikyō (literally: livelihood co-operatives; the translation 'Consumers' Club Co-ops' slightly misses the meaning). These co-ops openly tried to gain political influence and succeeded to some extent in local and regional elections. In view of the globally widening gap between the rich and the poor, these co-ops ideologically aimed at altering the life-style of their members and organising the joint purchase of healthy food. To these ends, they added three goals to their pursuit: developing from consumers (*shōhisha*) to individuals who were actively shaping their everyday life (*seikatsusha*); establishing a political power independent from parties by freeing themselves from the notion of being abstract national citizens (*kokumin*) by not electing representatives (*daihyōsha*) but deputies (*dairinin*); and connecting the 'consumer' in a direct way to the 'productively shaping' being. Starting from this point, the political scientist Michitoshi Takabatake developed his idea of *seikatsusha-citizen*. Thus, new perspectives for civil society in Japan were emphasised.

The will independently to conduct reforms in everyday life could also be a reaction against the appropriation of certain goals by politics, which—as it was perceived—emanated from political parties and big associations. Clearly, many citizens were no longer content with simply being 'roped in.' This is most apparent in the development of the popular movement Beheiren (Citizens'

Federation for Peace in Vietnam), a loosely-organized coalition of individuals in Japan that opposed American war efforts in North- and South Vietnam. For those actively involved or supporting the movement, the self-perception as an ordinary citizen meant to not view oneself as part of 'the masses' (*taishū*). Conversely, representatives of political parties often saw participants in the protest movements they led as 'the masses.'

The significance of *seikatsusha* for contemporary society

Amano also conceives of a potential role for *seikatsusha* in contemporary society. Certainly, her thought could be followed by a discussion about the behaviour and thought of citizens in highly industrialised countries. In this matter, two opposite tendencies can be observed. On the one hand, the 'colonization of the life-world' (J. Habermas) is progressing: instrumental rationality asserts itself to such an extent that bureaucratic and economic values determine the socialisation of individuals, their identity formation and social relations. These areas, such as arts, education and science, for which the economic logic is by no means constitutive, are gripped by a pervasive economisation and are transformed—often overriding their internal logic of action. On the other hand, many people try to withdraw their everyday life from this tendency, without waiting for a change accomplished by political forces. They encounter commercial promises of salvation skeptically, and independently control the quality of consumer goods and foods as far as they have room to do so. Or, they look for possibly independent sources of information.

Efforts for a good and appropriate life have to take today's ever-worsening economic situation for many people into consideration. Under contemporary conditions of a general increase of costs of sustenance, it might be difficult to maintain the level already achieved in quality of life. The challenge, however, does not only lie in adapting individual consumption. Rather, our view has to be on the *ordinary citizen*. An orientation towards everyday coexistence with people of the local community is needed. This includes those who are disadvantaged in many ways (the elderly, for example), but who are nonetheless integral members of this local community. As Amano points out in her work, it seems as if the spiritual and moral resources to accomplish that are more present in Japan than in Western countries.

Prologue: in search of the *seikatsusha*

The word in context

'*Oshiete yo/seikatsusha tte/dare no koto?* (Tell me/who do you mean/ when you say "*seikatsusha*"?)'

Such a *senryū* poem was published in the readers' column of the *Asahi* newspaper on 26 August 1993, the work of a housewife residing in Yokohama. One selector's critique said: 'I understand the idea of producers, consumers and workers, but is there such a thing as a non-*seikatsusha*, I wonder?'

If I look out for it, I see the word '*seikatsusha*' in frequent use around us. I try leafing through a newspaper at hand: there, I find introduced the topic of a housewife who, having checked the yearbooks of manufacturing firms, sent letters and faxes to their presidents, saying: 'Please buy into the *seikatsusha*'s perspective,' 'I want to improve the wet-rubbish container in the sink, which gets slimy,' 'If only I could operate the tap's lever with just one finger while cooking!' and 'How about a bathtub for elderly people?' (*Asahi shinbun*, 1996a). This was the success story of a housewife who succeeded in earning a monthly income of 250 thousand yen by submitting a string of ideas for solving the troubles that housewives confront in their day-to-day lives. *Seikatsusha* is used here to signify a possessor of 'kitchen sense' and 'housewifely sense.'

When the mass media write that 'that politician has "*seikatsusha* sense,"' they use it on the level of the politician catching a crowded train rather than riding in a limousine, or knowing the price of eggs, milk or rice. Here, the meaning of *seikatsusha* approaches that of someone with 'common-people's sense.'

There is also a different way of using *seikatsusha*. A certain university professor who conducted a survey to explore the typical image of volunteers who hastened to help after the 1995 Great Hanshin

1

Earthquake tells of the significance of the survey in the following way: 'One cannot omit from historical memory the volunteers who are able to carry out activities rooted in the *seikatsusha*, out of the administration's reach' (*Asahi shinbun*, 1996b). From the context, *seikatsusha* here can be seen to be employed in the sense of those who side with the elderly or disabled—in other words, 'the weak.'

A keyword for the age

When was it, one wonders, that the word '*seikatsusha*' thus made its appearance as a keyword for the age and began to be 'consumed' in such great quantities, without so much as a clear-cut definition? And when did the people who consciously 'consume' the image and atmosphere held by this word make their appearance?

In the 1990 Lower House elections, '*seikatsusha*-driven politics' became a catch-phrase, and it is still fresh in my memory how *seikatsusha* was used as a keyword for political reform. Komeito, especially, often used '*seikatsusha*' as a term promoting its party image in its electoral posters. As can be seen in that party's slogan: 'We will protect *seikatsusha*,' *seikatsusha* was used there as a collective symbol for people who sought defence of their livelihood, symbolised by opposition to the consumption tax. In this case, there would be no great difference even if *seikatsusha* were replaced by the word 'consumer.'

It was not only Komeito that did this: in the Tokyo metropolitan elections in 1993, Japan New Party hammered out '*seikatsusha*' across the board, promising 'community-building that prioritises the *seikatsusha*.' Nearly two-thirds of the candidates with official Japan New Party endorsement were people who had moved from other parties. For the New Party, a motley collection of members still without a clear-cut policy platform as a party, *seikatsusha* must have been an extremely convenient and valuable term. Here, *seikatsusha* only meant something like 'metropolitan residents who were living locally.'

As de-alignment progresses and party support becomes more and more ambiguous, unaffiliated voters are seen to be the ones holding the key to elections. For candidates, unaffiliated voters are people whose moves are difficult to apprehend. There are indications that the word *seikatsusha*, so comfortable to the ear, will become even more sought-after among politicians who strive to gain peace of mind by bestowing it upon floating uncommitted voters.

It is not only in electoral races that *seikatsusha* has been brazenly walking abroad. It made a 'career advance' even to the extent of being adopted as a keyword in a 1992 report from the Economic Council, a consultative body during the Miyazawa prime-ministership, entitled: 'The Lifestyle Superpower 5-year Plan: aiming for coexistence with global society.' While still in joint name, as '*seikatsusha/shōhisha* (consumer),' it had even progressed to being the title of one of its chapters (Chapter Five), under a basic policy that 'the awareness and action of business and individuals, as well as that of the government, must change from being business-focused, as hitherto, to having an emphasis on the perspective of the *seikatsusha*/consumer.'

Here, too, there is no definition of *seikatsusha*, including whether *seikatsusha* and consumer are the same or different. According to the Foreign Ministry's translation, both '*seikatsusha/shōhisha*' and '*seikatsusha*' are rendered by the blanket term 'consumer.' *Seikatsusha* appears to refer to 'people who are making their living in this country' = nationals = consumers.

In their use of the word *seikatsusha*, local government bodies are not outdone by the central government. 1996 saw the launch of a colloquium called 'Seikatsu toshi Tōkyō o kangaeru kai (Group for thinking about Tokyo, a lifestyle metropolis),' a private consultative body of Tokyo's Governor, Yukio Aoshima, which considered the way Tokyo should be in ten years' time from the vantage-point of '*seikatsusha*.' The 'Tokyo, lifestyle metropolis' declaration was positioned as the drawcard of the new policy Governor Aoshima was promoting. In it, *seikatsusha* are tentatively defined as 'metropolitan residents who seek latitude and abundance,' 'metropolitan residents who participate in and make proposals to metropolitan government,' and 'metropolitan residents who act autonomously and independently.' If the question is where specifically to find *seikatsusha*, however, it goes no further than to say they are 'people making a livelihood in Tokyo' = metropolitan residents = consumers.

The word *seikatsusha* is also making advances into business. Since the end of the 1980s, when the recession was prompting people increasingly to turn away from material possessions, there has been a proliferation of firms that promote themselves with the slogan: 'a company that is kind to *seikatsusha*.' In this case, also, there would be no harm at all in substituting 'consumer' for '*seikatsusha*.'

In the days when Japanese society was single-mindedly racing through its period of rapid economic growth, the word *seikatsusha* was not heard as widely as it is now. It was in the time from the late eighties into the 1990s that '*seikatsusha*' came into frequent use.

A modern 'verbal talisman'

'Who do you mean by "*seikatsusha*"?' If directly confronted with this question, the very people who copiously employ this term are sure to show embarrassment. What is the difference between *kokumin* (nationals; members of the nation) and *shimin* (citizens)? How do they differ from consumers? If *seikatsusha* is a word that encompasses everyone who has a life, then that will mean there is no such thing as a non-*seikatsusha*. If so, then there will no longer be any positive reason to go out of one's way use the term *seikatsusha*. Is it not for the very reason that it has some element that cannot fully be expressed by other terms, including consumer, that this word has been coined, chosen and used? The creation of any word is likely to see the existence of a new horizon that it carves out.

At this juncture, I try looking up '*seikatsusha*' in Japanese dictionaries, but cannot find it in any of them. Though the word *seikatsusha* is in frequent use as a keyword of the times, it is not sufficiently mature to be recorded in dictionaries. While it remains vague as a concept, or, rather, for the precise reason that it *is* vague, a variety of people, from politicians to business-owners, use it often. Is this not what Shunsuke Tsurumi calls a 'verbal talisman (*o-mamori kotoba*)' (Tsurumi 1946: 12–25)?

According to Tsurumi, each respective age has set up a kind of magical word system that would resist all criticism. During the Second World War, the Japanese intoned the slogans: '*taisei yokusan* (imperial rule assistance)' and '*hakkō ichiu* (all the world under one roof),' and shouted '*kichiku BeiEi* (American devils and British beasts).' After Japan's defeat, they made an about-turn, and vied with each other to use expressions belonging to a different system from that of wartime, such as 'democracy,' 'freedom' and 'equality.' The meaning of these words was not strictly questioned. By using these words, anyone could dodge criticism from others. In that sense, they constitute verbal talismans. People need only rely upon words which are like key symbols provided by the times. They are a sort of charm to ward off evil.

Tsurumi claims that the popularity of using words as talismans signifies the poor ability of the society in question and the people inhabiting the times to read the subtext of those words. If people are equipped with the ability to grasp a word's meaning concretely in terms of their own life-space and their own experience, and to appreciate its essence, then there would be little likelihood of their being bewitched by the magical power held by that word. What might 'hakkō ichiu (all the world under one roof)' mean? What is 'minshu (democracy)?' If those who use such expressions, and those to whom they appeal, both have the habit of taking words back to their life-settings and experience, and pondering their meaning, then they surely will easily see through such words as being nothing more than verbal talismans.

Is not 'seikatsusha' one of these modern verbal talismans? Numerous people employ this handy term without careful consideration. It seems to incorporate an easy, yet determined, calculation that nobody will be able to oppose them if they rely upon the verbal talisman of seikatsusha. Moreover, it is also probably necessary to note that other words linked with seikatsusha, such as seikatsu bunka (life culture), seikatsu no shitsu (quality of life), seikatsu taikoku (lifestyle superpower), and the like, are also in frequent use.

The fall of the Berlin Wall and the ending of the Cold War are not unconnected with the rise in value of the words seikatsusha and seikatsu. The ideological standoff which pressed for a choice between capitalism and socialism collapsed, and an environment began to emerge in which people could express their own claims and pursue their own interest freely and in diverse ways, but people are yet to reach the point of finding appropriate words to express themselves. Is it not the case that terms incorporating 'seikatsu' are ones chosen as substitutes in the interim, after the abandonment of perspectives that focused on the bigger picture, such as ideology, politics, economics and foreign diplomacy?

When we think thus, we start to see the scale of the problems contained in inundation by the word seikatsusha. The term seikatsusha is one worthy of particular attention, is it not?

From envy to sympathy

By way of example, we live in a reality such as the following: until some years ago, a train of foreign students used to come to Japan to delve into the secrets of its 'miraculous' post-war economic development. The numbers of those students have begun to follow a downward trajectory, however. Rie Kishida, who associates deeply with overseas students on a daily basis, points out that the cause for this lies not in the strong yen and stagnation in economic growth, but in the fact that the puzzle of Japan's success has been solved.

> What foreign students arriving in Japan experience first of all is the unbearable crowding in the trains every morning. Later, when they have understood that the special treatment and discrimination towards foreigners which they sense daily is due to Japanese people's fixation on identity, many of them return to their home country, but among those students who further overcome the high language barrier, there are some for whom such anger changes to sympathy, and they experience mixed feelings. They see the actual condition of Japanese people's lives, with their cramped housing and high prices, and yet low general income, and realise that the reason for Japan's success is that its people all have been working until late every night, not complaining even in such a severe environment. They come to understand that, *surprisingly, the secret of success boils down to something so simple* (Kishida 1995: 26, emphasis added).

One cannot suppress the thought that the realities of Japanese society, where the word *seikatsusha* is frequently used, are being plainly grasped in the process of foreign students' feelings of 'curiosity' and 'envy' eventually turning to 'anger,' and further developing into 'sympathy.'

Behind the burgeoning popularity of this term, there clearly exists some remorse over the mechanism of Japanese society having been too biased towards 'producer' supremacy. There is the question of why there is no feeling of leeway in the lives of us in Japan, which built up enough strength in the production aspect to catch up to the advanced nations of the West and almost overtake them; and far from there being any elbow-room, there is anxiety towards the accumulation of challenges such as urban problems, environmental-, safety- and resource issues within that 'abundant society,' and, furthermore, the sense that creaking has begun to be heard here and there in the very structure of economic society, whose construction was mainly centred on efficiency and productivity. This could be called a firm premonition that the 'obviousness of abundance' in Japanese society is starting to crumble.

The term '*seikatsusha*' was created from amid such remorse and doubts, and chaos imbued with anxiety and foreboding vis-à-vis Japanese society. It perhaps should be seen as a label for a new human typology, filled with people's desires and expectations. If that be the case, then rather than making *seikatsusha* simply a trendy term, soiling it though handling and discarding it, is there not a necessity to interrogate its essence anew, as a richly evocative word, for the precise reason that it is an ambiguous verbal talisman?

Towards an alternative horizon

I wish to dwell upon the word *seikatsusha*. This term is chosen and used not because it indicates people's mode of behaviour or attributes (consumer, worker, national, and so on), nor because it points to the characteristics of a level of sensibility, such as 'a housewife's perspective' or 'popular sentiment.' The reason seems to be that it focuses on the substance of people's behaviour and their behavioural principles. Maybe '*seikatsusha*' is being used as one 'ideal type' for persons who adhere to particular behavioural principles, or who aim to do so?

If so, then what sort of behavioural principles do people have to follow in order to be deemed '*seikatsusha*?' There is one group of people likely to give us a clue. They are people who, drawing a clear line of demarcation between themselves and the '*seikatsusha*' that have been heavily used in print and slogans and turned into mass-consumer goods, have continued to aim for a transformation in their very own lives—the people who gather at the Seikatsu kurabu seikyō (Seikatsu Club Consumers' Co-operative Union), one of the regional cooperatives based on the Consumer Co-operatives Act, and hereafter abbreviated to 'Seikatsu Club.'

As you will later see, the Seikatsu Club movement began with the joint purchasing of foodstuffs, 'from production, through distribution, and finally to disposal,' and developed even further into a *seikatsusha* movement directed at transforming everything in the whole of life that was relevant to all of such spheres as politics and labour. *Seikatsusha* in that context can be understood as beings who take on the following two definitions.

Firstly, there are '*seikatsusha*' as people who, being counterposed to 'workers' that speak from the site of production and 'consumers' that speak from the site of consumption, generate their ideas from their living sites, which include the aforementioned two, and strive to solve problems. Living does not only involve the consumption of goods and services, but also production and work as its prerequisites, and, on a most basic level, has a connection with human life and death, and their environment. The word *'seikatsusha'* indicates the kind of totality that life naturally has, and people as subjects who desire to place the whole of it into their own hands. This further goes on to link with a positive assertion which says that the thing called life is one that cannot be subdivided and segmented into work, consumption, politics, and so on, as a specialised society should be.

Secondly, there are *'seikatsusha'* as people who, while rooted in 'the individual,' endeavour through cooperation with other 'individuals' to choose 'alternative' ways of living from the one hitherto seen as self-evident. They are people who, through their approach to goods, focused on 'food,' the foundation of life, take responsibility for their own actions, while simultaneously building networks with others and striving to create a new way of living in counter to a 'normal' life. 'Individual,' 'cooperation' and 'alternative' are the key words here. Moreover, supposing one divides people's living sites into the four domains of individual, home, occupation and locality/citizen, then, for *'seikatsusha,'* their way of relating to the locality/citizen domain as a site transcending 'the private,' where people with divergent private interests according to each respective domain have repeated dialogue, will become vital.

Here, I will refrain from encroaching further upon a definition of *seikatsusha*, and will affirm just the two following points. *Seikatsusha* refers to: 1 a subject who grasps the totality of living; and 2 not a static form, but a dynamic, everyday practice that changes a way of living to that of a *'seikatsusha.'* The main theme of this volume is to go on to unravel what *seikatsusha* thus defined means, in concrete terms.

Visiting the source of *seikatsusha*

It was probably the group called Seikatsu Club that located the process of becoming *seikatsusha* itself as a movement, and installed it as the stout axis upon which all of their activities revolved. This does not mean, however, that no ideology or movement which made the term *seikatsusha* a keyword had ever shown itself in

Japanese thought or activism up till then. Neither did it suddenly appear as a keyword of the times in 1980s Japanese society. It has several sources within the various preceding ages. One should probably view Seikatsu Club as having discovered a problem-consciousness connected to its source, albeit still unwittingly, tapping that water vein and developing their movement while drawing energy from it.

In that sense, *seikatsusha* is both a word that has a certain historicity, and a concept. It has been generated amid particular temporal circumstances, repeatedly recalled, and has 'grown' as a term made to bear a specific meaning. Under what kind of temporal circumstances, and carrying what sort of issues and concerns, has the word *seikatsusha* made its appearance? What social class of people has it indicated, and to which other categories of people has it been counterposed? The tasks which I simply must first attempt in order to clarify the contemporary meaning of '*seikatsusha*' are to re-apprehend—in the context of its germination, and in the setting where the term was born and developed—the word and concept of *seikatsusha*, which has been prolifically used and begun to be soiled; and to trace its historical trajectory.

These, I propose, are indispensable procedures for restoring the term *seikatsusha* once more to a word brimming with dynamism, one that has a fresh and vibrant ring.

The structure of this volume

When one probes and traces the kinds of genres in which the word and mentality that constitute *seikatsusha* have been germinated and used in thought and movements thus far, they can be roughly summarised into the three following discourses:
1. Life culture
2. Consumer society
3. 'New social movements'

These three divisions almost overlap temporal divisions, without alteration. Of course, the three genres naturally have parts which intertwine in a complex manner within the continuing flow of time. Each period, however, has had its respective characteristic mainstream *seikatsusha* discourse. In this volume, I wish to set these three domains as the centrepiece in my pursuit of the temporal changes that have taken place.

In Chapter One, I discuss the individuals—Kiyoshi Miki and Itaru Nii—who, under the wartime regime from the late 1930s into the 1940s, used the word *seikatsusha* in ways not always appropriate to the mood of the times, and, in that connection, advocated life culture (*seikatsu bunka*). What meaning did this pair make the concept of *seikatsusha* assume when it appeared? How does it differ from the concept of '*kokumin* (nationals)' or '*rōdōsha* (workers)?' Also, while focusing on the kind of connection it had with contemporary thought, I will highlight the pre-war image of the *seikatsusha*.

In Chapter Two, I take up the period from the end of the war into the 1950s, which was for the Japanese precisely the age of focus on their 'living.' In this period, a unique life-culture theory was devised by Wajirō Kon, who established the foundations of modernology and lifeology. It was also in this age that the '*Shisō no kagaku* (Science of thought)' movement was developed, with the aim of fathoming a 'people's philosophy' in the life-world of common people who were not experts in speculation. Neither of these two moves used the actual word *seikatsusha* in a definitive form. Clearly, the *seikatsusha* image which Miki and Nii posed is carried on by 'the people (*hitobito*)' in 'people's philosophy' research, which was the instrument of Wajirō Kon's life-culture theory, and it exhibits a unique growth.

Moreover, in this period there was Yasuko Mizoue, who probed among the farming folk of the San'in region for the *seikatsusha* living the concrete reality of agrarian villages, and wrote a book called *Seikatsusha no shisō* (The ideology of the *seikatsusha*) (1961). Here, I wish to explore the historical significance of these three endeavours, by Wajirō Kon, the '*Shisō no kagaku*' movement, and Yasuko Mizoue.

In Chapter Three, I deal principally with Japan's period of rapid economic growth from the 1960s onwards, in which the word *seikatsusha* began to appear in the mass media. It was the economist Nobuyuki Ōkuma that first counterposed the concept of the *seikatsusha* to that of the 'consumer' in the realm of social science, and began to use the former as a concept which transcended the latter. Meanwhile, from the 1970s into the 80s, all kinds of consumer-society theories around the metamorphosis of the general public were unfolded in the world of criticism. Here, while sorting out concepts including '*taishū* (undifferentiated masses),' '*bunshū* (segmented masses)' and '*shōhisha* (consumers),' I will clarify the position of the '*seikatsusha*.'

In Chapter Four, I take up the so-called 'new social movements' which arose in the late 1960s and became firmly established in the 70s. What these movements had in common was that their participants called themselves '*shimin* (citizens)' or '*seikatsusha*.' Members of Beheiren (Betonamu ni heiwa o! Shimin rengō) (Citizens' federation for peace in Vietnam), which was launched in 1965 and laid the foundation for subsequent 'new social movements,' also called themselves '*seikatsusha*' almost as often as 'citizens.' Using Beheiren as an example, I wish to extract the elements that communicated with the word *seikatsusha* used in various senses within those several movements.

Next, I deal with the people gathering at Seikatsu Club, who, given the accumulation of such 'new social movements,' positioned the very 'process' of becoming *seikatsusha* as their movement, and established it as the sturdy axis running through the entire movement. My aims here are to inquire into the processes of everyday practice of these people's joint-purchasing activities, their *dairinin* (deputy) campaign (sending proxies to local assemblies) and their workers' collective activities (creating a new way of working on a self-management model), and to divine the characteristics of the logic of *seikatsusha*, its potential and its new challenges.

When one attempts an inquiry in this manner, it becomes clear that the word *seikatsusha* has threaded its way through a history spanning over half a century. Upon that word *seikatsusha* are projected not only the feelings of the 'individuals' who have employed it, but also the sentiments of the people in those respective 'times.' Now that *seikatsusha* has been mass-produced and consumed as a verbal talisman, let us first embark on a journey to visit the '*seikatsusha*' in history, in order to rescue the '*seikatsusha*' locked inside that verbal talisman, give it new life, and resurrect it.

1 Under a fascist regime

The *seikatsusha* is an artist: the life-culture theory of Kiyoshi Miki

Scholarship that lacks 'life'

Strictly speaking, it is not necessarily appropriate to begin a discussion of *seikatsusha* from Kiyoshi Miki (1897–1945) or Itaru Nii (1888–1951). This is because the playwright and critic Hyakuzō Kurata (1891–1943) is thought to have been the first user of the word *seikatsusha*. Over three days, from 27 to 29 April 1926, he published critiques entitled 'Seikatsusha to bundanjin (*Seikatsusha* and literati)' in the *Tōkyō asahi* newspaper. In addition, in May of the same year, he launched and supervised a magazine called *Seikatsusha* (Ōkuma Nobuyuki Kenkyūkai (ed.), 1990, no. 8: 2).

In '*Seikatsusha* and literati,' Kurata lamented that the literati in those days had come to see art and literature as 'enterprises' and to pursue 'profit,' and had begun to resemble politicians. He wrote: 'Proper art and literature must first start from the self as a *seikatsusha*. Before being a literatus, one must first be a *seikatsusha*.' Here, '*seikatsusha*' is explained as being 'a pilgrim in a life [that] has its roots in the depths of the soul,' a 'spiritual pilgrimage.' For Kurata, 'life' meant a chaotic earthly realm of worldly desires, disorder and violation, and '*seikatsusha*' signified seekers who controlled themselves with a stoic ethic in resistance to such worldliness. The magazine which he supervised, *Seikatsusha*, was also was a publication deeply imbued with religious atmosphere, brimming with seeker-like ardour.

For Kurata—who depicted the love and anguish, worldly desires and religious life of Buddhist monks Shinran and Yuien in his play, 'Shukke to sono deshi (Priests and their disciples)' (1917), thus triggering the start of the Taisho-era flowering of religious literature—'*seikatsusha*' indicated, above all, persons of religion who mastered 'the way,' still striving to cast away hesitation and be strictly introspective toward themselves in the midst of their unbreakable attachment to the present world. In that sense, '*seikatsusha*' had to be people who transcended and were liberated from *seikatsu* (life/lifestyle).

It was more than a decade later that '*seikatsusha*' was freed from such a religious hue and began to appear in the context of life-culture theories, as the bearer of actual 'life culture.'

From the pre-war through to the post-war, incidentally, Japanese intellectuals did not wake up to the significance held by the reality called '*seikatsu*' or '*kurashi* (living/livelihood).' Life-culture theory has not occupied an important position in Japanese thought and philosophy,.

Most intellectuals have not thought it possible for something like *seikatsusha* to be the object of serious speculation or investigation. Scholarship that comes with a 'weight' such as *seikatsu* or *kurashi* looks very primitive and 'immature' when seen from the perspective of studies that are unburdened by such a thing. Scholarship advances far more rapidly without the weight of living being attached, rather than with its attachment. Philosophers themselves have pointed out that the majority of philosophers have regarded the 'proper function of philosophy' as fulfilled by 'being separated from people's lives and disconnected from the social reality of Japanese society' (Nakamura 1989: 15).

Not only that, the very state of Japanese thought and scholarship has made it difficult for these to amass the necessary vigour to cross swords with people's actual lives. According to historian Sannosuke Matsumoto, Japanese scholarship and thought had begun to lose the vigour to respond to the suffering and thirst in people's actual lives as early as thirty or so years after the 1868 Meiji restoration (Matsumoto 1994: 13). Whether in philosophy or any other academic discipline, all established disciplines have poured much energy into the introduction and succession of leading theories and doctrines from the West. Japanese scholarship became a sort of 'branch store' for foreign scholars, disassociating itself from issues of actual people's lifestyle issues, and thereby being formalised and progressively losing its vitality.

Given the nature of such scholarship, the inevitable result was that 'life' fell away from life-culture theory, and there was hardly any expansion of cultural discourse that focused upon 'living' and 'how to run one's life.' In those circumstances, one of the rare philosophers to have developed life-culture discourse and theory on *seikatsusha* as bearers of life culture was Kiyoshi Miki.

Miki criticised the fact that conventional philosophy had severed the world of learning from the world of living, and isolated them. He writes:

> I want to ask whatever kind of philosophy the Japanese nation possesses. Here, philosophy does not mean the sort of philosophy that expert professional philosophers have been bringing into question all along. What I mean is the sort of philosophy or world-view that has been formed from amid national life and has permeated that national life (Miki 1940b [1967]: 349).

Miki's life-culture theory is none other than something born of such criticism and reflection towards the way philosophy had been hitherto.

Cultural life dependent on material things

In his 1941 critique, 'Seikatsu bunka to seikatsu gijutsu (Life culture and living techniques),' Miki begins with the following passage:

> Life culture is a new term that has begun to catch the eye somewhat these days. Up until now, mention of 'culture' always immediately brought to mind literature, fine arts and the like, and something such as life culture hardly ever became an issue (Miki 1941b [1967]: 384).

Miki firstly understands his 'life culture' to be something contraposed to conventional 'cultural life.' Ever since the Meiji era Westernisation movement, Japanese people's cultural life mostly had continued to be one of reliance upon material things, such as 'playing a record or listening to the radio, reading a book, or watching a film.' 'Culture' in this case referred to 'something Western-style, something exotic, or something in the latest fashion.' For that reason, Miki asserts, 'cultural life' was 'something that cost money,' and so it inevitably became nothing other than 'consumption-type culture.'

By contrast, life itself, such as 'language, cooking, socialising, customs—these completely ordinary things, so to speak, [constituted] an important and fundamental part of the culture that humans create,' and was something in the base layer of 'our old traditions.' Yet 'old traditions' does not indicate traditional sites for education and learning, linked to so-called '*dō*' such as *sadō* (the way of tea = tea ceremony), *kadō* (the way of flowers = flower arrangement) or *shodō* (the way of writing = calligraphy). It is important for culture to become a force in people's lives and be useful to those lives. While thus contrasting life culture to conventional cultural life, Miki attempted to define what life culture was.

Culture that has a body

According to Miki, life culture was 'not something that has been attached to culture from the outside,' but the 'form in which one shapes one's life.' In other words, the very fact of being alive here now is life (*seikatsu*), and life culture is something that one creates on the foundation of one's way of living, that is, culture that has a body.

Alternatively, one could rephrase this as follows: 1 everything that is generated from the positive transformation and reconstruction of lifestyles; 2 something which links people with other people, not merely a privileged few, as something public; and 3 something created from emphasis on day-to-day-ness itself—that is what life culture is, says Miki.

By means of the expression 'life culture,' which he contraposed to a 'cultural life' that was divorced from living, Miki was trying to advocate the necessity of an active and technical life culture which had a clear-cut self-awareness vis-à-vis the place where people lived on a daily basis, centred on the family and household and extending to its surroundings, and aimed for self-improvement there.

Moreover, Miki says that the very creators of such a life culture are '*seikatsusha*.' '*Seikatsusha*' does not refer to passive livers of 'cultural life' who are in 'a position to enjoy the culture that a minority of artists and scholars have made.' It is precisely the 'artists' who participate in the creation of life culture (productive culture) that constitute '*seikatsusha*.'

'In a similar way to how artists make works of art, we make ourselves and our lives. All *seikatsusha* are artists' (Miki 1941b [1967]: 386).

In other words, *seikatsusha* indicates action-oriented or technical humans who, while taking themselves and their lives as their raw materials, create another, independent lifestyle that is greater than the sum of its parts. Their own selves and their lives are things that have been fashioned by the 'structure' of society. *Seikatsusha* are not beings who merely settle for such given terms, however. They are no less than technical humans who, as subjects, remake those terms, or else destroy them and create a new mode of living. *Seikatsusha* were given the image of humans who, through an internal impulse, continually shaped and created new meaning in society.

What Miki wished to express by the word *seikatsusha* was, in plain terms, that which is described by the expression 'quality' of life: in other words, the figure of 'the public (*minshū*)' who search among the substance of living for ways to make a really 'meaningful life' for themselves, and put these into practice. What is important is not an abundance of material things in quantitative terms. Rather, it is an exploration and a search for meaning and value for the self who uses things.

That can also be appreciated from Miki's having cited firstly the common people's positive attitude towards their own lifestyle ('love towards life'), and secondly, a spirit of the times that was liberated from the 'evils of standardisation,' as the greatest prerequisites for making such practices possible—especially his repeated emphasis on the importance of the latter.

He says, 'Even in relation to life culture, standardisation will result in cultural poverty.' Standardisation does not merely regulate the state of political control over the exterior and interior. It even controls the condition of the lives of the general public. Moreover, it has even extinguished their spark of spontaneity in terms of their wanting to make their current livelihood a little better. Taking the side of the common people who were placed in a tense relationship with the state and social groups, Miki strove to find the potential of the *seikatsusha* in their aspiration towards a spirit of the times free from lifestyle standardisation.

Experiencing Marx

It is well-known that Miki read Kitarō Nishida's *Zen no kenkyū* (An inquiry into the good) in his student days at Tokyo's Dai-ichi kōtōgakkō (Japan's premier higher secondary school under the pre-war system), and was so moved that he entered Kyoto Imperial University and studied under Nishida. After that, in 1922, he went to Germany to study, and his eyes were opened to new intellectual trends from his encounter with Rickert and Heidegger.

From his student days until his later years, Miki's philosophical speculation was swayed by the inherent concerns and thought of the times in each respective age, and changed repeatedly several times. Nonetheless, if one were to summarise its underlying consistency, this would probably be 'people's cultural formation, done from a raw philosophical viewpoint' and 'the pursuit of the logic of historical formation' (1994: 18). And when examining Miki's thought from that angle, out of his books, which amount to an immense number, it is the two volumes *Pasukaru ni okeru ningen no kenkyū* (A study of humans in Pascal) (1926) and *Tetsugaku nyūmon* (Introduction to philosophy) (1940c) that are especially important.

The book on Pascal, his first publication after returning from studies in Germany, is one which endeavours to find philosophical issues not from out of the depths (mind and consciousness) of the solitary self, but within the very 'life (*sei*)' of people living the concrete reality of the same times; and there, 'along with Heidegger's influence, the starting point of Miki's own philosophical anthropology is displayed.' After that, in rapid succession, he published the fruit of his Marxist studies, including 'Ningengaku no Marukusu-teki keitai (The Marxist morphology of philosophical anthropology)' and 'Marukusu shugi to yuibutsuron (Marxism and materialism),' but from those papers it is possible to read 'an intention to give a material foundation to his own philosophical anthropology' (Watanabe 1988: 275).

His study of Marx was one that firstly tried to read Marxist thought—which until then had tended to be understood in a formal, fixed manner as the elucidation of objective principles—as a realistic theory in the process of development, in which humans are made amid history, and make history at the same time. It was also one that attempted to tie Marxism to the foundations of personal humanism which had been cultivated in Japan's philosophical circles since the Taisho era (1912–26), and to reconstitute it.

Through these two perspectives runs Miki's basic stance vis-à-vis Marxism, namely not to set up Marxist ideology as complete, absolute truth, but to take it as something to develop through scientific verification in the midst of reality. As is well-known, such attempts were severely criticised by 'orthodox' Marxists as having an idealistic bias. His *Tetsugaku nyūmon* (Introduction to philosophy) (1940c), bears the stamp of his Marxist experiences such as these, and the influence of Kitarō Nishida.

There, Miki has posed reality not as an 'object,' but as a 'live' stage where its actors work, think and die; and, while focusing there on the human being as a dualistic existence that is both subjective and objective, he has expanded the philosophy of the 'technique' of making history and shaping culture (1940c).

The source of Miki's assertions in a later paper, entitled 'Seikatsu bunka to seikatsu gijutsu (Life culture and living techniques)' (1941b), can be found in these two volumes. There, one can see a perspective pertaining to each individual member of the masses (*minshū*) who live within historical reality, and anticipation towards the image of *seikatsusha* as subjects who, unceasingly boosted by their internal life-force, expand themselves and create meaning in society.

The farmer as an archetype

The reason for Miki's life-culture theories having started in this way from the image of *seikatsusha* as subjects is not unrelated to his upbringing. Miki was born in 1897 in a half-farming, half-merchant household in Tatsuno City in Hyogo Prefecture. He writes:

> I preferred helping with the cultivation to business. In other words, I grew up as the child of farmers. I think it was when I was in the sixth grade that I saw a thing called a magazine for the first time...Even now, when I look back on my boyhood, the things I see in my mind's eye are the nature in my native place and all kinds of people, but there is not a single book (Miki 1941a [1966]: 370).

He also recounts as follows:

> Even now, the thing that captures my heart is the soil: not nature as a sightseeing spot, but nature as the soil. It is not even nature as landscape. Even Bashō['s haiku poetry] is too refined for me, as I regard the traditions of farming folk to be more precious than the tradition of elegance (Miki 1941a [1966]: 373).

For farmers, 'nature as the soil' is neither a famous place such as depicted in postcards or photographs, nor is it the scenery extolled in *haiku* or *tanka* poetry. It is the very reality in which they work, live and die. At the same time, farmers are an embodied, cultural presence, ceaselessly working on 'nature as the soil,' and nurturing and creating products in it. Miki may have discovered the archetype of the *seikatsusha* in the figure of the farmer working amid 'nature as the soil' in his native place.

If one rereads his life-culture and *seikatsusha* discourses now, they are too conceptual, too theoretical, and lack reality. They also appear only to have the meaning of enlightenment engendered by a philosopher's speculation. However, it is impossible to sense the reality of the meaning that his life-culture and *seikatsusha* theories hold without trying to set them in the temporal context in which they were written, namely the establishment of a controlled economy, for one, and the rise of fascism, for another. In what temporal circumstances, then, did Miki's *seikatsusha* discourse make its appearance?

A new human typology

Beginning from the implementation of the National General Mobilisation Act of 1938, control of the economy was continually intensified, with the start of a rice-rationing system the next year, in 1939, and, further, the introduction of a ration-voucher system for the purchase of goods. Amid the financial distress of daily life under the wartime regime, the lifestyle of the populace was about to usher in a time of collapse of the existing order, and its restructuring. The question of how to rebuild and protect one's own and one's family's livelihood, which was rapidly losing its freedom, in a day-to-day lifestyle that was increasingly regulated by the institutions of National General Mobilisation and materials-control, occupied central place in the general public's lifestyle-consciousness.

The realities of such a populace's actual living conditions and lifestyle-consciousness were published in the Shinano mainichi newspaper from 1938 into 1940, and can be read in the letters from rural youth compiled in a three-volume collection of lifestyle records, *Nōson seinen hōkoku* (Rural youth reports) (Kataoka et al. 1940; 1941).

Kiyoshi Tsutsumi, a reporter with the Shinano mainichi, who edited these records of life, wrote in his editor's afterword: 'What is most interesting is that all of the contributors are *seikatsusha* from agricultural villages, and the whirlpool of contradictions that germinate, develop and wither within rural village life in the situation are depicted concretely and without ostentation through the writers' experiences (Kataoka et al. 1940: 329). In other words, *Nōson seinen hōkoku* is a record of the contradictions of 'life in rural villages in the situation' by '*seikatsusha* from agricultural villages.'

According to Tsuneo Yasuda, who assiduously considered the 240 contributions recorded in the three volumes from the perspective of the 'lifestyle-consciousness of the general public during the war,' what is depicted here is the lifestyle-consciousness of farmers who, in the dual processes of reality comprising departure for the battlefront and rural migration on the one hand, and price-rises and material shortages on the other, while harbouring discomfort at the war regime, ultimately went on to accept it (Yasuda 1987: 223).

A letter from a woman who wrote and sent in 'To my younger brother at the front,' for example, conveys those processes well. The sight of even female students commuting by train to school shod in straw sandals 'touched her heart,' but the theory by which she finally convinced herself that she should accept such circumstances of a shortage of materials as 'a fine challenge' was something akin to the following:

> But if I think about the soldiers at the front, I cannot ask too much. I think nothing of trifling inconvenience...When I try to come up with something, I get all kinds of good ideas, and even rags are quite useful. And things become very precious. We have been given too much freedom up till now. I even think of it as a *good test bestowed on everyone equitably in the name of state policy* (Kataoka et al. 1940: 299; emphasis added).

This reasonable desire somehow to protect one's own and one's family's livelihood easily invites fascism, and leads to it. If confined only to oneself or one's family, a shortage of materials would be an unbearable misery. If it were a 'test' visited equitably upon everybody in the name of state policy, and, moreover, a test in a time of emergency in which people had to search for a way to escape from economic deprivation by their own efforts, then people would probably accept it as something 'natural.' Yasuda points out that, in that sense, people's efforts to protect their livelihood and escape from economic deprivation had a correspondence relationship with attunement to fascism.

Miki no doubt was fully aware of the contradictions in 'life in rural villages under the circumstances.' One can view his statement, 'Our lifestyles, which at present have been reduced by necessity, not only must have the opposite effect of giving impetus to new living techniques so that deficiencies are compensated for by the production of new life culture, but also must be made even more abundant' (Miki 1941b [1967]: 397), as having been an expression of the faint hopes he staked on the populace developing an autonomous life culture, amid the unrelenting expansion of the course of the war. The image of the *seikatsusha* was none other than one 'new human typology' that Miki had prepared as a prescription for conquering the 'anxiety' that he had continued to harbour since the Manchurian Incident of 1931, and, further, the start of all-out war between Japan and China in 1937.

Living through the dark valley

In his diary on 1 January 1938, the year after the outbreak of the second Sino-Japanese war, Miki registers the following wishes:

> This year, I would like to shut myself in my study and live a quiet life. I want to make my work in journalism as little as possible, and write good academic books and academic essays. I have to be wary of my tendency to be seduced by others, protect myself more, and have more faith in myself (Miki 1938b [1968]: 180–81).

Far from it bringing Miki back from the world of journalism to his study, however, the year 1938, which he ushered in with the investment of such hopes, conversely became an opportunity to push him out to the forefront of politics. A mere half a year after his new year's diary entry, he had to note as follows:

> There could be all kinds of criticism about what manner of situation gave rise to the action Japan is currently taking on the continent. But time is irreversible, and we cannot pretend that history did not happen. And if events were only of such a scale that we could just be standing by and watching until the end, then it would be all right for us to

remain onlookers, but in cases where they were events of a nature that would have weighty consequences, such as would drag all bystanders willy-nilly along with them, it would not be permissible for us to let them pass only on bygone criticism. *Regardless of how they arose, we must make efforts to find 'historical rationality' within the events that have actually happened* (Miki 1938a [1967]: 143; emphasis added).

One can simultaneously read into this Miki's attitude towards the war and his serious determination. Criticism of the war was forbidden, in terms of thought as well as action. Almost all those in Miki's milieu who were the central actors in thought campaigns or cultural movements critical of the war had been apprehended and thrown in gaol, and stripped of their freedom of expression. Under such circumstances, the only remaining choices were to keep completely silent throughout, or else to go inside the system, attempt a 'meaning-shift about the war,' and explore the risky path of resistance within the regime (Kuno 1967: 588). The one that Miki chose was the latter. The fact of his honoured teacher Heidegger's having joined the Nazi Party also functioned as an important impetus to his decision.

According to Shōzō Fujita, 'resistance' meant fighting with the prevailing spirit that formed the nucleus of the regime (1975: 221). If so, then the only way to carry through one's own ideas would be to push one's way inside the principle upon which the dominant spirit stood, expose the contradictions in the principle itself, and try to implement a shift in its meaning. To 'illuminate the truth by probing into the actual problem and constructing a philosophical concept from that position' appears to have been Miki's consistent problem-consciousness as he lived through the age of the dark valley (Miki 1941c [1968]: 338–339).

In the same year, Miki took part in the 'Shōwa kenkyūkai (Showa research association),' a group for study of national policy established as a 'brains trust' of Prince Fumimaro Konoe, who was in the position of Prime Minister. As the member in charge of the cultural division, Miki endeavoured to give a philosophical basis to the Konoe Cabinet's domestic and foreign policy and create a new meaning for the war, by such means as putting together the theory of an 'East Asian community' in Japanese foreign policy, and a manifesto called 'Shin Nippon no shisō genri (Principles of thought for a new Japan),' in domestic policy. The philosophy of 'co-operativism' which he created, by assuming Japan as the leader in terms of foreign affairs, and the Konoe Cabinet as the leader vis-à-vis domestic issues, turned into something which in principle repudiated the liberation of ethnic groups in Asia on the one hand, and the domestic labour movement, on the other (Miyakawa 2007: 124). At the same time, however, he was also a stout cosmopolitan in the sense that he regarded the doctrine of Japanese supremacy, which lacked self-criticism, as dangerous, and rejected it. His philosophy, which distinctly beats out a 'No' towards totalitarianism and the doctrine of Japanese supremacy from the vantage-point of world history, also had the character of a theory of resistance towards the ultra-nationalism of the military.

Resisting the discourse of national culture

Miki's critique, 'Life culture and living techniques' (1941b), was published after the total collapse of confidence in the Konoe Cabinet that touted the 'new regime,' but about a year before the establishment of the Tōjō Cabinet (in October 1941) and Japan's plunge into the Pacific War (in December of the same year). It was almost becoming obvious that the path of internal resistance to the regime, upon which Miki had wagered, was going to end in defeat. In that midst, he was still speaking of last 'hopes' vis-à-vis people's life culture.

Let us return once more to his life-culture theory. Nazi Germany, Japan's ally at the time, directed deep interest towards the formation of a national culture, and was advocating a nationalistic culturalism that held the spiritual culture of the German people to be supreme. Similarly, a debate aimed at the formation of a national culture was unfolded in Japan, too, by nationalistic polemicists sympathetic to Nazi Germany. A national entertainment discourse and national culture discourse for the elevation of national sentiment had begun to attract attention.

This same period saw the return of Yasunosuke Gonda (1887–1951), who once, as a researcher out of power, had recognised popular entertainment in the Taisho era as being a social reality inseparable from the lifestyle of the common people (*shomin*) under a capitalist system, and had penned the unique volumes, *Minshū goraku mondai* (Problems of popular entertainment) (1921) and *Minshū goraku ron* (Theory of entertainment for the masses)

(1931). Then, in complete contrast, he published 'Minshū goraku no hōkai to kokumin goraku e no junbi (The collapse of popular entertainment and preparations for national entertainment)' (1935) and from then on, he re-emerged in the new guise of a proponent of 'national' entertainment whose task it was to consider 'how best to guide...and control the entertainment lives of the national populace,' towards the 'guiding principle of national life,' namely, carrying the war through to its end (Terade 1982: 178).

'Cultural life' that had lost touch with daily living, and which Miki had contraposed to life culture, was none other than a 'paraphrase' for state-led, nationalistic national culture. One may see it as the most brazen expression he could employ under strict speech control. In opposition to the leadership-centrism and spiritual discourse preached by contemporary vocal proponents of national culture, Miki posed the subjective efforts made by the populace towards lifestyle-remodelling which were supported by spontaneity and rationality, in the form of a life-culture theory.

In regard to entertainment, he euphemistically criticised 'national entertainment' for the elevation of national spirit, and emphasised the value of entertainment in the sense of the populace 'enjoying things that are in their lifestyle' 'in the same manner as their daily meals.' He had not overlooked the situation whereby the notion of *kokumin* (nationals) in *kokumin bunka* (national culture) and *kokumin goraku* (national entertainment) had ended in the slogan 'for [nationals],' and could not extend to culture or entertainment 'made by [nationals].' Shōji Yoshino points out that 'Kiyoshi Miki, the rebellious liberal, probably thought that there was a necessity to rebut their [vocal advocacy of national culture]' (Yoshino 1986: 77).

'Lifestyle' refers to various objective conditions and the subjective business of the common people under such conditions. Miki strove to find a way for the common people to escape attunement to fascism in building their own autonomous lifestyles as far as possible—in short, their own life culture—under the various conditions imposed by the current situation. Alternatively, we could rephrase this as follows: Miki said that the common people would slide into fascism when they each relinquished their adherence to a lifestyle that they ought to protect, and wanted to treasure.

As such, Miki's sense of the times directly leads to that of Yasuji Hanamori in the post-war. In 1948, the third year after Japan had lost the war, Hanamori founded *Kurashi no techō* as a magazine on food, clothing and shelter. The initial intention in its foundation lay in nothing less than Hanamori's deep remorse towards himself for having been with the propaganda division of the Imperial Rule Assistance Association (Taisei yokusankai) during the war, and having waved the banner of waging armed conflict; and the 'memories' of his wartime experiences, having been caught up in war because every member of the populace, including himself, had failed to build a life of their own that they wished to protect.

Neither nationals nor workers

Faced with the perils of the age, the '*seikatsusha*' as a 'new human typology' that Miki had imagined now involved a call to become people of action. At its base lay Miki's deep problem-consciousness that, without an awareness towards 'lifestyle' constituting the space where people live from day to day, and efforts to create culture there, the common people would not be able to resist the trend of the times.

In that sense, in a context dominated by the image of the common people who were lumped together under the nomenclature of 'workers' or 'nationals,' the *seikatsusha* appearing in Miki's life-culture theory cut a remarkably conspicuous figure.

In terms of the work of thinkers, hardly any attempts had hitherto been made to reinterpret the common people as leaders of life culture, and as *seikatsusha* living the reality of Japanese society. According to Tsuneo Yasuda, most Marxists on the one hand had a 'tendency to foist the image of the worker or peasant as an ideal onto the common people of Japan, by relying on literature imported from foreign countries, while attesting to their own "theoretical correctness" by shining light only upon one facet of workers or peasants (the image of the struggling worker, or struggling peasant, for example), on the other' (Yasuda 1987: 284). There, the figure of the common people taking charge of their lifestyle was buried amid the concept of 'class' as a collective representation, and it was not recognised as an individual existence.

Though the common people, under the nomenclature of 'nationals,' were also subjects for waging total war, which was a state objective, they could not be the *seikatsusha* to which Miki refers. This was because nationals were completely incorporated into public life under the National General Mobilisation Act, and hardly anything was left of the part that constituted their quotidian private life.

The perspectives of life culture and *seikatsusha* were the standpoints that Miki, a deeply-committed Marxist, finally discovered while on the one hand maintaining a certain distance from them, and placing himself in the delicate position of attempting internal resistance to the regime, on the other.

Despair and hope

The hope and conviction that, even under objectively desperate conditions, there was likely to be some remaining latitude for people's subjective undertakings, were what comprised Miki's consistently-held view of humanity and the foundation of his philosophical speculation, from his 1926 *Pasukaru ni okeru ningen no kenkyū* (Study of humans in Pascal) to his *Kōsōryoku no ronri* (Logic of conceptual ability), which he started writing in 1937 and continued until 1943.

Human beings are internally torn between the intellectual and the emotional, between logos and pathos, and for that very reason are in the thick of anxiety and agitation. This contradiction that life harbours, this 'anxiety that unavoidably shadows humans due to their being an intermediate existence,' seeks the unification of logos and pathos, and gives rise to subjective and objective action, and that action shapes the self (Karaki 1966:121). The more dangerous a situation the times are experiencing, the more humans as an intermediate existence that acts and shapes itself will seek the fusion of logos and pathos, and continue to shake and question the order of reality, including themselves. Even in an age when irrational pathos prevails, rational logos will always start to look for a new synthesis. The humans whom Miki depicts as intermediaries are beings who confront such times and history, and take them on subjectively. What underlay his image of the *seikatsusha* was just such a view of humanity.

Miki wrote, 'always walking alone seemed somehow to be my destiny,' and he frequently cited the words of Pascal: 'We shall die alone' (1926: 22). Faithful to those words, he breathed his last, all alone, on the wooden floor of the Toyotama Detention Centre, from scabies, malnutrition and insomnia. It was on 26 September, 1945, forty days after the day of Japan's defeat.

Already, the times had begun to say the words '*jiyū* (freedom),' '*minshu* (democracy)' and '*byōdō* (equality),' each composed of two Chinese characters. Without a moment's hesitation, people who until recently had been singing the praises of militarism as the principal of a youth school or as the leader of a factory now touted democracy. This did not, however, lead to the rise of any public pressure or campaign for rescuing Miki, who had been thrown into gaol. In the age of the dark valley of fascism and militarism, Kiyoshi Miki recounted his hopes for active humanity, investing them in his life-culture and *seikatsusha* discourses. What will one draw from the experiences of that age; and how will one incorporate them into the essence of the present-day image of *seikatsusha*?—The meaning of the questions he posed is deep, as will be appreciated from simultaneous examination of his life-culture theory in 'Bunka seisaku ron (On cultural policy)' (Miki 1940a [1967]: 357–375).

The *seikatsusha* of the streets: the world of Itaru Nii

I am one of the common people

In the Suginami Ward Central Library, there is a corner devoted to the works of authors with a deep affinity to Suginami. Lined up amongst volumes by the likes of Masuji Ibuse, Osamu Dazai, Akatsuki Kanbayashi and Tatsuji Miyoshi, there are several books by Itaru Nii. I ask a passing librarian, 'What kind of relationship did Mr Nii have with Suginami Ward?' 'Hmm. If necessary, shall I try looking it up?'

I wonder how many people in Suginami Ward remember that Nii was the first democratically-elected mayor of Suginami in the post-war. Is he someone from so distant a past? It will later become clear that that is not the case. This is because Nii was the person consciously to use the word *seikatsusha*, which was out of step with the mood of the times, and advocate life culture in that connection, in the same age as Miki indirectly discussed the *seikatsusha* in connection with life-culture theory. Nii concludes his 1940 work, *Machi no tetsugaku* (Philosophy of the streets), with the following passage:

> The thought that has been occupying my mind of late concerns the desirable *seikatsusha*. I am thinking of such things as I gaze at the light

outside my window with its greenery. Before [I ponder] what constitutes a person of letters, [I wonder] what a *seikatsusha* is (1940: 406).

Here, the word *seikatsusha* is used in the sense of the 'common people' who have their feet firmly rooted in day-to-day-ness, and not the intelligentsia or the elite.

Unlike Kiyoshi Miki, Nii did not ideologically discuss *seikatsusha* and life culture with the objective of philosophical elucidation of a 'new human typology.' Nor did he approach it from the position of a detached researcher. By shedding light upon the realities that live within the everyday world of nameless people, and by carrying through his desire for freedom in his own life, he endeavoured to explore the identity of the *seikatsusha*. Itaru Nii, who tried not to 'discuss' the *seikatsusha* but to live as one, was—to borrow a phrase from Ryūji Komatsu—a '*seikatsusha* of the streets' (Komatsu 1982: 242).

Kizokujin versus the common people

According to Nii, *seikatsusha* are not '*kizokujin* (people who belong to institutions)' who 'place themselves in government service or major companies or banks.' In other words, they are not 'white-collar salaried workers.' They are people who 'organise and run their own lives themselves.' Compared to *kizokujin* who live under the protection of the system, *seikatsusha* have the power to determine their own lifestyle 'however wretched and transient their lifestyle might be.' They differ from *kizokujin*, whose loyalty to institutions is tested, in that 'though lacking ambition, [*seikatsusha*] have a spirit of independence.'

From this emerges a lucid definition of 'common people,' in other words, *seikatsusha*, as referring to Nii himself. In that aspect, he is an extreme contrast to Kiyoshi Miki, who defined himself as an intellectual, and from first to last took the stance of a torchbearer from his intelligence and conscience as one who did philosophy.

I am no kind of scholar. Nor could I become a scholar, and to become one would be repugnant...to remain a rustic, a man of the streets, from first to last: that is my great ideal (Nii 1940:18).

I am a literary hack. I am the same as a rice-merchant, a fishmonger, or a greengrocer. I may be a more inferior being than they simply because literary hackwork is not a daily necessity, but I am a member of the common people, having them put up with me and getting them to admit me to their circle on the streets. And in that I am trying to forward my own life by my own hand alone, I am at least the same as they (Nii 1941:135).

In that he does not live by labouring, but feeds himself with a single pen, he is nothing more than a literary hack. And as long as he keeps on placing his free self outside the systems called the literary world and the academe, he is also a 'common man.' By thinking thus, Nii gained the necessary foothold for scaling the barrier that was the dichotomy between the intellectual and the 'common man.'

This suggests that, in order to elucidate what Nii was trying to express by the words *seikatsusha* and life culture, one needs to pay attention to his own way of life and living style, rather than to his *seikatsusha* 'theory.'

Nii was a prolific writer. Even the current-affairs critiques and social statements of his which, not having been arranged into a single volume, have been completely forgotten, amount to a prodigious number. While their content is also diverse—ranging from politics, literature and thought to customs, social issues, labour unions and lifestyle co-operatives, and from free love to female suffrage—their writing style is varied, too. Based on the style of personal notes, there are diary-like pieces, travelogues, and ones in the vein of miscellaneous thoughts or short short stories. Consistently sketched there, however, are all kinds of people without titles, as well as the story of the man called 'Itaru Nii,' told through his relationship with them.

They say, 'If one were to ask what constituted Itaru Nii's true worth, it would tell more about him to say 'anything and everything,' rather than to say what it was' (Akiyama 1974: 277). The following epitaph, contributed upon Nii's death by Isaku Nishimura, his friend and President of Bunka Gakuin, is deeply interesting in its confirmation of that.

> I have asked Nii what he was studying and what he was doing. I did not know his occupation, or what he was specialising in. And yet he had a wife, and had raised several children to adulthood. I think that his speciality was anthropology, and his profession the business of humanity. I like that sort of person; I think that experts are mundane,

and that it is valuable for ordinary people to lead fittingly human lives and think fittingly human thoughts (Wamaki 1991: 73).

Based on such multifarious forms of expression that he was said to be 'anything and everything,' and on a philosophy that said it was sufficient to live as an 'ordinary person' and end that way, Nii made continuing inroads into the reality of the lives of the common people.

It was into the late 1930s that Nii began consciously to use the words *seikatsusha* and life culture in his writings as expressions with vital significance. As mentioned in the section on Miki, that age was the one in which a national general mobilisation scheme was established, and everything converged towards a system of all-out war. While forces worked to impel obedience to the will of the state, for Nii, the *seikatsusha* perspective was the last refuge for living without misrepresenting oneself. Embedded within the expression *seikatsusha* was his idea that however temporal circumstances may change, the thing that forms the foundation, what is certain, is the fact that one is living here, right now.

A cheerful anarchist

Nii was born in 1888 in Tokushima Prefecture. One of his cousins was the Christian social activist, Toyohiko Kagawa. For the record, Kagawa had great influence on Nii's consistent involvement in consumer unions and the consumers' co-operatives movement through both the pre-war and war years. It is well-known that, not long after the war, Kagawa proposed the creation of a 'new Japanese union state' through the reorganisation of the neighbourhood associations that had existed during the war into a mutual-aid type of consumer union which would carry out fair production and distribution on a nationwide scale (Tsurumi et al. 1961: 150–151).

Having studied under Kiheiji Onozuka in the Politics Department of Tokyo University's Faculty of Law after attending the Seventh High School in Kagoshima, Nii was called a 'young Kant,' and was expected by those around him to progress along the path to becoming a scholar. One of his classmates was Eijirō Kawai. Personality-wise, however, being a thoroughly free spirit, and extremely disliking being constrained, Nii disdained to be confined by an organisation called a university or a learned society, and entered the world of journalism. Apart from his ten years of life as a reporter, beginning at the Yomiuri newspaper, and his one year somewhat later on as a ward mayor, he lived by his pen in a life unrelated to the world of '*kizokujin* (those-who-belong = salarymen).'

If one were to attach a label to Nii's ideological standpoint, it would probably be 'anarchism.' In actual fact, in the 1920s anarchist–Bolshevik dispute in the realms of literature and art, he sided with the anarchists, and developed an arts theory which argued that literature should not be subordinate to politics.

For Nii, who was not going to acknowledge that state authority was absolute, the state had a light presence. This does not mean that he was a principlistic, stubborn anarchist. In him there is no 'dark' shadow of Russian anarchism from the late nineteenth to the beginning of the twentieth century, nor the bloody shadow of the sort of Japanese-style anarchism that rabidly desired life in nirvana, which was prominent in the 'age of winter' after the Great Treason Incident. To that extent, Nii stood on the side of cheerful, rational, anti-authoritarian, anti-statist thought.

In contrast to one representative Japanese anarchist, Sanshirō Ishikawa, who deeply involved himself in rural villages and farmers' livelihoods, lived a semi-rural life himself in the Tokyo suburbs, and nurtured '*domin shisō* (native thought)' (advocating self-government for farming people) as an ideological practice, Nii loved the freedom of the city and the hubbub of the streets, and his utterances somewhere always were accompanied by a refreshingly unrestrained breath of fresh air. Nii, who would appear in Ginza or Shinjuku with a light heart and spend hour upon end in spirited discussion while enjoying a cup of coffee at a café, even had the nickname of 'salon anarchist.'

The word '*sakei* (left-leaning)' is his neologism. It made its appearance for the first time in his initial book in 1921, *Sakei shichō* (Trends in leftist thought), and amid the sudden rise to power of socialism and the labour movement in the Taisho era, it promptly became a buzzword. Nii's 'kid brother,' Sōichi Ōya, likened Nii to the 'first fruit of the season' (Wamaki 1991: 77), and one can see that Nii was blessed with a keen sense of smell that quickly sniffed out a hidden trend of the times and named it.

What Nii emphasised above all was the mutual relationship between subjects in which each person valued the irreplaceable 'I,' and their autonomous connection in the form of mutual aid by each individual standing on their own worth. In that respect, his 'anarchy' meant not a rejection of politics, but a denial of authority that ignores the intrinsic value lying at the base of the lives of the common people, and imposes state-sponsored values in opposition to it. He did not deny the order in families and communities, but problematised the absence of liberty to criticise that order, or of a free relationship between leaders and members. What was important for him was the freedom for ordinary humans to live life, which took precedence over any kind of state authority.

The fact of Nii's having endeavoured to discover thought within the day-to-day way of life of the common people, and his having consistently involved himself in a practical manner with consumer co-operatives in the post-war, was not unrelated to his unique perspective on anarchism, which took as its basic principle his freedom and mutual solidarity as one such common man.

Culture that life recounts

'Life culture' was the name Nii gave to the 'suitably lifestyle-like lifestyle' of the common people, that is, *'seikatsusha.'* According to him, life culture was the common people's way of living. Culture only begins to live and work when it returns to *seikatsu*—the lifestyle from which it originally sprang. The pattern for each person to make a guide for their own way of living, adjust their course, and relate it to those of other people living side-by-side, constituted what he called life culture. The lifestyle of ordinary, unostentatious common people unconnected with fame, wealth, or position was 'nothing more than monotonous repetition when seen on an individual basis.' The way that the common people each assume responsibility for their livelihood, however, overflows with free and diverse originality and ingenuity.

He cast a critical eye upon the contrasting lifestyle of people who, as *kizokujin*, were of middle-class and above. When, under the slogans of 'You cannot expect to be extravagant' (1939) and 'Luxury is the enemy' (1940) as part of a national spiritual mobilisation campaign, there was an unfolding of state-led calls for lifestyle reform (prohibition of long hair for students, abolition of permanent waves, et cetera) and the New Life Movement (abolition of year-end exchange of gifts and banquets, postponement of tailoring of new clothes, and so on), Nii asserted that the target should not be the lifestyle of the common people, but that of the middle-class and above, who belonged to an 'extraterritoriality club' that stockpiled goods. Nii was also critical of the command to 'sacrifice oneself for the nation (*messhi bōkō*),' suggesting that the ones to whom 'the day's urgent business was to clarify the notion of public versus private' applied were the public officials who nonchalantly used the public office telephone for private calls, or wrote private correspondence on official stationery (Nii 1943: 286).

He also aimed critical arrows at the 'neighbourhood associations (*tonarigumi*)' which characterised daily life under the wartime regime. The *tonarigumi* system is considered to have been proposed to the mayor of Tokyo in 1938 by Noboru Tanikawa, head of the City of Tokyo's ward administration section, taking a hint from the Edo-period system of '*gonin-gumi* (groups of five household heads)' and from the neighbourhood voluntary mutual-aid organisations conceived by Sontoku Ninomiya (1787–1856) in the late Tokugawa period (Tsurumi 1982: 171).

Though the neighbourhood voluntary mutual-aid aspect of the latter was not implemented, the *tonarigumi* system of the time, planned and established in 1940 as an apparatus of the Imperial Rule Assistance Association, had the twin aims of 'top-down,' that is, conveying the will of the governing to the governed, and 'bottom-up.' For that very reason, it gained people's widespread, spontaneous support in its early stages, but, in reality, it was organised to overlap with bureaucracy, and government officials and military personnel consequently controlled people's personal lives down to the last detail, and it grew into a thoroughly 'top-down' organ that ensnared the populace in a war involving the whole nation.

At the point when the *tonarigumi* system was proposed, Nii seems already to have spotted such limitations, and have seen through the character of the all-out-war regime. He asserted that such things as '*tonarigumi* or *chōkai* (town block associations)' should not be made to carry political significance. They only gained a *raison d'être* by becoming simply the basis for 'co-operation for mutual economic assistance,' a 'symphony of civic life' (Nii 1941: 86).

Intensification of the controlled economy and shortages of goods spawned fine opportunities for black-marketeering and profiteering. The egoism that kept secret the black-market route for supplies occupied a central place in people's lifestyle-consciousness in this period. If, as Nii had proposed, the *tonarigumi* system in those times had functioned in a lively manner as a space for exchange of goods and information necessary for people's mutual livelihood, without state direction, then it could truly have been called a cultural revolution.

In that sense, his life-culture theory was a criticism of moves by the government and military to fit the lifestyles of the common people into a frame, through a New Life Campaign that was akin to state policy. Under severe regulation of thought, Nii, in the same way as Miki, also tried to resist the state-policy-like New Life Campaign by advocating the necessity of culturedness (originality and cooperativity with neighbours).

The wisdom of the common people

At the base of Nii's life-culture theory, there lies a feeling of fellowship with the common people, and an unrestrained, affirmative and optimistic view of humanity in their regard.

Nii had the routine of going out into the streets almost every day. 'The streets are carpeted with lessons to learn.' When municipal assembly elections were looming, the slogan '*Kiyoku, tadashiku, kiken sezu* ([Vote] cleanly, correctly, and without abstaining)' blanketed the district. Why, then, in spite of that, were the common people 'indifferent' to elections? Why were the amusement quarters so bustling? Why was there more vomit? Why were there more accordion-players in the wining-and-dining streets? As he strolled around the town, Nii kept his ears open, observed, and pondered, discovering the common people's 'nonchalant' way of living within such urban phenomena, and identifying their negative resistance towards the worsening of living conditions under the wartime regime. He even said that 'now that today has come, there is need for a new nonchalance' (Nii 1940: 89).

In an age when everything was on a ration-voucher system, the common people had an unending struggle over 'lifestyle.' 'There are contradictions, there is irrationality, there is selfishness, there is egotism, and there are things such as misunderstandings, distortions, suspicion, jealousy, envy, anger and quarrels'—that is how common people's lives are, says Nii (1941: 139). Yet there is self-moderation and order. Unlike *kizokujin*, the common people, not being protected by the system, have to make decisions about and take responsibility for their own lives. Because there is a need for mutual aid between themselves and others with whom they live side-by-side, they cannot unendingly pursue their self-interest. The common people have uncertainty over their livelihood, which makes it all the easier for them to gain 'wisdom' to do with living, Nii observes (1941: 139).

Creation of an image of the future

One other feature of Nii's life-culture theory lies in its anti-centrist orientation. For Nii, it was small localities like villages and city wards and their life culture that deserved attention and expression. Localities are not things that gain a *raison d'être* by being connected to the centre. They are open towards the world because they have concreteness and identity as spaces where people live their daily lives. Such assertions go on to link directly to the idea of now so-called 'decentralisation of authority,' or rather 'regional sovereignty.'

On the other hand, politicians pride themselves on always aiming for the centre, drawing nearer to the centre, and having a wider area as their electoral turf, and they take a centrist stance. They strive to ascend from the bottom up in a hierarchy with the emperor at its pinnacle, down through elder statesmen, cabinet ministers, members of the House of Peers, members of the House of Representatives, prefectural assembly members, city councillors, to members of ward assemblies (or town block associations). It can be seen from Nii's post-war footsteps that he took a standpoint very far removed from that. Even with the onslaught of the mighty swell of democratisation after the war, Nii had no need to hide or alter his own pre-war and wartime tracks, unlike the majority of other cultural figures. After having declined a membership invitation from Dai-Nippon genron hōkoku kai (Great Japan patriotic journalism society), which was a state-policy body of journalists during the war, he writes as follows:

> I consider that participation in political trends belongs outside [my] limits, and that to rank among ordinary citizens is more fitting to my station than to hobnob with all the dignitaries in society. But citizens' philosophy, however modest, has a human flavour, and is something preferable (Nii 1940: 375).

When the war showed deepening signs of defeat, Nii avoided Tokyo with its strict control of speech, and evacuated to Izu to divide his time between working in the fields in fine weather and reading when it rained. Renting a small, abandoned temple, he wrote 'Kōgakuan (Hermitage for scholarly contemplation)' on a piece of board and hung it at the gate; and when he tired of reading, he would cultivate some wasteland in a bamboo thicket and plant sweet potatoes, and visit farm-houses to have a chat—such was his daily routine. For the record, as he had all but ceased writing, seeing that he had not changed his pacifist principles, he only had thirty yen in the currency of the day to live on each month. After the defeat, when he returned home from his place of evacuation looking thin and wasted, he apparently shocked his family and acquaintances.

Nii's having thus kept his pacifist stance, not having curried favour with the military, and having abided by his perspective and position as a *'seikatsusha* of the streets' until the bitter end made the impact of the defeat a small one. He makes clear his own continuity of thought in an appendix to his 1948 translation of Carl Friedrich's *The New Belief in the Common Man* (1942).

Amid the poverty following defeat, in an age when the shape of the future was strongly sought, utopian concepts were being explored in a variety of localities. In areas within the Japanese archipelago where self-sufficiency was possible, such as Hokkaido, Shikoku and Kyushu, there was even talk of dreams of secession from the state (Tsurumi et al. 1961: 100). In such a mood of the times, for Nii, too, democracy signified not a word but a revolution in ways of thinking and behaving, a cultural revolution—and, first of all, his own cultural revolution.

The world's Suginami Ward

Having stood as a candidate for the mayoralty of Suginami Ward and become Japan's first popularly-elected ward mayor in April 1947, Nii issued specifications upon his assumption of office to the effect that he wanted to make Suginami Ward not one part of metropolitan Tokyo or the Japanese state, but a similar kind of cultural community as Weimar in the days when Goethe was Privy Councillor. In it is clearly laid out an aspiration to reinterpret the small locality called Suginami Ward as an area freed from the conventional framework of 'region' as opposed to 'centre,' and one which has a cultural universality linked to the world.

> I dislike flimsy, cheap, no-fuss types of plans. I think that it would be better to have none at all than to have such a one, because the half-baked and the make-do are the enemies of culture. Prices need campaigns to bring them down, but in the case of culture, it is important to have campaigns to elevate it as far as it will go. Culture in the post-war has deteriorated markedly. We must not allow that to continue. My culture plans are none other than a campaign to elevate culture. I want to make the area we inhabit into one imbued with the fragrance of the arts (Nii 1975: 110).

His dream to make 'the world's Suginami Ward' had no bounds—art galleries surrounded by greenery, cultural centres for enjoyment of music and theatre, libraries where people could casually stop by, station plazas as speakers' corners, agricultural land where urban *seikatsusha* could appreciate nature, streets afloat with the scent of tulips. Yet at the same time, his vision was truly concrete.

His cultural revolution soon began. Shouldering a placard that said: 'Contact Person for Suginami Ward Office,' out would go Nii into the streets, wearing a tatty old deerstalker hat, asking people if they had any requests. The Ward Mayor's seat was virtually a reception desk. 'As he would report to work every day looking like a local fishmonger or something,' everyone could feel comfortable bringing their own problems into the mayor's office. In place of framed calligraphy by a politician bearing the words '*Shisei hōkō* (Sincere devotion),' he hung a painting of a female nude by Ryūzaburō Umehara. A Nii constitution was created and strictly observed: however esteemed the officials who came from the metropolitan government office, Nii entertained them with nothing more than a cup of tea and a snack. Nii himself was not a drinker, but he was a person who could spend hour after hour in discussion while munching on fresh Japanese sweets, becoming intoxicated on the atmosphere just as if he were a drinker. On Saturdays, he would bring a hoe on his shoulder from home, and drop by his field on the way back from the ward office. When he felt like it, he would head for a dance hall in Ginza, in the same garb.

A sower of seeds

This unconventional ward mayor, who himself appeared posing as the protagonist in Courteline's novel *Le commissaire est bon enfant* (The commissioner is a good guy), was inevitably frustrated after only a year in office. Nii was a totally 'unconventional' mayor in the eyes of the ward officials, who thought that suitably mayor-like mayors were those who exerted themselves in 'having an understanding' with local bosses and central officials; who poured their energy into reaching agreement with the ward assembly; who prided themselves on winning even a little larger budget than other wards; and who wined and dined on a daily basis one way or another. And it was not only the ward officials, either. When Nii came into contact with his 'beloved' common people, too, in a relationship of mayor to constituents, what was revealed in them was a disposition sensitive only to their own interest, which Nii found hard to reconcile. He is said to have recollected to someone close to him: 'I wonder if the *minshū* (populace) which I have in mind only exists in the ideal' (Nii 1975: 280).

It is hard to say that Nii had a sufficient sense of direction and concrete strategy to bring forth a new quality of politics and make it bear fruit, while confronting the concrete realities of the locality in the thick of the 'old' local interpersonal relationships and administrative structure, while bringing these into the picture, too. The 'sower of seeds,' as he dubbed himself, did sow seeds, but in terms of a concrete methodology for raising them, he was far more of an idealist than he was a politician. Therein lies his deep tragedy.

Nii transcended Miki's conceptual *seikatsusha* theory by definitively establishing '*seikatsusha*' not as intellectuals or the elite, nor as middle-class, but as 'the common people' who had the roots of their livelihood even further down. At the same time, though, he shares common ground with Miki in having emphasised life culture as common people's originality, nurtured in the family and subregion, and strove to see the figure of the *seikatsusha* among people who distanced themselves to a certain extent from the lifestyle framed as national policy under the strict wartime regime.

In 1951, three years after vacating the seat of ward mayor, Nii passed away. His dogma of linking with the world by means of his subregional cultural revolution temporarily lost its sparkle. Now, however, the local utopia for which he forever hoped appears to be being drawn up into the 'local' emphasis of the Seikatsu Club, which I shall discuss later, and into their idea and activities of 'cooperative' action.

2 Towards a post-war departure

A dialogue with 'ways of living': the life-culture theories of Wajirō Kon

From attention on 'lifestyle'

The age called the post-war was one that offered the Japanese an unparalleled opportunity to look squarely at 'lifestyles.' It was a time when people fought and quarrelled fiercely over their 'living.' In the cities, several households-worth of families lived cheek-by-jowl in houses that had escaped war damage, and it was hard to meet even their daily needs in life. It was an age when everyone in their own way experienced the pain and the pleasure of what constituted 'a livelihood.'

As children trained their eye to discern which wild plants were edible and mothers made efforts to obtain food to fill their families' stomachs, they learned the difference in exchange value of those respective articles. Amidst the cries for democratisation, they playfully distorted the English word 'democracy (*demokurashī*)' into expressions like '*demo kurushii* (but it is painful)' or 'but [what about] the livelihood? (*demo kurashi*),' and a determination to look obliquely at their extremely reduced circumstances and laugh them away was born. For the Japanese, the decade or so from the end of the war until the mid-1950s arguably was the age of '*seikatsu* (life)' in its simplest and strictest sense.

Moreover, it was in that age that another unique life-culture discourse by Wajirō Kon (1888–1973), who built the foundations of modernology and lifeology, made its entrance.

In 1948, the third year since Japan's defeat, Wajirō Kon was in charge of lectures entitled 'Life-culture Theory' at the evening division of a certain technical college. It was a boys' school with three-year courses in the social sciences. There were many ambitious students with the desire for upward mobility who were aiming at politics or business. Faced with a class of three or four hundred students who had finished their daytime jobs and ridden a crowded train to the school, Kon started his first lecture in the following manner:

> If in future you are going to become a Diet member or a village mayor, don't you think that the issue of the lifestyle of the national or regional populace is one of today's most significant issues? And it won't do to suggest leaving it up to the female parliamentarians. Still, until this day, you probably have never had the opportunity in any school to learn about things like the nation's food, clothing, and shelter…The question of whether that will do is my primary motivation for starting these lectures. In terms of a daily routine familiar to you, say, for example, you are in your room at a boarding-house—whatever kind of life do you lead there? …You frequently encounter the opportunity to sense and think that if only things were a little more something-or-other, or if you did such-and-such, don't you? In actuality, every member of the nation is being made to feel such things acutely day after day. The plea for someone to do something about today's livelihood is a cry from every citizen's heart of hearts (Kon 1949a [1971]: 43–44).

Whatever the case, Kon apparently never shouted eager assertions. For that reason, the spirit that Kon poured into his life-culture theories comes across all the more strongly from surviving transcripts of his lectures in oratorical style. Here, 'life-culture (*seikatsu bunka*)' is alluded to merely by the ambiguous expression 'food, clothing and shelter.' What is important, though, is that Kon enthusiastically employed the word 'life-culture' when confronting those male students to explain that problems related to living, namely those of food, clothing and shelter, were at the foundation of politics and economics, and that everything began with attention to and recognition of that fact; and especially that it was of utmost importance to wake up to the enormous significance that the reality called 'living (*seikatsu*)' had, and to investigate that *seikatsu*.

The starting-point of democracy

In those times, many Japanese, including politicians and intellectuals, were busy 'discussing' democracy. Certainly, for post-war Japan, the building of a democratic society would have been more important than anything else. The majority of such discussions, however, was limited to abstract theories in law or politics about democratisation. In their midst there were also advocates of democracy such as Takeyoshi Kawashima, author of a 1946 paper, 'Nihon shakai no kazoku-teki kōsei (The family-like composition of Japanese society).' Based on his own experiences as an evacuee in a rural village from wartime through to the post-war, Kawashima critically scrutinised the traditional family system that had supported the fundamental character of Japanese people's lifestyle, concretely questioning its relationship with the principles of democracy, and preaching its full-scale denial. Such advocates were few in number, however.

In Kon's view, democracy was not a political or economic issue, but above all one of a way of 'living,' and furthermore was not something to 'discuss,' but something that meant precisely a 'revolution' in lifestyle. He thought that, in order to press democratisation forward, it was important first for the Japanese each to confront the reality of their distressed lifestyle, redefine their own lifestyle, and to get on with the job of drawing new meaning from it. In a piece called 'Seikatsu no kakumei (A lifestyle revolution),' Kon speaks as follows:

> We have now come face-to-face with a predicament where we must embark in earnest on a lifestyle revolution. Without that being undertaken, no matter how well-ordered the political mechanism might have become, if politics and lifestyle are not completely integrated, then a desirable world will not burgeon as something that is alive. This is because unless politics and lifestyle, and the external and the internal, are not ordered according to the same concept and the same tone, nothing but renewed abjectness and fresh contradictions can be expected to eventuate (1947a [1971]: 50).

For Kon, a 'lifestyle revolution' did not mean giving a negative interpretation to everything in the poverty-stricken life of wartime and post-war Japan. He tells of the importance of having a new appreciation of the positive lifestyle aspects deriving from material shortages: straightforwardness, simplicity and rationality; and of sifting through, sorting out and reselecting the bundle of customs relating to one's way of living—including associating with neighbours, welcoming guests, and exchanging gifts—according to the criterion of need vis-à-vis one's own lifestyle.

While most scholars and intellectuals, as if in a kind of avalanche phenomenon, regarded Japanese people's lives in a negative light as being 'warped' or 'retarded' from a modernist viewpoint, Kon clearly took a different position. He did not unconditionally reject the traditions of people's way of living, but by revisiting them and reconfirming their necessity, he strove to explore the possibility of reassembling and remoulding Japanese people's lives and Japanese society.

The phenomenology of peripatetic scholars

In September 1923, when Tokyo turned to burnt-out ruins due to the Great Kantō Earthquake, Wajirō Kon, shod in *jikatabi* (construction-workers' typical footwear), with sketchbook in hand, and accompanied by his pupils, walked around the disaster-hit areas. For the record, the thirty-five-year-old Kon's outfit, namely an undershirt-type top and the split-toed, rubber-soled cloth shoes called *jikatabi* (later replaced by canvas shoes), subsequently became his trademark. Whether at a party held by some embassy or at an academic conference venue, his casual style, consisting of no necktie, an undershirt-like top and canvas shoes, was a familiar sight.

In such a style as Kon's, it is not hard to find the archetype of the style common to 'peripatetic scholars' including the folklorist Tsunekazu Miyamoto (1907–81) or Yoshiyuki Tsurumi (1926–94), a scholar of South-East Asia. In a similar manner to Miyamoto, who noted having notched up 273 days of travel in his most prolific year, Kon also often strolled urban streets and rural villages, with the method of walking field-sites on his own two feet as his motto.

Kon's style differed greatly from the formal outfit of his teacher, Kunio Yanagida, in his 'crested *haori* jacket, *hakama* trousers and white *tabi* socks.' Rather, it was close to the travelling garb of the ethnographer Tsuneichi Miyamoto, twenty-six Kon's junior, with his 'staple fibre jacket, corduroy trousers, gaiters, canvas shoes, black fedora, grubby rucksack and black umbrella hanging from its sling.' For the record, after his graduation from Tokyo School of Fine Arts, Kon had knocked at Kunio Yanagida's door, receiving instruction from him and undertaking the collection of materials from an old folk dwelling. Kon's deep interest in dwellings as life-sites is presumed to have emerged from his experience of collating data from this old residence.

Similarly, as ethnographers, both Yanagida and Miyamoto were constantly travelling. Norio Akasaka says, however, that their journeys were decidedly different in atmosphere, as were their travel preparations. Most of Yanagida's journeys combined observation with a lecture tour as an official. By contrast, Miyamoto, in his 'penniless-looking' travel garb, had not a single title worthy of the name. All he had was the fact that he was 'a farmer from Ōshima, Yamaguchi Prefecture,' and when he said that, people would open their hearts to him (Akasaka 1995: 19). Miyamoto, who claimed he was often mistaken for a Toyama medicine-peddler, writes: 'I was comfortable cutting such a penniless-looking figure; and the people with whom I came into contact were also at ease' (Miyamoto 1971: 215).

The travel outfit of Yoshiyuki Tsurumi—who says that he hardly used any source materials apart from Tsuneichi Miyamoto's *Wasurerareta Nihonjin* (The forgotten Japanese), and maps of South-East Asia and Japan in his lectures at Kyoto's Ryūkoku University— seems to overlap that of Miyamoto. Clad in a light jacket, jeans or shorts, canvas shoes and a hat, Tsurumi's field-survey style was to 'walk, look, listen,' as well as to take detailed field notes every day. It is still recent memory how he focused attention on things familiar to the Japanese such as bananas, prawns and sea cucumbers, and blazed an imagined trail for reading South-East Asia.

Amateur collectors

To return to Wajirō Kon: the shacks that people who had been burnt out of their homes built by gathering up sheets of corrugated metal and pieces of wood as they pleased, to keep out the rain and dew after the Great Kanto Earthquake, are preserved in Kon's sketchbook. Among them, there is even a hut put together from wooden grave tablets picked up from a temple graveyard. The age of those shacks soon ended, and what appeared next were barracks. Though arguably somewhat better than the huts, these were truly crude structures in terms of places to live. Soon, however, former merchant houses began to be rebuilt in smart, Western-style guise amid those barrack communities, too. What Kon saw in the burnt ruins was people's hardship that was staked on their change of residence, their robustness in rebounding from that and making efforts in pursuit of a better lifestyle, and, furthermore, the brimming energy of those who, in a constant quest for 'newness,' continued to transform their current situation. The result of Kon's 'research,' in which he diligently sketched the process whereby homes changed from being burnt corrugated metal to barracks, and then to modern buildings, and made a collection of them, later went on to bear fruit as modernology. Kon explains the origin of its nomenclature by saying that if interrogation of antiquity by studying ruins and artefacts from the past constitutes archaeology, then modernology is a discipline that considers the 'modern' from people's 'lifestyle gestures,' namely the lifestyle commodities (food, clothing and shelter) and customs that are so new that they have not yet been recorded.

As previously mentioned, Kon did not totally deny all of the traditional aspects of people's livelihood. At the same time, though, he always kept a curious eye on the changes that were taking place in front of him. Not being satisfied with the shape of the conventional world of architecture which called for degrees of completion over adventure, Kon perceived within those things that were constantly changing a will to live from people who were sensitive to newness and fashions. In later years, in answer to disputants who interpreted fashions negatively as being expressions of the vanity hidden in the hearts of people unwilling to fall behind others, Kon wrote on trends (*ryūkōron*) (1959), stating flatly that fashions were things which were an expression of people's life ambitions and consciousness of the times, and not things to despise.

The technique of what Kon called modernology is an amateur collector's methodology, close to the enumerative methods of natural historians who venture out into the fields with butterfly net and botanical specimen case and go around collecting every last thing that catches their interest. It involves collecting, organising and analysing the 'external forms' that are visible to the naked eye, from people's clothing and hairstyles to their belongings, ways of walking and sitting, detailed physical habits and so on. Kon's idea was that only through these things would it be possible to explore the interior of people's morals and consciousness of the times which lay at the root of people's lives.

In *Seikatsu bunka ron e no shōtai* (An invitation to theories of life-culture), Kōji Terade points out that Kunio Yanagida's folklorist methodology basically entails endeavouring to close in upon 'the heart' through the collection of things written in 'words' (1994: 117).

What is important, according to Terade, is that gathering 'things' by means of one's 'eyes' is a far easier method to master for amateur collectors than collecting by means of 'words.' This can also be appreciated from the fact that participants in these modernology surveys included not only scholars but also numerous amateurs such as students from Motoko Hani's Jiyū Gakuen (Freedom School) and readers of her magazine *Fujin no tomo* (Women's companion). They keep on collecting things and events of interest with their own eyes as a starting-point, without presupposing a cumbersome conceptual framework. From that practice, the unconsciously overlooked realities of their own livelihood become visible. To borrow Kōji Terade's words again, modernology was 'none other than a "study in self-acknowledgement" enabling people to keep firm hold of their own violently-changing lives with their own hands' (1994: 117).

Dwellings are a way of living

Just as modernology was born from the blackened ruins of the Great Kanto Earthquake, Kon's lifeology, too, was spawned from a spotlight on the facts of the concrete 'lifestyles' of people living through the post-war period of turmoil. Both modernology and lifeology focused attention upon the lives of people who robustly survived the Great Kanto Earthquake and the pre- and post-defeat period of confusion, and were born with the support of Kon's realistic problem-consciousness which strove to find a path towards restoration and regeneration there. Lifeology made its start from the observation and recording of facts connected to 'lifestyles,' such as how a certain household's living schedule differed between summer and winter, or what kind of action a housewife in a farming family took at breakfast-time. Kon's initial use of the word 'lifeology' was in a 1951 newspaper article entitled: 'Seikatsugaku e no kūsō (Musings on lifeology).'

> So, I start wanting to envision a new sort of lifeology which, by *starting absolutely afresh from the question of what entertainment means*, continuously re-examines what relaxation means, what work means, and so on; and scientifically studies and philosophises as to how they are intertwined, and pursues and orders such forms as food, clothing and shelter which constitute the material aspects of life so that they can be controlled by those means, thus enabling their delineation (Kon 1951 [1971]: 17, emphasis added).

Terade points out that Kon's aim in advocating lifeology is symbolically illustrated by the phrase, 'starting...from the question of what entertainment means' (1994: 127). This is because a new conception is alive there, the kind that endeavours to force a Copernican transformation in the basic standpoint of orthodox life research which approached life from the perspective of reproduction of the workforce; and strives to understand lifestyles in a more comprehensive manner, from the aspect of the non-work domains of entertainment and relaxation.

Life research in Japan was begun and developed in the period from the second Sino-Japanese war through to the Pacific War as studies on national life—in specific terms, as economic research on poverty, and on the minimum cost of living, in social policy theory. Work such as Junzō Nagano's *Kokumin seikatsu no bunseki* (Analysis of national life) (1939), for a start, and that of Kazuo Ōkōchi, Keizō Fujibayashi and Takashi Kagoyama, fall into this category.

These studies did not always look at things from the same research angle. They did, however, have points in common, namely their attempts to apprehend the financial difficulties in national life caused by soaring retail prices during wartime and the deterioration in bodily posture brought about by the extension of working hours that accompanied the intensification of production—not as individual, private issues, but as questions of the reproduction of the workforce in connection with working life. The principal question there was what constituted the conditions for enabling the reproduction of the workforce, with consideration as to 'lifestyle' also mainly being undertaken from the perspective of the consumption of the workforce = the process of capital production; and this was not something which sufficiently embraced the very life-process of the workers themselves.

In *Seikatsugaku no teishō* (Advocating lifeology), Noboru Kawazoe positioned Kon's lifeology, which the latter began 'absolutely afresh from the question of what entertainment means,' as a proposition from 'a standpoint from the flip-side of conventional scholarship, one that turns it on its head, so to speak' (Kawazoe 1982: 188); and that, as Kōji Terade notes, was certainly no exaggeration.

The actual idea of Kon's lifeology had already clearly appeared in papers entitled 'Jūseikatsu (Dwelling life),' published in 1945, just before the war's end, and 'Hito no sumu jūkyo (Houses where people live),' written in 1946, immediately after the defeat. In these papers, Kon pointed out firstly that dwellings have a base-like element which encompasses all lifestyle aspects such as rest, entertainment, social interaction and housework; and secondly, that they are intimately connected to the lifestyle, consciousness and feelings of the people who live in them, commensurate with their social stratum. Here, one can see Kon's fundamental way of thinking, namely that 'dwellings are a way of living.'

For coalmine workers, for example, a dwelling is literally a place of rest. What is important is primarily a spacious, uncomplicated room layout rather than such interior decoration as intricate work on walls and fittings or delicacy of colouration. By contrast, in the case of people engaged in 'brainwork,' rather than the spaciousness of the dwelling, it is such details as the craftsmanship of the walls and fittings, the changes of light, and the colour of curtains and floor-coverings that have a great influence upon their mental and physical tranquillity. The view is emphasised there that even though these both constitute places for rest, the difference in housing conditions must be determined according to the inhabitants' respective 'lifestyles.'

Kon says that in order to understand dwellings, one must first gain a comprehensive grasp of 'lifestyle' itself. There, one can see the fundamental idea of lifeology, which endeavours to separate the realities of 'lifestyle' into its various elements and aspects, to compartmentalise and capture them; and which does not peg 'labour' as the starting-point for apprehending 'lifestyle,' but strives to understand the abundant integrity that 'lifestyle' itself intrinsically possesses, on its own terms.

Moreover, Kon's life-culture theories eventually formed the basis for this lifeology.

Lifestyle as a 'macrocosm'

It is in Kon's paper, 'Seikatsu no kōzō (The structure of lifestyles)' (1947b) written en route from his 'Dwelling life' and 'Houses where people live' to his ultimate 'Musings on lifeology,' that the framework of his life-culture theories is clearly shown. There, Kon deems the four elements of work, rest, entertainment, and 'cultivation (kyōyō)' to be the basic elements comprising a 'lifestyle,' and he defines a lifestyle as consisting of the interconnection of these elements. In other words, a lifestyle in that context is seen as a 'macrocosm of activities' that is not restricted to activities for the maintenance of life in a biological dimension (the reproduction of the workforce), but extends even to leisure- and spiritual activities.

Nowadays, a way of understanding life that views it comprehensively is taken for granted. As already mentioned, however, most of the life research prior to Wajirō Kon interpreted human lifestyles only from the perspective of the workforce and its reproduction, and it was usual for such studies to approach from fields like social policy or economics. There are times in human lives when they are 'absentmindedly' doing nothing. Spending time 'absentmindedly,' in the sense of enjoying it for its own sake, might include entertainment-like elements peculiar to the person in question. Yet from the vantage point of economics and social policy studies, this will be positioned as preparatory action for working, or as rest-like behaviour. There, even human action that does not fall into a particular category is understood to be embedded in the framework comprising the workforce and its cycle of reproduction.

By contrast, Kon thought it necessary to interpret a life domain such as cultivation, entertainment or rest as something that had intrinsic meaning in itself which transcended the function of reproducing the workforce. He also considered that one should, conversely, shine new light upon the meaning of work from the viewpoint of entertainment and spiritual fulfilment.

Kon's way of thinking, which sought to grasp life in its totality, was later further deepened, and in 1949, his paper, 'Seikatsu no bunkateki dankai (The cultural stages of living)' was penned (Kon 1949b [1971]: 23–27). In it, 'life' is classified into the following three stages:
- The first stage: a life revolving only around work and rest
- The second stage: a life revolving around work and rest, with the addition of entertainment
- The third stage: a life revolving around work, rest and entertainment, with the addition of cultivation

In this paper, Kon points out that it is only in the second stage, when work and rest are guaranteed, that the primary cultural need (= primary life-culture) called 'entertainment' makes an appearance; and further, in the third stage, where work, rest and entertainment are guaranteed, the secondary cultural need (= secondary life-culture) called 'cultivation' appears; and he deemed the third stage, which has the addition of 'cultivation,' meaning logicality and sensibility, as being the level of 'an ideal life.'

His argument, namely that after 'survival needs' are satisfied, 'cultural needs' come into being in this way, can be seen as having pre-empted—rather than being a Japanese version of—A.H. Maslow's Hierarchy of Human Needs (1954), in which only after the satisfaction of lower-order needs (hunger, thirst, safety) can higher needs (esteem and self-actualisation) appear.

Kon's assertion that people can only qualify as creators of culture when entertainment and cultivation are guaranteed in their lives was something launched from the then-current reality of deprivation in the lives of workers who were pushed down to the very edge of survival amid inflation and unemployment caused by bankruptcy, as well as material shortages and population increase. People tried to survive by evading death from starvation or malnutrition by sacrificing their enjoyment of entertainment and spiritual 'luxuries.' For Kon, the problem was not economic 'poverty,' but want of a 'lifestyle' as a macrocosm which poverty brought about; and his lifeology proposal to start 'absolutely afresh from the question of what entertainment means' was something rooted in the reality of such workers.

From 'living' to a 'way of life'

Kon divided life-culture into primary and secondary stages, and deemed the latter to be life-culture in its original sense. He says that this life-culture in a narrow sense is one which only comes into being when the needs for rest and entertainment are satisfied. Even here, there is no clear-cut definition as to that life-culture. His particular methodology lay in how Kon puts himself in that position, thinks, and uses language more closely aligned with everyday life rather than defining the concept he uses and developing a systematic lifestyle theory.

Kon is thought to have used the word 'cultivation (*kyōyō*)' as something with the same meaning as 'life-culture.' His 'cultivation' meant culture spawned from the midst of living, such as the way to use money in the family budget, or how to use goods effectively (in the consumption process), for example. When one is making desperate efforts to fulfil the most basic needs of working, eating and sleeping, the use of money and the way to consume goods are predetermined. There is no margin for pondering ways of consuming goods to suit one's own style, or suchlike. Only when the material conditions necessary for survival are met can people's thoughts turn to their own particular mode of consumption, and have the leeway to make a choice. Life-culture is something that is progressively formed as intangible stock through such ways of consuming goods and enjoyment, and the way that people make good use of things shapes individuality in lifestyle.

By establishing 'stages' from a lower-order to a higher-order lifestyle in this manner, Kon suggested the necessity for a life-culture that comprised 'quality' of life for workers, and, by that avenue, attempted indirectly to access workers' lifestyle issues. This vastly differed from the then-current dominant approach to workers' lifestyle problems, which emphasised above all the securing of working conditions and the guaranteeing of a minimum standard of living.

Kon also directed his concern towards the question of the formation of people with the capability to apprehend the totality inherent in a lifestyle, in a self-aware manner. One of his papers written in 1956 is 'Seikatsu ni okeru kokoro to mono (The heart and goods in lifestyles).' According to that paper, lifeology is the study of consumption, but is not a discipline that simply aims to analyse the consumption of goods. Kon says that it is the 'study of consumption in human life' which pursues the relationship between people, who are the consuming subjects, and the things that are consumed. He claims that the lifestyle-consciousness of the people who use them (their cultivation or life-culture) is projected in goods, which are one configuration of material culture (Kon 1956 [1971]: 64–74).

In that paper, there is emphasis on a positive stance towards people's lifestyle and its practical workability, such as doubts over a stereotypical lifestyle, and a consciousness of 'wanting to make their lifestyle into something better.' His idea that life-culture is rooted, above all, in people's spontaneous desire and activity towards 'making their lifestyle into something better,' automatically led to theories on the improvement of living conditions.

In a paper entitled: 'Seikatsu kaizen ni tsuite (On improvement of living conditions),' Kon writes:

> When people have the desire to make their lives into something better, out of a self-awareness of wanting to respect and take care of themselves, and that is expressed as action to any extent, that will mean that the germ of life-improvement has been seen (1963 [1971]: 492).

The actors in life-culture, which was rooted in people's 'self-awareness of wanting to respect and take care of themselves,' and people as the subjects in the improvement of living conditions—they were where Kon sought to find the '*seikatsusha*.' The uniqueness of Kon's life-culture discourse lies in his having grasped *seikatsu* (life) as a macrocosm of all activity, his questioning of the quality of life not as 'the fact of being alive,' but as 'a way of living,' and his having preached the raising of workers' impoverished lifestyle to a life-process that included entertainment and cultivation.

Along with the end of the post-war '*seikatsu*' times, people stopped paying attention to and exploring '*seikatsu*' just as if there had been no such thing as the age of '*seikatsu*.' Then, onwards towards the present, via the period of high economic growth—people in a time of the 'all-Japanese-are-middle-class mentality' are living life surrounded by material things, as if there never was an age when food was given precedence over clothing or shelter, let alone things like friendship or loyalty. If that be the case, then that might be all the more reason for us now to return to the starting-point of the life-culture discourse and re-interrogate it in order to resurrect the dimension of abundance that '*seikatsu*' once had.

Seikatsusha ideology: 'Science of thought' and 'the people's philosophy'

A Copernican transformation in philosophy

The same period when Wajirō Kon was zealously expounding his life-culture theories and trying to see the *seikatsusha* in its bearers saw the beginnings of the birth of research into 'the people's philosophy,' which strove to discover the power of thought within the lives of nameless people who were no specialists in speculation. This constituted the Shisō no kagaku kenkyūkai (Institute for the science of thought) founded in May 1946 (hereafter abbreviated to Science of thought), a study circle focusing on a journal with the same name.

According to the fourth inaugural issue of *Shisō no kagaku* (publishers having changed several times), it was not until 1959, thirteen years later, that 'Science of thought' was to use the word '*seikatsusha*' in a definitive form, and declare its wish to 'mine the hidden seam of thought' amid 'nameless *seikatsusha*.' However, 'the people'" in 'the people's philosophy' had meant '*seikatsusha*' from the start, and 'the people's philosophy' was nothing other than '*seikatsusha*'s thought.'

While Miki, Nii, and then Kon, had tried to clarify who was meant by the *seikatsusha* from the latter's connection with life-culture theory in which *seikatsusha* were the actors, and to elucidate their attributes and the characteristics of their behavioural patterns, 'Science of thought' was greatly distinctive in that it directed its focus upon the thought of 'the people,' that is, *seikatsusha*, and conducted repeated methodological experiments in order to discover that thought. Here, let me shed light on the image of 'the people,' or, in other words, their *seikatsusha* image, through tracing those methodological tracks.

If one looks at the chronology of 'Science of thought,' it says 'began "the people's philosophy" around December 1946.' The study of 'the people's philosophy' was the main theme pursued all the way through, from the launch of 'Science of thought.' By whom and with what intent was this research, which later came to have great breadth and depth, inaugurated?

'Philosophy is a matter of concern to all people. It is the sin of professional philosophers that it has been cut away from common people' (Kenkyūbu 1948b: 43).

> Now, since the defeat, when Japan is trying to throw its old plans away and start afresh, and to make new plans in various quarters, it is even more vital to reinterpret the philosophical thought of the general public, who constitute both the material for those plans and the ones to carry them out (Kenkyūbu 1948a: 1).

This passage, which shows some fighting spirit, conveys the youthful enthusiasm of the fledgling 'Science of thought' coterie (Mitsuo Taketani, Kiyoko Takeda, Shigeto Tsuru, Kazuko Tsurumi, Shunsuke Tsurumi, Masao Maruyama and Satoshi Watanabe), who aimed at a Copernican transformation for resurrecting philosophy.

Japanese philosophy, which had developed as a professional philosophers' discipline, and an imported one, to boot, was unable to evade the impact of the war in a variety of senses. In spite of this, 'without a skerrick of reflection' in that regard, its philosophers 'now came to wave the philosophy of democracy and suchlike nonchalantly around.' And that was not all. Logic unintelligible to ordinary people was spun there, such as 'the mediation of non-mediation, or discontinuous continuity, from fascism to democracy.' Mitsuo Taketani (1946) observes that the habit of philosophers in which words just ran around in circles was still dominant, as ever.

It was already difficult to expect that the philosophy of philosophers would face the historical experience of 'war and defeat' head-on. Supposing that the goal of the new philosophy lay in the pursuit of happiness by people living in day-to-day-ness, was it not necessary precisely to seek it among both its new bearers and the 'general public = ordinary people' who did not make speculation their occupation? The ordinary people who had endured a harsh and painful life from wartime to the post-war—in their midst, would it not be possible to find a robust power of thought whose nature differed from that of the intelligentsia? Such a hope was alive there.

The shape of regret

It was in February 1946 that the seven had their first get-together, from a 'totally coincidental, individual association.' What appear to be the rules for this gathering, seen in the 'Aims of the inaugural issue,' are just these two: 'to try not to say things that we ourselves do not understand' (the clarification of meaning); and 'not to close the door on a way of thinking, whatever it may be' (organisational pluralism). In that can be seen bitter regret and self-criticism, namely that firstly, they had not arrived at the point of having a habit of thinking from their own experience, having been led astray by the magic of words (verbal talismans); and, secondly, that diversity in ideology had been eliminated, and that the wartime thought-space, which had lacked a site for ideas to hone each other through dialogue, had opened up the pathway leading from war to defeat.

The harsh wartime experiences that ordinary people had lived through were also experiences of the same nature for the seven in the 'Science of thought' coterie.

> Of the four who returned to Japan on the first repatriation ship, Shigeto Tsuru had wartime experience of being a contracted clerk with the Foreign Ministry, a researcher with the Tōa keizai kenkyūjo (Research institute of East Asian economies), and so on; Kazuko Tsurumi was enrolled in the School of Philosophy at Tōyō University, pondering the post-war; and Kiyoko Takeda, while working at the YWCA, had

experience on the home front toiling alongside young people in the dormitory of a special steel factory in Shimizu City in Shizuoka Prefecture. Shunsuke Tsurumi had war experience in Indonesia, as is widely known; while Satoru Watanabe is sure to have endured Tokyo University academism in the wartime years. Additionally, Masao Maruyama wrote up his research on Sorai Ogyū and Norinaga Motoori almost as a farewell note, and was involved in an educational call-up in Pyongyang, Korea. In between two experiences of imprisonment, Mitsuo Taketani was involved in nuclear research at the Nishina Nuclear Research Laboratory at the Institute of Physical and Chemical Research (Riken), while barely continuing to lecture at Tokyo University of Science and Literature (Yasuda and Amano 1992: 7–8).

It was not only their wartime experiences. Of the 1946 coterie, who appeared to be a spirited group of researchers, it was only two, Masao Maruyama and Kiyoko Takeda, that had regular jobs, and even that pair was trying to live their respective post-war lives while pressed for food. Their focus on 'the people's' philosophy, and hopes and expectations towards the latter, arose from amid their shared experience of an age in which nobody could survive without some connection with basic pursuits for maintaining life.

One could cite a deep fixation on other irrational things that pierce the foundations of humanity and society—weakness, ambiguity, unsteadiness, and brittleness—as a model for speculation shared by this group. A poetic nature which, freed from a speculative pattern that apprehended 'weakness' negatively in comparison with 'strength,' inherently grasped the potential of 'weakness' itself, could be seen especially notably in Shunsuke Tsurumi, Masao Maruyama and Kiyoko Takeda. This brittle, unsteady 'sensitivity' that constituted their poetic nature further developed into the power to open up the depth of the life-world of 'the people' living through the same times.

Pragmatism as a method

The early 'Science of thought,' as is generally understood, was not preoccupied with the 'importation and introduction' of American philosophy, or pragmatism, in particular. Its aim was to discern whether these could be useful as tools for analysis or criticism of Japanese society.

According to the *Shinpan tetsugaku [and] ronri yōgo jiten* (New edition dictionary of terms in philosophy [and] logic), edited by Shisō-no-kagaku kenkyūkai (1995), pragmatism refers to an 'idea-clarification movement with a metaphysical bent.' It began with C.S. Peirce's proposal: 'Consider what effects, which might conceivably have practical bearings, we conceive the object of our conception to have. Then, our conception of those effects is the whole of our conception of the object' (Peirce 1992: 132). Called the pragmatic maxim, it took the following form: 'In order to gain a clear grasp of the meaning of a certain concept, one should think what kind of actual outcome would inevitably arise if that concept were true.' Pragmatism is a movement to clarify ideas, or a methodology of ideas, based upon that maxim. At the same time, the ideologies that are spawned by means of this method (utilitarianism in an ethical aspect, and empiricism in a logical aspect) are also called pragmatism (Shisō-no-kagaku kenkyūkai 1995: 346).

The originality of 'Science of thought,' and particularly that of Shunsuke Tsurumi, lies in their having striven to hone pragmatism not by understanding it as thought or as the 'substance' of an ideology, but as applying it to Japanese reality.

'Pragmatism as a method'—that was Tsurumi's philosophical position. He first tried to render obsolete the word 'true,' as in 'true' ideology or 'the sole true' answer within himself as a thinker. He regarded pragmatism as the operation of thought that would actually guarantee, in all cases, the fundamental 'freedom' to begin speculation or action, to sustain and develop it, and to make mistakes and correct them. He saw the characteristic of pragmatism as being 'a "mistakist" disposition that always apprehended things provisionally and responded to later revision' (Tsurumi 1956 [1975]: 300).

For the record, immediately after the war's end, when Marxism made a brilliant comeback centring upon the Japan Communist Party, 'Science of thought' was neither pro- nor anti-communist, and, drawing a clear line of demarcation between itself and such partisanship, it maintained its position as a group of thinkers that on the one hand accepted ideological challenges from Marxism head-on, while being open to people of a variety of ideological positions, on the other, this also relying on a pragmatic way of thinking. Movements oriented in the direction they considered correct for reforming the present situation met with resistance from other movements that thought yet different directions were correct, and were further deepened. In that sense, 'Science of thought' and Marxism were placed in a relationship of adversarial co-operation.

Secondly, pragmatism for 'Science of thought' needed, above all, to be a way of thinking that could be put to effective use in the setting of everyday life—not as a method by which professional thinkers would analyse people's lifestyles, either, but as a way for ordinary people to use effectively themselves. If one takes a pragmatic standpoint, then a particular theory or ideology will be recognised as 'science' only when the validity it has in action by real people has been confirmed. In that context, ideology means a method or tool for people to use in order to live, and to live well. Study of 'the people's philosophy' was none other than a practice for deepening such 'pragmatism as a method.'

The philosophy that ordinary people have—in other words, the thought of the general populace—is not something fixed and static. It is something that is expressed as concrete action in the midst of people's lives, and which is ceaselessly changing. It is something that lives in day-to-day lifestyles and is opened up in that process. In addition, people's thought is often ambiguous, and buried in delicate emotions without taking on a distinct shape. If one endeavours to replace it with a thesis and understand it in the abstract, it will overflow. This means that a unique method is required in order to approach 'the people's philosophy.' How would it be possible to scoop up the living, breathing ideology hidden within people's lifeworld, note it down, and fix it on paper as something tangible without losing its original form? 'Science of thought' was one space of experimentation in which to grope for such a new methodology.

Let us first start by looking at who 'the people (*hitobito*)' are.

Philosophy of the common man

Traced back via pragmatism to its source, 'the people's philosophy' which 'Science of thought' set forth arrives back at the 'philosophy of the common man' expounded by the nineteenth-century American poet and philosopher, Ralph Waldo Emerson (1803–82). It was in 1837, in a speech called 'The American Scholar,' that Emerson asserted that Americans, having left Britain and started to live in a distinct natural environment and society, should spin out a distinct type of thought which differed from that of Britain. This has been called America's 'Intellectual Declaration of Independence.'

What is important in regard to Emerson's assertion is that it was one which proposed a 'common man's philosophy,' or, in other words, a 'philosophy of ordinary people' which would become the matrix and wellspring of America's new culture. 'Not out of those on whom systems of education have exhausted their culture comes the helpful giant to destroy the old or to build the new, but out of unhandselled savage nature' (Emerson 1837). Emerson says that those giants will be created from the lives and everyday utterances of untutored people unrelated to the over-educated.

Country folk with no connection with refined 'cultivation' quite ordinarily say, 'My philosophy is...' Within the things that such ordinary people think are hidden weighty truths, because it is only when thoughts are returned to the original space called life where they were spawned that they come alive and have the power to work. Emerson is deemed to have had a great influence upon the pragmatists James and Dewey through his 'common man's philosophy' (Tsurumi 1984: 21–25).

Moreover, just as the 'common man's philosophy' had been an intellectual declaration of independence from Britain, 'the people's philosophy' in 'Science of thought' was none other than an ideological declaration of independence from professional philosophers.

Who are 'the people'?

The word for 'the people' in 'the people's philosophy' was written not as '*hitobito*' in Chinese characters, as is the norm, but spelt out as *hi-to-bi-to* in the native syllabary. Why did 'Science of thought' do that? The expression, which now has a mysterious ring, was imbued with the unique sentiment of the 'Science of thought' coterie, and the core of the question: 'To whom does *seikatsusha* refer?' is hidden in the very meaning of the word.

Firstly, it contained a clear intention to understand people who live ordinary lives not as a mass or a 'lump,' as suggested by the terms '*jinmin* ('people,' as in 'People's Republic of...),' '*jinmin taishū* (the people's masses)' or '*kokumin* (nationals),' but as 'scattered' individuals; or, additionally, not as 'one person in the masses' but as 'one person's masses.' It assumed an image of members of the nation or the masses, 'one by one' facing up to the violent historical change that was Japan's defeat—an image poles apart from that of '*taishū*' as in *taishū rosen* (the popular line), who all slid one way. In an interview, Shunsuke Tsurumi remarked: 'As for the feeling of the word, "*hi-to-bi-to*" feels more scattered than "*hitobito*." This meant that we wanted to understand the common people not as a solid mass, but as 'individuals' whose respective faces were visible.'

Kazuko Tsurumi, in turn, commented: 'I hate the word *taishū*. People like me have been criticised with the expression "*taishū shinkō* (popular religion)," but they understand *taishū* as "mass." It refers rather, to each individual person, as a *seikatsusha* (Tsurumi, 1992: 176).

At the same time, this is inseparably tied to the view that seeks to grasp philosophy or thought not as a 'system' or 'generality,' but as 'everything that each person thinks in getting on with her or his own life,' or 'the entirety of each person's thoughts about living.'

In anyone's case, in common people's experience there will be inscribed thoughts that have arisen from lifestyle necessity. Firstly, through such an understanding, 'Science of thought' members became able to obtain a method for transcending the dichotomous interpretation of the conventional masses and intelligentsia, who saw *minshū* (*taishū*) as being a group with retarded consciousness that should be enlightened by intellectuals; and gain a pluralistic perspective that emphasised dialogue and intercommunication with 'people' with extremely different ways of feeling and thinking, in order to know themselves and confirm their own thought.

Secondly, also in connection with the first feature, in the way the common people understood it, the word '*hi-to-bi-to*' was one clearly demarcated from the then-prevalent concepts of '*jinmin*,' '*jinmin taishū*' or '*taishū*,' and it had great significance. Kazue Morisaki speaks as follows on the immediate post-war opinion situation.

> The way we understood [the idea of class] around the time when labour unions had been formed under instruction from the Occupation forces, and the labour movement had started to flourish, was very sketchy, a 'such and such a price for one heap' kind of feeling—just like giant radishes or soy beans. I kept on thinking that something was wrong, though. It was as if I had been obsessed with the idea that there was something that the Marxist concept of class could not explain....

At the time, the reality was that one's words would not reach their target unless one was on the common conceptual footing called class (Yasuda and Amano 1991: 105; brackets added).

Words like '*jinmin*,' '*jinmin taishū*' and '*taishū*' were used as things that coincided with the concept of a 'class' in terms of the subjects of social upheaval and leaders of socialist revolution. By contrast, the word '*hi-to-bi-to*' was one that refused to be easily reduced to a class concept as a collective representation. It brings out from within each individual person's lifestyle her or his self-styled ideas as to what to do to attain more 'happiness.' It signifies the importance of the quality of individual experience, which is never integrated into the group.

In these two senses, the concept of 'the people (*hi-to-bi-to*)' ends up occupying the position of a keyword that prescribes the direction of the 'Science of thought' movement.

Serial biographies of common people

The intention of 'the people's philosophy' which had started like this was clear-cut. By comparison, the methodology for grasping it as an entity could not escape being vague. This was due to a complete lack of research and scholarship that could be a methodological model. What is more, it was not as though there was any mutual understanding as to what kind of 'people' to take up, and what sort of framework to use to explain their ideology, either.

Based on a questionnaire put together by borrowing a ready-made framework from Western philosophy, repeated attempts were made by trial-and-error to record accounts of the living conditions of homeless people and returned soldiers at Tokyo's Ueno station. Running through this was a have-a-go sort of pragmatic attitude that said that any seemingly useful philosophical framework would do; and as for methodology, that it would suffice to use it as a temporary tool and gradually remodel it into something better. By such a process of not being afraid to make 'mistakes' and 'attacking from as many routes as possible, from all directions including highways and byways,' several directions eventually became visible. Here, I will take up: 1 the compilation of 'biographies of common people'; 2 the life-recording movement; 3 the analysis of 'personal consultations'; and 4 research into popular arts.

'The people,' or, in other words, *seikatsusha*, do not necessarily behave in a clearly logical manner. The ideas and philosophy of 'the people' operate not within expressed language, but in as-yet unexpressed circumstances that have blended into the chaos of everyday life. There are important truths within day-to-day-ness that are expressed by people's way of living, but cannot be put into words. Perhaps one should better say that the world of meaning is hidden within the truths that are disheartening them. What kind of issues emerge within circumstances that 'the people' cannot discuss; and through what ways of living will these be resolved? One of the methods worked out amid interrogation of 'the people's philosophy' from such a vantage point was the method of biography-creation called '*shomin retsuden* (serial biographies of common people).'

This was an attempt to plumb the depths of the existence of 'the people' in the street who had no voice, and to sketch their ideological portraits. Why compile biographies of common people? The compilation of biographies has meaning not only for 'the people' who are written about, but also for 'the people' who write the biographies. In *Minshū no za* (The seat of the masses), Shunsuke Tsurumi writes: 'Biography-making is interesting because it makes us understand ways of thinking and ways of living that differ from our own...and because it pulls our thought out of a cul-de-sac and takes it to a place where we can try to put our own thought into perspective' (1955: 5–6).

One writes the biography of a person completely foreign to oneself who is in one's vicinity; the interchange of thought emerging from that process deepens the writer's thought; one emphasises dialogicality; and, by that means, a new breath of air is blown into the writer's very thought: these were the major characteristics of this method.

> Around when we began compiling the biographies, every time we went to a new place, we made efforts to invite new writers in. Now, there are a number of groups in places like Kyoto, Okazaki, Tokushima, Marugame, Yonago, Osaka and Tokyo. The work gathered here is all composed of things read aloud and made into a final manuscript by these various groups (Tsurumi 1955: 6).

The venue for the readings was on the *tatami*-matted floor of a certain temple in Kyoto; and the biography writers comprised a diverse range of 'people,' including students, various tradespeople and researchers. Naturally, in a period when all travel was inconvenient—nothing like the Bullet Train being in existence—it would have been no trivial matter for people to gather at a Kyoto temple not only from Tokushima and Tottori, but from all parts of Japan. One person wrote 'Sensai furōji (War vagrant child),' while another wrote 'Nōmin (Farmer),' and they brought these along and read them aloud. 'Byōnin (Invalid),' penned by a patient at the National Sanatorium Nagashima Aiseien, was read by someone else because the author could not participate.

Michitarō Tada reminisces: 'We would debate for hours on just one cup of tea, and when evening came we would slurp *udon* noodles at a makeshift *udon* place with the quirky name of 'Ayashikaran (Not dubious)' in the grounds of a temple in Uraderamachi' (1986: 80).

Another person to join the members sitting in a circle on the tatami mats in the dimly-lit temple was Fuyuko Kamisaka, a clerical worker at Toyota Motor Company in Aichi Prefecture who would later go on to pen *Shokuba no gunzō* (The group at the workplace), which was serialised in *Shisō no kagaku* (1959). The work of compiling biographies gradually progressed in the direction of writing up the group of a particular cohort (a workplace, family, hamlet and the like), and common people's groups. *Shokuba no gunzō*, which dynamically depicted the ecology of white-collar workers who waver between companies' ingenious labour-management policies and the labour movement, was one product of that attempt. Kamisaka later recounts: 'I could not even begin to imagine what I was seeking, or which direction to go, but my will alone dazzlingly took the lead...For me, the temple in Kyoto was an irreplaceable starting-point' (1986: 96).

In this manner, the job of compiling biographies did not stop at the dialogue between the ones doing the writing and the ones being written about, but accomplished unique expansion in terms of intercommunication among the writers and collaborative work.

The whereabouts of egotism

The 1950s, when the biographies started to be compiled, was an age in which the necessity began to be emphasised for the creation of a new academic tradition of 'serving the common people, and learning from the common people,' one based on reflection over the way scholarship and research had been up till then. It was also in this period that Tadashi Ishimoda's 1952 book, *Rekishi to minzoku no hakken* (The discovery of history and ethnicity), which rhapsodised about 'joining the ranks of the common people and writing history along with them,' was published, and 'joining the common people' became a password for 'progressive' scholars and students. These same scholars and students were still maintaining a position that sought to instruct and enlighten 'the common people' politically. Yoshimi Usui, the chief editor of a magazine called *Tenbō* (Perspective), recounts as follows:

> Just as I could not stand the shrill voice of the Right that incessantly scolded, threatened and cajoled the nation during the war, I could not tolerate the same sort of shrill voice—albeit one that had changed direction—from the Left in the post-war. I could not help the feeling that even if one argued that Right and Left were not the same, they were still shrill voices, and were no different in their determination to flatter and use the members of the nation (1964: 130–31).

Amid a proliferation of the sort of words and action that would curry favour with and incite the people/general populace/common people, on the one hand, and movements and debates that took the position of enlightening and instructing the people/general populace/common people, on the other, where the biography-making group in 'Science of thought' was aiming was clearly a different direction. This was because it was a movement that aimed not so much to go 'amid the masses,' but to go 'among the masses of distinct individuals' and, further still, to go 'among the *seikatsusha*.'

'The people' and 'the people's' philosophy contained in the biographies thus written were diverse. What they had in common, however, was that they did not cut out and discuss 'the people's philosophy' which had survived through the violent upheavals of wartime and the post-war as a ready-made ideology, but tried to bring it out 'in one lump,' including all of its guile and exclusivity, brittleness and weakness, and potential and expectations, together with the human energy that supported and gave direction to it.

Katsumi Watanabe's 'Coalminer,' for example, is the oral transcript of 'the lifestyle and thought of Ichizō Ashida,' a man who spent twenty years working as a coalminer at the Chikuhō coalfield prior to its cutback (Watanabe 1954: 2–8). The thoughts of one adaptable coalminer who should perhaps be labelled a Japanese kind of *petit bourgeois* are brought into sharp relief while pursuing his trajectory from being a dirt-poor farmer with a mere three *tan* of land to becoming a coalminer; his firm belief that, while giving credit to the union movement and strike action for his post-war wage rise, it was a miner's duty not to go on strike but to go down the mine and work; his wish to take voluntary retirement, open a little shop near the coalmine using his severance pay as capital, and live a life of ease; how he had been satisfied with his own way of living, seeing that he had been disfavoured by 'the soil,' gone broke in his native place, and been saved by the coalmine; and his attachment to and reluctance to leave the coalmine which were thus engendered. That probably was an ideology common to the majority of workers of the same generation.

A cheerful pessimism

In social surveys that use statistical methods, only the image of a 'general' or 'average' coalminer can be captured. With historical recording methods, accent is placed on the 'retrospective' dimension in which a coalminer looks back upon past events, and rationalisation towards the past tends to operate. By contrast, the biographical description method stresses the 'prospective' dimension in which an individual, while differentiating as much as possible between the way things were seen when they happened, and the way in which those past events are looked back upon now, faced an uncertain situation of not knowing what would happen in the future at those respective points in his life.

It sketches the form of thinking created when a coalminer is at a loss whether to take part in a strike ordered by his union or to go down into the mine and work, and vacillates between the alternatives, as a 'process.' Moreover, by those means, it enables the grasping of a 'typical' individual's ideological portrait. This biographical description method later went on to bear fruit in the documentation of individuals' personal history in a three-volume joint study entitled *Tenkō* (Conversion) (1959–63).

The oral transcripts from 'the people' who have different lifestyles and live different lives from oneself certainly make interesting reading. In many cases, however, the things depicted there are various aspects of the egotism that 'the people' exercise in order to survive. What relation do such techniques for 'the people' to make their way in the world and their cunning have with 'the people's' wisdom? Is it not that they merely have an affirmative attitude towards their present livelihood, and are insufficiently critical of the current situation, lacking any feeling of tension towards it? Shunsuke Tsurumi writes as follows, as if to anticipate such doubts and criticisms:

> It is a mistake to expect wisdom from the common people in the form of superior insight vis-à-vis trends in world history, or progressive opinions about social structure. In the context of contemporary Japanese society, designs for a new society, better images for life, and schematic drawings of historical trends are all the wisdom of a child. A mild form of guile is what constitutes an adult's wisdom. When children become adults, they forget their childhood wisdom, but when they are still children they cannot have the wisdom of adulthood. The sharpness of this divide comprises a major ideological problem for modern Japan. *There needs to be correct judgement as to the trends of world history, and the good intentions to head in the direction of progress, and a reconstitution of the common people's artfulness and inventiveness in a way that relates to the preceding, does there not?* (1955: 15–16; emphasis added).

Within 'the people's' egotism there is a vigorous ability to make a living, and a sober gaze that reads reality. As these directly link with their 'self'-assertion, they are not easily hoodwinked by the lies told by those in power, and have the capability to disobey the imposition of authority from above. One can see there a directionality that strives realistically to apprehend the antiquity and cunning that 'the people' harbour, and, without rejecting it for rejection's sake, tries conversely to turn it into a positive opportunity through its rejection.

There are subtle differences in the respective stance of the respective writers towards 'the people,' as seen in their biography-making. Their images of 'the people' depicted will vary according to the extent to which the writers make those things that 'the people' whose biographies are being written interpret as being 'worthy of repudiating' overlap with the same qualities in themselves, and understand as things to which to respond. For Tsurumi, the egotism of 'the people' corresponded to that within himself, and that was none other than his own problem.

One could paraphrase it thus: a kind of resignation, which said that 'the people' who live their actual lives could not be expected to continue to have pure 'children's wisdom,' had the opposite effect of making Tsurumi bet on the limited potential that 'the people' had. A cheerful pessimism: that was a contrasting direction from the way that the 'progressive' intellectuals of the time assumed an optimistic view of humanity and pinned their romantic hopes upon the wisdom of the people's masses, and also from Itaru Nii's unreservedly glorified understanding of the *seikatsusha* as common people.

The life-recording movement

If one tracks the compilation of biographies back in terms of the history of thought, one will hit upon the '*seikatsu tsuzurikata* (lifewriting)' movement that had been going since the Taisho era. This *seikatsu tsuzurikata* movement was both a civil education campaign and an ideological movement, begun by teachers who were not satisfied only with education that centred on the imposition of uniform concepts through state-designated textbooks; and its aim was to have children express experiences and discoveries from their own lives in their own words, and give them the power to create ideas rooted in their everyday lives. Having suffered severe repression during the war, it was revived in the 1950s and began to be used not only by children but also by adults as a method for creating their own style of expression and thought. The life-recording (*seikatsu kiroku*) movement which came to extend over a wide range, from farming villages to factories was just that. Moreover, it was 'Science of thought' that played the role of vanguard in respect to that movement, also.

Kazuko Tsurumi describes the impetus by which the methodology of the children's 'life-writing' movement came to be passed on the adults' life-recording movement, as follows:

> In 1952, the Japanese Composition Association (Nihon sakubun no kai) held its first conference on composition education in Ena, in Gifu Prefecture. That was the start of the post-war revival of composition education. I was asked to give a talk there, and I was interested, so I went. That was the direct impetus. I realised that this was the way for ordinary *seikatsusha* to hone their thought within their everyday lives. From there, I went into the life-recording movement together with housewives from uptown and downtown Tokyo, and female factory

hands working in textile mills. When you are on the actual spot, you realise that the most important things are the problems which every individual comes up against while being alive, the ideological issue of how to solve them, and individuals, don't you agree? You start to feel that what is important is not something like grand [Marxist] theories or inevitable principles (1992: 175).

In 1950s Japan, terms imported from America, such as 'democracy (*minshu*; *demokurashī*),' 'freedom,' and 'human rights' were abundantly used. In most cases, however, these did not extend beyond the realm of clichés, and were not things that took deep root in the everyday lives and cultural traditions of 'the people.' Furthermore, recording and expressing one's own opinions and statements in written form was still the privilege of just a tiny handful of urban residents. What should be done in order to make the series of actions of 'writing, reading and speaking' not just the privilege of a few, but to spread them among 'the people,' turning them into a means for 'the people' to assemble thought according to their own needs and make new values their own? That question was the starting-point of the life-recording movement.

One example of such a movement was that of female factory employees at Tōa Bōshoku, a spinning and weaving factory in Yokkaichi City. In the process of writing down the realities of work and their workplace, romantic love and their own dreams in a shared notebook, and deepening their deeper discussions, they liberated themselves from 'antiquated' commonsense, gained new ways of thinking and living, and even went so far as to compile an anthology of their mothers' histories (Kinoshita and Tsurumi 1954). This had great significance in that it illustrated that whoever 'the people' might be, and however scant their vocabulary, if they construct a method for thinking firmly of things, in language connected with their own experience, then they will be able to participate in the job of rewriting modern history.

When an adults' life-recording movement loses its tension in relation to the times and circumstances, there is a danger that it will fall into the trap of recording passive sentiments. Study of 'the people's philosophy' was a methodological experiment in 'spelling-out of life' for adults.'

While the production of biographies that sketch the figure of 'the people' with both affection and criticism is the building of 'histories of others,' so to speak, life-recording is the making of 'self-history.' Just as finding out about other people's way of living links to knowledge of one's own way of life and a solid self-recognition, one can only have a deeper understanding of other people's way of living by coming to have self-styled concepts and expressions of one's own. Such moves became an even greater flow, and were theorised by Daikichi Irokawa in 1975 as 'attempts at self-history (*Jibunshi no kokoromi*)' which subjectively confront contemporary history.

Biography-production, which began as a method of discovering 'the people's philosophy,' went on to open up new prospects as a movement called life-recording, a movement for 'the people' to construct self-histories which expressed their own thoughts in their own words.

The genealogy of 'the people's' unhappiness

The next stage of development seen by attempts to explore 'the people's philosophy' consisted of research on contributions to personal advice columns in newspapers and magazines. Though various researchers later attempted to employ the approach of trying to discover an inherent framework for 'the people's' way of living within personal consultation columns (Mita 1965), it was 'Science of thought' that first undertook it. The novelty lay not in the latter's simply having taken up personal advice as their raw material, but in it having been thoroughly infused with a methodological awareness that sought to grasp the real figure of the *seikatsusha* within the 'unhappiness' of 'the people.'

Personal advice (*minoue sōdan*) is a setup by which 'the people' complain to somebody else of troubles they cannot solve by their own efforts, and venture to get an answer.

According to Akio Saki's article, 'The origins of personal consultation' (1953: 2–7), its original form can be found in what Tenrikyo—a new religious movement at the end of the Tokugawa Period—calls '*mijō tasuke* (helping personal matters).' What Tenrikyo refers to by '*mijō*' is mainly the body, and '*mijō nayami* (bodily troubles)' meant illness more than anything. On this point, it differs considerably from the '*minoue* (personal circumstances)' in *minoue sōdan*. At the same time, though, both '*mijō tasuke*' and *minoue sōdan* share the aspect of taking troubles that the party concerned cannot solve by their own efforts alone to some other person. Many of Japan's new religious movements may be said to have developed with this personal-consultative element set as the focus of their religious salvation, and in that sense personal consultation can be seen as something native to Japanese society.

The founder of Tenrikyo, Miki Nakayama (1798–1887), was a housewife in a wealthy farming family. As was the case with many farm wives, the days of being pursued by work and domestic labour under the traditional household (*ie*) system were heavy pressure for Miki. In addition, she was enduring the double and triple distress common in well-to-do farming families, namely a decline in the family business and the defection of indentured servants. In the autumn of her forty-first year, the worst trial assailed her, in that her son had a recurrence of foot pain, Miki herself had severe back pain that coincided with menopause, and her husband had eye trouble. Left on her own, Miki took refuge in God, accepted her troubles as they were, and sought to resolve them by her own efforts. And from that, she went on to become the contact-point for people's '*mijō tasuke*.' She had the realisation that she herself was 'one who ails,' and for that very reason, when a person came looking for something, Miki was able to compare that with her own anxiety and loneliness. Miki's '*mijō tasuke*' was mutual healing in the name of reciprocal treatment, so to speak.

To live means to shoulder some sort of burden. There are all kinds of questions that one encounters on a road of life trodden with the kind of burdens one cannot evade as long as one lives, and various questions which arise from one's search here and there for the source of troubles that leave one at a loss. The process of confronting those problems within oneself, confessing them to someone, and accepting the given answer with satisfaction—in that process lies the true philosophy for 'the people' to go on living, and that is where its original form is hidden: that is how 'Science of thought' apprehended personal consultation.

One of the coterie, Kazuko Tsurumi, had already taken note of the issue of personal consultation in February 1951, and understood it as being one type of 'the people's' everyday thought that connected with the 'logic of inquiry' in Dewey's philosophy. How can one achieve happiness? 'The people' do not seek the answer to that compelling question by reading books or learning things. They come up against a problem, grapple with it, doubt their previous ideas, discard them, and bring forth new ideas as they open up the situation. Tsurumi argues that this very process constitutes 'inquiry,' and that personal consultation is nothing if not the practical process of that 'inquiry.'

Between two views of history

In regard to the research into personal consultation, there was a debate within the study group over the realistic appraisal of personal consultation itself. In abstract terms, this probably boiled down to a clash between pragmatic and Marxist views of history. In other words, it was an issue of 'individual historicity' which directed its focus upon how 'the people' could pursue happiness, and 'social historicity' which focused upon the lawfulness of the kind of social development that was hard to avoid. Within the group there was a clash of standpoints over this—one emphasising 'juncture' by trying to tie the two together, and the other that thoroughly adhered to individual historicity.

In regard to the former position, while observing the 'process' that was personal consultation and valuing the self-liberation and the refreshed feeling of having said one's piece that can be gained by 'daring to expose one's secret anguish to public scrutiny,' Akio Saki pointed out that there was a *'petit bourgeois'* limitation in that the way the problem was resolved remained at the level of the individual, without overstepping the boundaries of a 'personal matter.' Hidetoshi Katō also indicated something similar from the standpoint of communication theory. Thought that derives from co-operation between multiple people, mediated by communication—in short, the party asking for advice and the party supplying it—certainly has the potential to become the 'driving force for building a new society.' He suggests, however, that in actual practice, both the person writing in for advice and the one replying trivialise the problem and confine it within a narrow perspective; and that ideas are going around in circles with no connection to what actually exists in real Japanese society (the family system and non-modern social relationships) (Katō 1953: 49)

What Saki and Katō have in common is that they both attempt to repudiate the kind of monistic argument that immediately looks to reform of the social system for the solution to problems appearing in personal consultation, and take a pluralistic position. Among the contents of the personal consultations, that is, what is troubling 'the people,' there are many pressing problems of what to do today or tomorrow about this individual's unhappiness, the sort that cannot wait until social conditions change. There are questions about karma: a family's or the surrounding people's coldness—'Why must I be the only one to suffer?'

In answer to a problem in the vein of: 'How can I get him to notice me?' nothing will be solved by saying something like: 'Wait until the social system changes.' No small number of such problems can be solved by changes on an individual level, such as altering a habitual way of looking at things, or reconfiguring interpersonal relationships. That being said, even in the case of individual, small-picture problems, if they are explored in the context of communication and thought by multiple people, then they will always lead to greater contradictions and big-picture issues inherent in society and the system. In the position that emphasised 'juncture,' there was a strong problem-consciousness of wanting to trace the small-picture problems of 'the people' down to big-picture issues involving the system and tying these together, with personal consultation its strategic grounds.

What about the position that insisted on individual historicity? In 1956, *Minoue sōdan* (Personal consultation) was published as the fruit of collaborative research by 'Science of thought.' The authors were Shunsuke Tsurumi, Sadako Yokoyama, Yoshiyuki Tsurumi, Hiroyuki Gotō, and Hiroshi Hanzawa. Divided into categories such as 'male–female relationships,' 'romance,' 'heartbreak' and 'married couples,' the book elucidates how the problem situation changed over the four periods comprising Meiji, Taisho, early Showa and the post-war, and by doing so, outlines the history of 'the people's' lifestyle ideology. No problem-consciousness vis-à-vis how to 'join' the small- and big pictures can be seen in this volume. Taking a thorough position of individual historicity, the aim there is to shine light upon the process of trial-and-error in which 'the people' confront their respective problem situations, deepen their awareness towards the latter, and, in addition, try to shake themselves free of habitualised patterns of thought and behaviour.

In the personal consultation research that takes this stance, there can be seen a strong methodological orientation towards digging down to deep layers of consciousness to find the history of 'the people's' quotidian ideas, and making clear the reality of 'the people's' thought which had been missing from the conventional history of thought.

It was an 'alternative' history, a history of 'the people's' lifestyle ideology that was the direct opposite of a book published at approximately the same time, *Shōwa-shi* (A history of Showa) (Tōyama et al. 1955), which was written pivoting on the abstract concept of 'class struggle.' According to Katsuichirō Kamei, in *A history of Showa* 'there were only two sides: the military, politicians and entrepreneurs who had enforced the war; and the communists and liberals who were suppressed for opposing them, with no sign of the layer of nationals that oscillated between them.' Why, it was not only that there was no 'sign of the layer of nationals,' but also that the very historians who wrote it made no appearance on any stage of *A history of Showa* that focused upon 'objective history' (Kamei 1956: 63).

One must not look down from high in the sky with the eye of a bird—with an insect's eye, one must confront each of the troubles of 'the people' who crawl along the ground. Within the standpoint that perceives 'the people' there is a clear recognition that the starting-point of history lies only in 'the people' becoming the determiners of the micro-situation in which they themselves have been placed, and their becoming the subjects who themselves will propel that micro-situation. 'The people' will be slow to realise this, but once they have realised it, 'the people' will also be the ones who will guard that discovery and nurture it. In that, one can see a strong sense of trust in 'the people,' namely, that only things which they have spontaneously thought up can become ideological power, and 'the people' constitute an existence that has such potential power.

The genealogy of 'the people's' happiness

If we suppose 'Science of thought's' research on personal consultation to have been something that delved into the genealogy of 'the people's' unhappiness, then the group's studies on popular arts were an attempt to find the genealogy of 'the people's' happiness. An even clearer image of 'the people's philosophy' should arise when these two are examined in mirror fashion. Research into popular arts, as a realistic expression of the desires and wishes at the root of 'the people's' livelihood, was invested with such an aim.

As seen in the pre-war Imperial Rescript on Education and military training, 'the people's' thought had been intentionally channelled in one direction by systematic teaching. That was not the only thing to have shaped 'the people's' thought, however. 'The people' also had different thought from that intended, and they went on equipping themselves with it in an unplanned form. One vital source for the formation of thought that outsmarted that intentional education was none other than popular arts and popular entertainment.

Many intellectuals had given negative appraisal to such popular arts and popular entertainment. Yet even as early as the Taisho era (1912–26), there were certainly people like Yasunosuke Gonda (1887–1951), too, who, by means of observation of films, comic storytelling and the like, positioned entertainment and amusement as something indispensable in the lives of the common people, and sought to see in it the common people's independence as subjects of cultural creation. That, however, was a complete exception, and entertainment and amusement had been left behind as realms never properly discussed by intellectuals.

This was because they had been considered firstly to be something vulgar and low-class that gave the populace a fleeting diversion and dissipated their stress, and dulled their critical powers vis-à-vis society; and secondly to be a means of edifying 'the people' in response to the demands of capital and those currently in power.

Objectively speaking, popular arts perhaps do fulfil such a role. Is that the only thing that 'the people' accept from popular arts, though? Moreover, are they simply a passive existence that unilaterally accepts what was intended? That is unlikely to be the case. 'The people' have a subjectivity rooted in their lifestyle, discover things within popular arts that touch upon the subtleties of their own way of living, resonate with these, and by sharing delight, anger, sorrow and pleasure, participate in the creation of popular arts, do they not? As their raw material, 'Science of thought' went on taking up pulp fiction and popular songs, *Naniwabushi* narrative singing and *yakuza* movies, as things that projected the desires of 'the people.'

The Janus-faced 'pretence of obedience and secret betrayal'

Taking up the subject of popular historical novelist Eiji Yoshikawa, Kiyoko Takeda explored the way of thinking and feeling of 'the people' projected in his works such as *Taikōki* (Taiko: an epic novel of war and glory in feudal Japan), *Miyamoto musashi* (Musashi) and *Shinran* (Shinran the priest), from the three angles of historical perspective, social perspective and values (Takeda 1984: 8–20). According to that paper, in Eiji Yoshikawa's world, the 'warrior's lifeworld' which placed supreme value upon 'career advancement' towards the ruling class of the time and 'victory' coexisted in contrast to the 'common people's lifeworld' (or 'townspeople's lifeworld') which affirmed 'life' and placed value upon living a carefree life. In the case of the former, ethical and value standards were set in hierarchical relationships between people, while in the latter's case, they were set in 'raw humanity' itself. Protagonists Hideyoshi, Musashi and Shinran were all torn between these two lifeworlds, and were placed in an ambivalent position, but essentially they were more strongly attracted to the 'common people's lifeworld' as an ideal, or else as an actual way of living. Takeda views the way of life of these popular novels' heroes that were moulded by Eiji Yoshikawa as fascinating and pleasing 'the people.'

In the 'common people's lifeworld,' social advancement and victory are by no means the greatest values. Advancement and victory are certainly values that people desire to obtain, but they find it repugnant to have imposed on them the kind of virtue from the feudal order that would make them wear a samurai's ceremonial costume and commit suicide. Even Hideyoshi, who conquered the entire land, makes 'a big family where everyone was lively, worked hard and laughed often' his ideal, and even the sword-fighting practitioner, Musashi, yearns 'still more to throw away his sword and live a townsman's life with [his lover] O-tsū.' As a different world, the easiness of the common people's lifestyle is filled with charm. What 'the people' like about the priest Shinran, too, is not the figure of a Shinran steeped in faith who says that the only way to salvation is by chanting the name of the Buddha. Rather, it is the image of Shinran as a meat-eating, married priest in his natural human form, one who approves of a secular way of life and lives that way, himself.

'The people' were in sympathy with Eiji Yoshikawa's world that so affirmatively depicted the lifestyle of the common people, drawing from it a vigorous energy oriented towards tomorrow. In it, Takeda saw the figure of popular arts that 'the people' create and nurture.

This oppositional schema between the 'warrior's lifeworld' and 'common people's lifeworld' deftly captures the dynamism of the lifestyle principle of 'the people.' The 'warrior's lifeworld' is not something which literally points only to a lifeworld where feudal norms have currency. It indicates a sphere where the norms and morals that the ruling powers in each respective age expect from 'the people' operate. It does not mean that 'the people' live only in a 'common people's lifeworld' that is completely cut off from the 'warrior's lifeworld,' in that sense. The moral perspectives and set of values that support society's dominant powers infiltrate the common people's lifeworld of 'the people,' while 'the people' in turn nonchalantly allow them to mix. If they saw that their opposite number had overwhelmingly strong authority, and that there would be no chance of winning even if they did oppose them, then, while outwardly submitting to the other's will, inwardly they would depart from that and search for a way of living faithful to 'their true selves.' In this overlapping of the two lifeworlds, Takeda sees the robust dual nature of 'the people' who, while outwardly meeting the social norms, with the idea: 'If you can't beat 'em, join 'em,' inwardly take a strategy of defiance while feigning obedience. What 'the people' perceive in the novels written by Eiji Yoshikawa is their own life-view. They project this onto the way of life of the heroes who are active in the novels, and draw from it the energy to live.

While sharply pinpointing the Janus-faced nature of 'the people,' Takeda simultaneously read within 'the people's' artfulness a realistic gaze that could interpret reality and a source of strength to go on living; and, furthermore, a potential to shape an awareness that would link with demands for the right for 'their true selves' to live openly in actuality. For Takeda, 'feigning obedience while secretly betraying' signified one model of resistance by 'the people' which stopped them from being linearly subsumed by public influence. For the very reason that it is not an extraordinary type of resistance, such as a revolution or a rebellion, but an everyday one, it is a sustained model of resistance. Takeda focused her interest on that point.

The creativity of self-criticism

Gradually, such research into popular arts also grew from being the work of intellectuals like Takeda who specialised in writing to that of a new type of intellectual born from among 'the people' themselves. One of 'people' who began to express his own thoughts not as a mere object, but as a subject, was Tadao Satō (1930–). Born in Niigata Prefecture as the youngest of eight children, Satō was four when he lost his father, who had been a ship chandler. After leaving higher elementary school, Satō attended night school while working for Japan National Railways, for Nippon Telegraph and Telephone Public Corporation as a repairman, and so on. Having been a young movie buff since seeing an American musical film the year after the war, he submitted to *Shisō no kagaku* a critical analysis of the psychological characteristics of 'the people' who demanded *yakuza* movies, based on his own feelings as an audience member. Entitled 'Ninkyō ni tsuite (On chivalry),' it was published in August 1954. The twenty-three-year-old Satō, a 'factory worker,' was apparently 'skinny, with an unsavoury look in his eyes, and quite defiant' (Tada 1962: 84).

In 'On chivalry' there is a keen appreciation of the dual nature of 'the people's' consciousness which, while glorifying and exciting empathy for *yakuza* that 'foil the strong and help the weak' and their distinctive model for human relationships, in the end drives these 'lovable *yakuza*' 'outside' the social order. That directly sums up Satō's own psychological tendencies. While nestling close to the feelings of *yakuza*, from his own insider perspective as an enthusiastic fan of *yakuza* movies he simultaneously dispassionately criticised the brittleness of the 'spirit of chivalry' of *yakuza* who would make a bee line for the strong.

From an external viewpoint, it is all too easy to criticise 'the people' who are attracted to *yakuza* films. Is it not important, though, while presupposing such 'people's' sentiments, to find and nurture a critical gaze towards the self who is seized by the old conventions and irrational aspects within them? Satō's 'On chivalry' drew attention as a unique discourse on 'the people' that highlighted the feelings of 'the people' raised amid popular cinema, and turned an internal critical eye upon them.

When the 'Science of thought' coterie aimed at a Copernican transformation in the bearers of philosophy, from the philosophy of professional philosophers to 'the people's philosophy,' what they envisaged there as the ideal form of 'the people'—in other words, the '*seikatsusha*'—was the image of the *seikatsusha* as an 'individual' facing up to the unprecedented historical process of 'war and defeat.'

What was depicted in the personal consultations was the figure of *seikatsusha* who, through starting to recount their troubles and sufferings frankly amid the same generation's problem situation and consulting with others, were trying to find guidelines for their own way of living. The life-recording movement teaches us that a major characteristic of the post-war *seikatsusha* image, as seen in comparison to that of the pre-war, lies in its heightening of self-expression. Moreover, what the *shomin* serial biographies and popular arts research revealed was the 'weak' yet 'sturdy' *seikatsusha* image which had to be Janus-faced in order to survive. The initial 'Science of thought' sought to read new potential for the power of thought within the lively expressiveness and livelihood skills of *seikatsusha* who were endeavouring soundly to survive.

The frames of reference and methods which 'Science of thought' opened up in its attempt to gain proximity to *seikatsusha* thought (transcribing oral accounts, life recording, analysis of personal consultations and popular entertainment) are now widely generalised. It might no longer be possible to perceive any novelty in them as methodologies. More than a half-century ago, in the age immediately following Japan's defeat, however, when there was hardly any scholarship or research that directly posed the thought of the populace that comprised the *seikatsusha*, 'Science of thought' offered an arena where a wide range of people with different ways of thinking, positions and ways of living—from Marxists to un-Marxists, workers and housewives, and from students to researchers— could participate and hold repeated dialogue, testing methodologies as they aimed for the thought-formation of the *seikatsusha*'s day-to-day life.

Now, when the word *seikatsusha* is prolifically used, and appears to be drifting through the age without its substance or foundation being questioned, there is a need to re-interrogate the original intention and methodology of 'Science of thought,' which tried to dig up the *seikatsusha*'s potential for thought, their life's soil and all, is there not?

A *seikatsusha* image with regional origins: the world of Yasuko Mizoue

The phantom people

Whatever their mentality, objectively speaking, most of those in charge of the 'Science of Thought' movement which endeavoured to find a 'philosophy for living' among 'the people,' or, in other words, among *seikatsusha*, were city-bred upper-middle-class intellectuals, that is, urban culturati. In an essay he submitted, 'Ninkyō ni tsuite (On chivalry),' Tadao Satō, who had trodden a path from being a 'worker' to an 'intellectual' as a film critic, writes as follows.

> Due to my having been a worker employed as a factory hand in a regional factory, for a while I was a topic of discussion. What delighted me more than anything was having received a long, long letter of ten or so pages from Mr Tsurumi. It described me as a writer with the ability to do theoretical analysis. After that, I had pieces published in *Shisō no kagaku* several times, and usually came to be called a *jikkan-shugisha* (one who prioritises sensations over facts). This was not meant in a negative sense, for I was apparently being praised, but it seems to have signified a person with a different perception of daily life from that of intellectuals, because of being a worker; and I was not always comfortable with that (Satō 1986: 94).

To put it the other way around, the very fact that Satō became 'a topic of discussion' because his submissions had come from a 'worker employed in a regional factory,' tells of the extent to which 'Science of thought' was a collection of homogeneous people. Though 'Science of thought' advocated interchange between people with differing viewpoints in both ideological and class terms, as one of its movement objectives, it still remained such a homogeneous group that the appearance of a heterogeneous member became a huge talking-point. It is hard to deny that, regardless of the 'sincerity' of each member who was trying to create their own thought through interchange with others, the class-related and geographical bias of such leaders was imposing a certain limit upon 'the people's' objects and perspectives.

The following letter, sent by Ryō Ōmura, Chief Editor of *Iwate no hoken* (Iwate health) (an official publication of Iwate Prefecture health-preservation groups, founded in 1952) to the editorial division of *Shisō no kagaku*, hints at that:

> I wonder if the editing of *Shisō no kagaku* is being done with tangible people who exist in this world inscribed inside its editors' eyelids. I have had the impression that it might be being done with nebulous, phantom people as its subject matter (Tsurumi 1954: 284).

Taciturn farmers

Ōmura is the author of a 1958 book, *Mono iwanu nōmin* (Taciturn farmers). It was in late 1946 that he was repatriated from the Okinawa battlefront. For the subsequent four years, he walked around the farming villages in his native Morioka as a travelling salesman of used clothing. Even the farmers who would not speak to outsiders talked to this 'piddling' travelling salesman in a tone unlike the one reserved for guests. Later, having become the editor of *Iwate no hoken*, Ōmura came to retrace his steps to the villages he had once visited with his bundle of second-hand clothes, only this time carrying notebook and pen. Ōmura's idea was that though medical services for curing farmers' illnesses and managing their health were also vital, what was even more important was to look to the very 'lifestyle' of farmers who, even when they did become ill, could not say they were ill. For rural folk, sickness and everyday life are connected issues. In order to find out about the hidden realities of life, he resolved first to get 'taciturn' farmers to open their mouths; and to jot down the 'fireside chats' in which villagers' daily livelihood and ways of thinking would make their appearance unadorned.

From country folks' murmured comments exchanged at the fireside at the words of a daughter-in-law from a farming household, who responded to someone calling a hello by coming out and saying, 'Nobody is home,' he was determined to grasp the reality of the life hidden behind their backs. To Ōmura, the 'Science of thought' movement—which it would be hard to describe as understanding the concrete image of the people (*minshū*), in spite of claiming to be 'from the inside' of the people—must have seemed such a hypocritical and theoretical thing.

This was also a strident criticism vis-à-vis 'Science of thought's' 'people's philosophy,' which strove to find the image of the *seikatsusha* in the print world of agony columns and popular literature, or *seikatsusha* thought within biographies of the masses compiled with paper and pen. Ōmura felt that the figure of 'the people' who were living in reality had been left behind.

In this way, when research into 'the people's philosophy' lost interest in depicting the concrete figure of *seikatsusha* due to the limitations of those in charge, as if to correct that bias, an attempt to reinterpret farming people, and especially the women, as '*seikat-*

susha' who were living the reality of rural villages was coming into being. Its originator was Yasuko Mizoue (1903–90), author of *Nihon no teihen: San'in nōson fujin no seikatsu* (Japan's margins: the lives of women in San'in rural villages) (1958), *Junan-jima no hitobito: Nihon no shukuzu, Okinawa* (The people of the suffering isles: Okinawa, a microcosm of Japan) (1959), and *Seikatsusha no shisō: zoku Nihon no teihen* (*Seikatsusha* thought: Japan's margins, continued) (1961); and its place of origin was Matsue, in Shimane Prefecture.

About seven years after beginning her life in Matsue, Mizoue was then on the teaching staff at Shimane University, where she lectured in pedagogy and home economy. Mizoue, who made time to 'head east and west, into the mountains and out to solitary islands, to give talks' on such subjects as 'democratisation of the family' and 'livelihood improvement,' appears to be an extension of the lineage of those torchbearers who toured post-war farming communities preaching anti-feudalism, democratisation and modernisation. The impression which her listeners gained from Mizoue, however, was more like that of an obliging 'auntie' addicted to writing letters and who loved chitchat, than that of a 'university professor.'

Wishing to know in what form the message she had delivered in her talks had reached the women from farming households, Mizoue handed round a notebook after the end of each talk and had participants write down their names, addresses, occupations and the like. She continued her 'selfish touting of goodwill,' saying: 'As long as there was nothing special to do, every morning I would drop a line to two or three, asking, "Please write down your thoughts and opinions about even the most trivial things in your everyday life."' The real voices of farming women who came thus to be vividly reproduced in her books were 'precious treasures' that the author had mined from amid associations that were 'as long as seven years, or as short as one,' with a single postcard as a bridge (Mizoue 1958: 319).

The question of *seikatsusha* on the margins

Mizoue understood '*seikatsusha*' first to be inseparable from the expression 'the margins (*teihen*),' and secondly in terms of their connection with 'being women.'

Her 1958 book, *Nihon no teihen* (Japan's margins), popularised the word 'margins' in academic genres of the likes of the history of thought, and went on to trigger a so-called 'margins boom' that included 'from the marginal vantage point,' 'uncovering experiences of the margins,' and 'the history of marginal women.' 'The margins' in this margins boom pointed above all to the 'lower classes' in society who had been left behind economically in the shadow of historical development, and, more broadly, to 'all the rest' who supported the handful of elite at the top.

For Mizoue, though, what 'the margins' meant was not mere economic poverty. She writes that she felt 'anxiety' at 'the margins' in the margins boom being 'accepted as if it referred only to the stratum that simply was not blessed with money' (1961: 268) She could not resist feeling bitter at the attachment of expressions such as 'languishing' or 'gloomy memories' when the term 'margins' was used. For Mizoue, 'the margins' did not indicate 'all the rest.' It meant people who, though nameless, had proper names at their respective living-sites.

This is not to say that Mizoue was refuting the very existence of 'the margins' that Japan's modern age had spawned since the Meiji era. Yet what Mizoue posed was not a question vis-à-vis 'the margins' in such a sense. 'What could one do so that one's life would improve?' 'What should one do to have a livelihood that was even a little bit better than at present?' In Mizoue's words, 'poverty' prompts people to raise questions about their actual situation. While extremely unsophisticated, those questions are really important, compelling ones about the lives of people living on the margins. Those questions finely hone people's sensibility towards 'human rights,' and continually shape and create their lives. People do not have human rights because they are entitled to them. For Mizoue, human rights meant things that only became fixed when they were produced and advocated by people who needed them when they wished to lead an even slightly more satisfying life.

According to Mizoue, it was not that poverty always led people to a 'philosophy of resignation.' Rather, one should focus upon the very potential for the breadth and depth of lives that was hidden in the questions arising from that poverty. Mizoue considered 'the margins' to be the mother-body of 'primordial energy' that gave birth to such questions, and *'seikatsusha'* to mean people who, in the midst of such a reality, posed questions and created lifestyles from within those questions.

Crossing boundaries

One of these people to make an appearance was Shōko Hashimoto (aged 34 at the time), a housewife in a farming household that cultivated 120 ares of farmland on the southern shores of Lake Shinji (Mizoue 1958 : 93–111). In the midst of her life in an extended family, cohabiting with her husband's parents and younger brother, Hashimoto has the desire to attend and learn from the lecture presentations and workshops held at the local community centre. The place of a daughter-in-law in a farming family, however, is as a 'labourer.' If she leaves the house for even two hours, the farm-work will fall behind by that much. If she absolutely wants to go out, she must employ a variety of wiles, exerting herself at her chores for several days previously, and looking out for an opportunity to obtain permission while keeping an eye on her mother-in-law's and husband's countenance. If she thinks that effort to be too much trouble, or if she becomes discouraged, then she cannot go to the meeting.

It is also possible to depict such a life as Shōko Hashimoto's as the tale of a pitiable farm housewife who lives out her days amid the residuum of the *ie* (household) system and harsh farm labour, but the Shōko Hashimoto in Mizoue's book appears as a being quite distant from such a tale. On the impetus of Mizoue's lecture, she begins to keep a diary. In the midst of her hectic life, she records the daily farm-work, the children's growth, the prices of things, and her own feelings towards that day's events and her family. For a moment before going to bed, even in the face of her husband's sarcastic comments that it does not earn her even a penny, she goes on filling notebooks from cover to cover.

What is it that impels Hashimoto to fill the notebooks? Of course, the purpose is neither for showing to Mizoue nor for publishing them somewhere. How can she have a bit better life; and what should she do in order to live as one human being? She writes to ponder those things. By focusing on the life of the farm household, where a daughter-in-law is nothing but 'labour,' she endeavours to grasp the lived realities of family and society as a relationship: asking what she need do to improve her life a little more, and scrutinising her life in order to find an answer to the question by herself, and inscribing that as a daily record in her notebooks. In the process of self-expression that comprises taking a pen and writing her own opinion, she extricates herself from being the 'undifferentiated individual' within the community called the 'household.' In that, Mizoue strove to see the form of the *seikatsusha* who grows amid daily life and draws up new meaning from it.

Seeing such a *seikatsusha*, Mizoue's viewpoint further crossed 'national borders' and expanded into a perspective that reflected Japanese society from Okinawa prior to its 'return to the fatherland,' and the lifestyle in Shimane, where she lived. In 1958, as an invited lecturer at Ryukyu University, she visited Okinawa carrying government-issued identity papers saying 'Yasuko Mizoue, Japanese'; and in the three months that she spent physically in the midst of 'the lives of ordinary people in Okinawa,' Mizoue realised that reportage on Okinawa from 'the mainland' was something which, rather than conveying the life-sized figures of Okinawan people, instead implanted a sentimental feeling into 'mainlanders' that 'the people of Okinawa were miserable and pitiable,' and, as the reverse of that, a sense of superiority over them. In her life in Okinawa, she writes: 'I even felt that *I*, living in Shimane Prefecture, was the more wretched' (Mizoue 1959: 337).

> I mean that the lifestyle issues on this island are all ones found on the Japanese mainland. The fact is that there is no single lifestyle phenomenon specific to this island. It is merely that because it is isolated, the problems are more clearly apparent than on the mainland; and, furthermore, because [Okinawa] has been placed in a unique position in the post-war, its problems are just all the more conspicuous. That is why I came to Okinawa and looked at the mainland. It is vital to acknowledge this fact (Mizoue 1959: 346).

Mizoue thus discovered that the perspective of *seikatsusha* living the reality of agrarian villages in the San'in region had a universality common to the standpoint of people living in every locality.

All-together-ism

Here, too, I wish to emphasise the use of '*seikatsusha*' not as a collective representation, but in the sense of 'each respective' *seikatsusha*. What is depicted in both *Japan's margins* and *The ideology of the seikatsusha* is the modest lifestyle of each individual *seikatsusha* and the figure of each *seikatsusha* who gives forth questions within her (or his) own life. In that sense, Mizoue's 'marginal *seikatsusha*' meant one who had something in common with the image of 'the people' used by the 'Science of thought' movement in contrast to 'the public (*taishū*)' as a mass.

Not long after its publication, *Japan's margins* provoked a great reaction, with arguments both for and against. There was also a lot of criticism. A shared feature of the critical book reviews was their pointing out that 'this book concerns itself with individual people. It must not end at this. The question is precisely what must be done to tie it all together and make it helpful to society' (Mizoue 1961: 270).

At that time, the slogan of the culture movement based in rural villages and factories was: 'Better that a hundred take one step than one takes a hundred,' and inside the movement 'solidarity' and 'unity' were emphasised. Mizoue responds to such criticism as follows:

> You say 'if we join hands and sing songs, consciousness of our union will grow. If we hold demonstrations, our solidarity will strengthen,' but is that true? Because the group always takes precedence there, it is hard for each member's individual awareness of responsibility to surface. The *ori* (the old constitution of farming villages) that has settled on the floor of history will not budge an inch unless each returns him- or herself once to 'the world of the individual' before being integrated into the group through unity and solidarity, with 'anti-feudalism' and 'reform' as its slogans (1961: 270).

Here, for Mizoue, the 'individual' meant each person's self that went on taking responsibility within the 'framework of an inevitable livelihood.' Only when there is responsibility to be assumed in life, as such individuals, does it become possible for 'everyone' to be connected from the inside. One course also might be to connect directly with a 'democratic' or 'reform' group, and aim for transformation of the old constitution and poverty of agricultural villages by means of 'solidarity.' Yet that, by itself, could not become a force for changing rural society from its core. What Mizoue consigned to the words 'marginal *seikatsusha*' was the importance of and possibilities in cultivating a firm sense of 'human rights' within daily life in keeping with the reality of one's own livelihood and opening one's eyes to society without losing sight of poverty and obsolescence. Her ideas, which had been born 'from the root' of a lifestyle, were in that sense more radical.

For the record, in the two decades since writing *Japan's margins*, Mizoue developed the marginal *seikatsusha* into the notion of a '*jinrui* (human) *seikatsusha*' (1978). When asked her title, Mizoue herself says she answered, 'I am a human *seikatsusha*' (1992: 210). The question of *seikatsusha* on the margins has the potential to transcend national borders as something universal to 'all humanity.' Mizouc's hopes and desires were bound up in her declaration of being a 'human *seikatsusha*.'

When Tokyo-bred thought and culture movements were caught up with an ideological image of farmers, and were unable to tie this to a substantive form, Mizoue's *Japan's margins* and *Ideology of the seikatsusha* drew wisdom up from within the life experience of rural women and attempted to explore the possibilities of 'people's philosophy' emanating from a regional area.

What is being a woman?

For Mizoue, being a *seikatsusha* meant above all 'being a woman.' This was because in agrarian society, which was persistently governed by traditional values, the realistic contradictions and challenges tied to the compelling questions within its lifestyle were things that women, more than anyone else, had to confront.

Just as the medicine-peddlers of Toyama would visit every house in even the deepest mountains, in the post-war, the word 'democracy' was 'issued' to every farmhouse tucked away in the valleys, however remotely situated. The word was less efficacious than those Toyama patent medicines, though, as the gap between people's actual lifestyle and the expectations held towards democracy grew all the wider due to the ballooning anticipation that 'this now being a world where democracy holds sway, even women (daughters-in-law) [can]…' In textbooks and newspapers, as well as on the radio, it was a simple matter to sweep away conventional 'common sense' and rewrite it differently. Within real life, though, a shift from the old to the new inevitably involves conflict and struggle. Such a situation gives rise to the question: 'Things were not supposed to turn out like this, so what went wrong?' This then raises a consciousness vis-à-vis human rights. In each individual woman, Mizoue endeavoured to find the power inherent in such a question, which sought to reform the realities of agrarian villages and farming households.

The impetus for Mizoue to discover the image of the mountain village *seikatsusha* in women rather than in men was the way of life of two women—her own mother and another called Ura Shibahara.

Mizoue was born in Hiroshima Prefecture in 1903, as the eighth child of a middle-class farming family. When pregnant with Yasuko, her mother harboured the secret worry that 'if this child again is a girl…,' and so she attempted to 'flush away' the child in her womb by such means as jumping from a great height, or deliberately chilling her abdomen. In later years, when Mizoue was at a loss whether to continue her life of research or to marry and live the life of an ordinary woman, her mother said: 'I feel so sorry to think that you cannot make up your mind because when you were in my tummy, I did not know what to do, not wanting to give birth to you.' Mizoue writes that this was her first experience of being made to realise the same-sex continuity that transcends the parent-child relationship of mother to daughter, through the medium of the irrational discrimination suffered by the female sex.

'Go get yourself a "foundling"'

In the pre-war period, when limitations on female advancement to higher schooling were great, Mizoue progressed from girls' normal school to the Nara Women's Higher Normal School, and further to Tokyo University of Arts and Sciences; then, on top of that, after the war, she entered the graduate school of Kyoto University. In her taking such a pathway, a significant role was played not only by her mother, but also by Ura Shibahara. Around 1922, when Mizoue had graduated from Girls' Higher Normal School and was working as a teacher in the city of Onomichi, Ura Shibahara, a native of a neighbouring village, was practising as a midwife in a fishing community near Onomichi. She became an adviser to the fishermen's wives worried about their poverty being exacerbated by their having many children, and she went around expounding the necessity for birth control. It was not until 1922 that the birth-control movement was initiated in Japan by people like Shidzue Kato and Isoo Abe, in response to Margaret Sanger's visit to that country. That being the case, then Ura Shibahara, who already had been enthusiastically going around giving guidance from the mid-1920s, could be named as one of the pioneers of that movement.

It was Shibahara's habit to say to Mizoue: 'Yasuko, you mustn't become a person who goes around in pursuit of money. Be someone that money itself chases after, begging you to use it!' It was due to Shibahara's encouragement and financial aid that Mizoue quit her teaching job in 1923 and entered Nara Women's Higher Normal School.

In 1934, at the age of thirty-one, Mizoue made up her mind to go on to Tokyo University of Arts and Sciences. In contrast to her father, who feared for her future, demanding: 'What is the use of studying so much?,' her mother cheered her on, saying that if Mizoue herself were prepared to take the responsibility, then she should go on studying as long as she wanted. Her mother had been unable to read or write, but at the age of sixty-eight, when she ceased farm work, she started learning to become literate. Once, her mother said to the unmarried Mizoue that she should 'go and get herself a "*hiroigo* (foundling)"'—in Hiroshima dialect, the word *hiroigo* means an illegitimate child. 'I'm still in good health, so I'll help you to bring up the child. If there's a child around, it'll cheer me up, as well, and I'll have something to look forward to,' the mother said. 'You and I would raise it, so nobody would have any complaints' (Mizoue 1980, p. 96). This was at a time when Mizoue was spending her days living in a rented room in Tokyo, with barely enough to feed herself.

In this day and age, to suggest bearing an illegitimate child does not sound particularly bizarre. As an expression used by a woman seventy-five years ago, however, it had the ring of a bold challenge towards the 'common sense' that underpinned the traditional *ie* (household) system. If only one had the will to shoulder the responsibility oneself, then anything would be permissible—here is expressed a strong self-assertiveness as a *seikatsusha* that precedes the words 'human rights' or 'right to self-determination.' With the idea that the condition for being a *seikatsusha* was whether one continued to have the desire and will for freedom of spirit, whatever the circumstances, behind Ura Shibahara and her own mother Mizoue saw the potential in many rural women to be such *seikatsusha*.

The lifestyle that Mizoue saw in agrarian villages and farming households in the 1950s was still changing at a slow pace, being that of an age when their stagnation and feudal nature were becoming central topics. Amid such temporal conditions, Mizoue endeavoured to see the *seikatsusha* within the form of each one of the women living in rural villages who were making efforts to divine the direction of change in the midst of the realities of their lives.

It was into the 1960s when, along with the rapid growth of the economy, rural villages and the way of life there began to undergo a drastic transformation. The age of high economic growth, on the one hand, promoted the rapid modernisation of agriculture in the direction of increasing mechanisation → off-farm employment → dual occupations, while on the other hand accelerating fragmentation of 'the margins' itself by spawning subgroups of people left behind—those who had abandoned agrarian occupations, and long-term domestic migrant workers.

More than thirty years later, in 1994, twenty-three percent of people carrying on agriculture in Japan were men aged over sixty-five, while a mere seventeen percent were men under sixty-five, with women making up sixty percent (Nōrinsuisanshō 1994). The potential for women who are the ones in charge of the changing 'margins' to become *seikatsusha*: that is the issue now being freshly called into question.

3 Negotiating consumer society

Farewell to the consumer: Nobuyuki Ōkuma's economic criticism

The *seikatsusha* declaration

In the realm of economics, the first person to have contraposed *seikatsusha* with the category of 'consumer,' and use it as a concept which transcended the latter, was the economist Nobuyuki Ōkuma (1893–1977). 'In handing the word "consumer" back to economics, I venture to stand in a position of new awareness that we are *seikatsusha*' (Ōkuma 1963 [1974]: 191).

It was at the beginning of the 1960s, when the Japanese economy had begun to race along a path to high growth, that Ōkuma expanded his *seikatsusha* theory in earnest. His initial use of the word *seikatsusha* had been earlier, however, in articles penned during the Second World War, including 'Seikatsu no genron (Principles of lifestyle)' (1940) and 'Shin kaseigaku (New domestic science)' (1943). There, it is pointed out how important it is for all disciplines, including economics, to consider human beings in the context of their lifestyle before any scientific consideration, and to look hard at the concrete day-to-day-ness of '*seikatsusha*' who are lifestyle practitioners. The notion of *seikatsusha* thus was none other than one spawned from Ōkuma's methodological attitude of trying always to envisage scholarship from the realities of life.

Such a *seikatsusha* discourse of Ōkuma's was seriously developed against a backdrop of the emergence of what Walt Rostow calls 'the age of high mass consumption,' in which a diversity of products began to be the target of popular demand in large quantities. It was in 1958 that the government's 'White Paper on the Economy' employed the expression 'consumer revolution' for the first time, and emphasised the fact that ownership of the 'three sacred treasures (*sanshu no jingi*),' namely a washing machine, a refrigerator and a black-and-white television, had begun to spread among the middle classes. By the mid-sixties, these were further augmented by a car, a telephone and a colour television, and dreams of an affluent life of consumption went on to shape people's new desires, spurred by various advertising techniques and the popularisation of loans. This was also an age in which the new field called marketing grew in the world of economics, and consumer research by firms who saw people as 'fair game' began to gain momentum.

Those were times when a nationwide effort was made to raise GNP, that is, to double income, under the catch-phrases of 'Investment breeds investment,' 'Catch up and overtake,' and 'It is good to be big,' and the industrialist values of mass production and mass consumption were unconditionally accepted. It is important that, in such an age, Ōkuma dared to come out with the '*seikatsusha*' concept, and present it as a task for academic inquiry.

Product-oriented economics

Essential works for examining Ōkuma's *seikatsusha* discourse are his paper 'Ningen seimei no saiseisan riron (Theory on the reproduction of human life)' (1974); and *Katei-ron* (On the home) (1963), his new discussion of the home whose proposals were based on the former theory. These writings constituted a grand summation of the thinking that Ōkuma had consistently pursued and accumulated since the wartime years.

His *seikatsusha* theory first starts with criticism of the conventional economic approach that analysed and understood the cycle of production and consumption from a 'product'-oriented (material-oriented) perspective. His basic viewpoint was to try to re-apprehend the cycle of production and consumption from a 'human'-oriented standpoint, as a total life-process involving the maintenance and continuation of life.

Economics, as a representative social science, has developed its scholarship on the foundation of classifying the human preoccupations of maintaining and continuing life into the two activities of production and consumption, and coming to understand them. Economics further seeks the theme of its analysis in 'the cyclical process of material reproduction, which centres upon capital.' Placing capital at the centre in this way means that the production of goods becomes the major research issue. As humans are also problematised there from a product-oriented perspective, they end up being 'classified into the two categories of producers of materials, and their consumers.' Economics 'labels *seikatsusha* (us) as "consumers," calls our life-materials "consumption goods," calls our home economy the "consumer economy," and calls our consumption "final consumption." Ōkuma asserts that uncritically bringing such an economic mentality into our everyday consciousness means 'humans lose sight of their lifestyle.' He says that such an economic mentality has locked people's 'lifestyle' within consumption, and narrowed the meaning of lifestyle (Ōkuma 1974: 180).

According to Ōkuma's way of thinking, simple consumption and simple production do not exist as single entities. To work is to produce things, but at the same time it is also the consumption of life; to eat is to consume things, but simultaneously it is the production of life. Given that the word production has two meanings, the word consumption also has a dual significance; accordingly, the only thing that actually exists is a 'lifestyle' as a united whole consisting of production and consumption. The 'economy' in economics thus will mean living by means of a cycle of production and consumption: in short, a '*seikatsu* (lifestyle).'

If the economy itself indicates a 'lifestyle,' then it is possible to give a fresh definition to the word '*seikatsu*,' as follows: in other words, it is the 'cyclical relationship of eating in order to work, eating and giving birth, with those that are born working in order to eat. The objective is not to eat, nor is it to work. To go on living, and to sustain life through those cycles,' is the goal.

In other words, a lifestyle is none other than the entire process for maintaining and expanding life as a human being, the very process of reproducing oneself. In that process, consumption for the sake of the reproduction of life also becomes 'productive consumption,' and we become not consumers, but '*seikatsusha*.' Here, one can probably see the origin of Ōkuma's theory of the reproduction of life, which argues that the business of human life, that is, '*seikatsu*,' must take priority over everything.

Between needs and wants

The second reason for the importance of Ōkuma's *seikatsusha* theory is the concept of the 'needs' and 'wants' in a lifestyle. As long as one-sided, materially-oriented thought prevails, enterprises will always strive to make what people 'really need to want to purchase' indeterminate, so that they will never be able to escape from a condition of frustration no matter how much they buy. In that context, the only answer to a question as to the purpose of consumption will be to fulfil 'wants.' Never will the reply be given that it is for the fulfilment of 'needs.' In such a situation, while still ignorant of their own spontaneous desires, people are made aware of their lifestyle needs as being 'wants,' and satisfying these becomes the measure for 'happiness.' 'Happiness' thus depends on its providers, and grows to be something mostly heteronymous that is regulated by production. Without anyone taking a moment to revisit the question of whether eating tomatoes in the depths of winter signifies a life of abundance, *voilà*, there on the midwinter dining table, arrayed with other foods, are tomatoes, these having become a lifestyle 'need.'

If one assumes that the true nature of a lifestyle lies in maintaining and sustaining life, as previously mentioned, then leaving the question of what is 'needed' for that purpose and how it will materialise up to others, Ōkuma argues, will mean discarding an important part of living as human beings. Naturally, the criteria for judging what comprises a 'need' will probably differ according to the times and the individual, but deciding on the 'lifestyle materials and lifestyle conditions considered the minimum necessary for humans to go on living in the fullness of life, both physically and spiritually' is the first challenge for '*seikatsusha*,' and what is important is 'their consciousness of the "minimum" and, on occasion, its testing and enforcement' (Ōkuma 1974: 202).

Amid the poverty-stricken lifestyle of the post-war, it was Wajirō Kon who asserted that people's 'fittingly human lifestyle' began at the point where it transcended mere 'necessity.' In the thick of rapid economic growth, Ōkuma considered that people's 'fittingly human lifestyle' started not from the satisfaction of 'wants,' but from each individual *seikatsusha* having the ability to decide 'what the absolutely necessary things for life were.' Both could be said to be concepts of 'needs' that probe the essence of lifestyles in their respective ages.

From such a 'theory' of Ōkuma's, the following kind of *seikatsusha* image can be drawn. In other words, *seikatsusha* refers to people who are 'aware of the fact that [the basis of lifestyle] is human self-production,' who 'establish "*needs*" and "*freedom*" in terms of time and money, always making a distinction, and forever abiding by "*needs*," and who 'try by their own efforts to minimise their being consumers as objects of commercialistic strategy' (Ōkuma 1974: 197, 201; emphasis in original).

This definition of Ōkuma's could also be paraphrased as follows. The value of goods for human beings is not something that is determined by their exchange value (the value for which a certain good can be exchanged for another good). It depends upon the ability on the human side to accept, utilise and appraise the goods. Ōkuma says that, regardless of their exchange value, things which are of no use in the sustenance, fulfilment or expansion of life are worthless, and *seikatsusha* are the people with the lifestyle-consciousness to seek, in a positive manner, the enlargement of a lifestyle domain built on utility value. In any case, let us confirm the following three points, namely that:

1. *seikatsusha* is a concept contraposed to 'consumers' as the target of commercialism;
2. the behavioural principle of *seikatsusha* is placed not in exchange value in monetary terms, but in utility value set at the core of the reproduction of life; and
3. whether people are *seikatsusha* depends upon the extent of their ability to accept, use and appraise goods

If we summarise the characteristics of such *seikatsusha*, the result will be as in Table 3.1.

Ōkuma's *seikatsusha* theory, which started from a criticism vis-à-vis economics that drove 'lifestyle' away from 'production' and locked it up in 'consumption,' was unable to achieve the status of a majority opinion in the Japanese society of the time. Never did there emerge any economists who accepted his problem-raising as a challenge to economics, nor any people perceptive enough to see that his assertion of '*seikatsusha*' as contraposed to 'consumers'

Table 3.1: Comparison of consumer and seikatsusha (1)

	Consumer	Seikatsusha
1	Actor in consumption	Actor in '*seikatsu* (living)' as a united whole of production and consumption
2	Object of commercialism	Subject of commercialism
3	Emphasis on exchange value as a behavioural principle	Emphasis on utility value as a behavioural principle

was ahead of its time as a task to tackle 'from here on.' It was not until the early 1970s, when shadows began at last to fall over high economic growth, that the industrialistic value of mass production and mass consumption itself came to be called into question.

The age of popularisation of housewifery

Ōkuma's standpoint, which propounded a shift from economics centred on the production of goods to economics focused on human beings, expanded to the rediscovery and reappraisal of the home and family, the space for the operation of human life. Seen from what was common sense in economics at the time, this meant quite a revolutionary shift in thinking.

Under the macroscopic methodology of classical economics, typified by Marx's *Das Kapital*, microscopic theoretical categories such as the family and the home are ignored. Modern economics, which adopts a microscopic methodology, by contrast, sees the enterprise and the family as the two basic economic units that comprise a national economy. Moreover, as previously mentioned, taken from the conventional wisdom of economics that regards the production of goods to be the main axis of an economy, the enterprise comes to be ordained as the unit of production, and the family (family budget) as the unit of consumption. Into the world of economics, where such orthodoxy reigned, Ōkuma carried his proposition that 'the family is the unit of reproduction of human life.'

Seen from this proposition, the family, as the unit of production that gives rise to human life, must be re-positioned as the economic agent of foremost importance. That is a natural conclusion from Ōkuma's viewpoint, which sees production as meaning not only the producing of goods, but also the renewal of human life; and his family theory went on, as was, to tie with the discourse of the housewife as the main actor in the reproduction of life.

Just as in the case of his *seikatsusha* discourse, Ōkuma's family and housewife theories, also, were ones born from a stern confrontation with 'the times,' amid a tense relationship with the latter. In that sense, Ōkuma's family- and housewife discourses cast deep shadows over the temporal situation from the end of the 1950s into the 1960s. Let us look for a while at what kind of age the 1960s were for families and housewives.

A fall in the ratio of people engaged in self-employment (from 56.5 percent in 1955 to 39.2 percent in 1965) (Cabinet Office, 'Labour-force Survey') and an increase in employed workers (from 43.5 to 60.8 percent over the same period), was a process in which the *omote* (outward-facing side) of the household—which, for families, had been open to society through the operation of a family business: a semi-public life-space, one might say—was drastically pruned, and it brought about a huge change in the position and role of the housewife within the family. The majority of housewives who had hitherto managed things inside the house by themselves, and also had run the family business along with their husbands in the production space at the front, now went on to assume a home-bound existence in which they supported their husbands who were full-time breadwinners working as salarymen, while the wives mainly took charge of housework and child-rearing.

Wives' domestic labour in the modern family (nuclear family) changes into what Ivan Illich (1980) calls 'shadow work'—that which, out of sight in the shadows, supports the husbands' socially-approved labour. Shadow work signifies 'unpaid servitude' in the private domain: labour which does not receive a fair wage assessment. It was in the Taisho era (1912–26) that the term '*shufu* (housewife),' referring to a wife who devotes herself to housework and child-rearing, came into general usage, but the birth of the housewife as a distinct social 'stratum' and her popularisation was none other than a product of the sudden proliferation of the urban salaryman family in the period of high economic growth. The age of the so-called 'professional housewife (*sengyō shufu*)' was not to continue for long, however.

The consumption revolution whose mainstay was the diffusion of electrical appliances, which advanced in the high-growth period, was something that greatly altered people's lifestyle, but it played the role of splitting the stratum of housewives in urban salaryman families in two directions.

On one hand, against a background of the increase in demand for female labour, out from among the housewives whose housework burden had been lightened by the consumer revolution there began to emerge some women who ventured outside the home and entered employment (*kengyō shufu-ka*—the part-timisation of housewifery). On the other hand, housewives who had been cut off from a local community because of progressive urbanisation came to have an even more house-bound existence, and there was increasing fixation of their role as housewives (*sengyō shufu-ka*: the full-timisation of housewifery). The majority of *kengyō shufu* were of the re-employed type: housewives who had quit their jobs for a time upon marriage or childbirth, and had re-entered the labour market around the time their children started school, the dominant pattern of their employment being as part-timers. In the case of full-time housewives, the 'privatisation' of the family (known by the hybrid term 'my-home-*shugi* (my-home-ism)') was accelerated amid competition between families over the acquisition of 'affluence,' symbolised by the purchase of material goods, and, at the same time, there emerged a stratum of housewives all the more strongly tied to the housewife's role. As they had swiftly begun to lose their human relationships at the front of the house (*omote*) which had been a semi-public space, as well as in the life-space that constituted the local community, many women who occupied a housewife's position intensified their feeling of social isolation.

Later, division in a further two directions arose among full-time housewives. One was that of the housewife as a leader in civic movements that grappled with such issues as peace, consumption and welfare; while the other was that of the mother who poured the spare time and energy arising from the spread of household appliances and the rationalisation of housework into her children. That marked the emergence of the 'education mother (*kyōiku mama*).'

Out of these, it was probably the *kyōiku mama* that expressed the full-time housewife's feeling of social isolation particularly strongly. It was after the dawn of the 1960s that the sight of mothers accompanying their children to university entrance examinations began to meet the eye, as the symbol of mothers who had high interest, expectations and estimations in regard to their children's academic achievement. Those mothers, having an excessive concern for their children, confirmed their own existence through looking after their offspring, trying to gain vicarious satisfaction from setting their children onto an elite course. It was from around this time that housewives complaining of being troubled by loss of identity began to appear and proliferate in a personal advice column entitled 'Jinsei annai (Life guidance),' which had run for half a century in the Yomiuri newspaper.

Changing men to be like women

Great transformations in the state of the family and the position of the housewife engendered bewilderment and confusion among people. From the end of the 1950s through to the mid-60s, there were dramatic changes like these in the times and in society, as the backdrop for the unfolding of the housewife debate and family debate.

The housewife debate (*shufu ronsō*) which had a vital significance in the development of post-war women's and family theory was touched off by Ayako Ishigaki's 1955 paper, '*Shufu to iu dai-ni shokugyō ron* (On the second occupation of being a housewife),' and it unfurled centring upon the pros and cons of housewives' entry into the workforce, and whether full-time housewifery was necessary. This is called the First Housewife Debate. Opinions were divided over Ishigaki's paper, and lively discussion unfolded with such opinions as Tadao Umesao's '*Tsuma muyō ron* (On the non-necessity for a wife),' one that argues that 'because the housework clung to by the housewife is being taken over by enterprises through the expansion of capitalism,' the wife should stop hanging onto unnecessary housework and have a job; Keiko Shimizu's 1955 view in her article, 'Shufu no jidai wa hajimatta (The age of the housewife has begun),' which emphasised the significance of full-time housewives' participation in movements, saying that the age of the housewife who took charge of all kinds of campaigns for 'preservation of peace and happiness' had arrived; and, further, Kyū Eikan's 1957 opinion, in his 'Danjo bungyō ron (On the sexual division of labour),' that the division of labour between men and women is natural providence.

The Second Housewife Debate opened up in 1960 and continued into the next year, pivoting on Fujiko Isono's 1960 paper, 'Fujin kaihō ron no konmei (The mess in the women's liberation discourse),' which argued that housewives' domestic labour should be paid; and counter-arguments from economists to the effect that housewives' domestic labour generated utility value but not exchange value. One could say this debate was one that aimed for a radical reinterrogation of the value of housework which the increase in working housewives (such as part-timers) had brought about in a way that was hard to avoid. Amid this series of housewife debates, Ōkuma ended up energetically developing his own theories on the family and the housewife.

The originality of Ōkuma's family theory lies firstly in its valuing of the home and family as a space where there exists the supreme principle of co-operation: 'From each according to his ability, to each according to his need.' This principle is the ultimate ideal in socialist thought, but there has yet to be any state on earth that has achieved it. Inside the family, however, this principle is alive and well. Nowhere are there parents who do not feed their children just because the children do not work. In the home, everyone simply needs to say, '*Gochisō-sama* (Thanks for the feast).' The world where everything is for free only exists in reality in the home. For human lifestyles, there is abundant meaning within the workings of the home that cannot be understood only in terms of monetary value.

Even if the productive functions that had been assumed by the pre-modern family were to be outsourced to companies, its educational functions to schools, and its entertainment functions to entertainment facilities, the modern family's *raison d'être* would not disappear. Far from it: Ōkuma argues that the function called the 'unceasing renewal of life' appears in an even more refined form as the essence of the unchanging family (1961 [1963]: 98).

Secondly, having faced the advent of the nuclear age under the paradigm of the Cold War between East and West, Ōkuma regards states that can become armed groups of 'death' as evil, and sheds light on the *raison d'être* of the family, which is at the opposite extreme. Behind Ōkuma's state view, which deems the very family which brings forth and nurtures life to be none other than the bearer of a new value called 'life' to supplant the state, there is hidden his own 'war and defeat' experiences, as I will later elaborate. Ōkuma stressed that the thing one must thus protect is not the state but the family; the direction one should take is not one of 'self-annihilation for the sake of the nation,' but of 'annihilation of the public for the sake of the private;' and the ideology one ought to learn is the idea that 'it is precisely private life that is an ultimate value for human life'—in other words, a 'family'-centric way of thinking.

Thirdly, in his advocacy of such a family discourse, Ōkuma positively championed the housewife's *raison d'être*. The reproduction of humanity that constitutes childbearing and raising children goes without saying, but if one compares the entire process of food 'production' to a relay race, then the last person to be handed the baton is the housewife in a family.

'Even in the present day,' says Ōkuma, 'the duty of a housewife lies not in consumption but in production, from start to finish. All the care taken in the kitchen to carry out that duty is essentially a *seikatsusha*'s care' (1961 [1963]: 232).

Seen from his standpoint which aims at a shift in values from the property-centric to the life-centric, the 'housewife's duty' becomes extremely important. As long as one adheres to a way of thinking that centres on the production of material things, the housewife will be a 'consumer' and the family's activities cannot amount to anything greater than a 'consumption economy.' By contrast, if one adopts a way of thinking that centres on human life, then the housewife will be a '*seikatsusha*' who takes on the dual aspects of consumption and production, and the activity of the family will become a 'lifestyle economy.' In her running of her daily livelihood, the housewife develops into a '*seikatsusha*.'

It probably should not be overlooked that Ōkuma's housewife discourse was not one that simply championed the housewife, but one that advocated 'changing men to be like women.' Claiming that there is a need 'to change men to be like women' in order to establish a set of values that centre not on the public (enterprises or states) but on 'the private,' Ōkuma comments as follows:

> Men's dedication, too, should turn and head for home. Men have until now been convinced that all kinds of competition and struggle are what makes life worth living, but now that war itself has come to mean the self-destruction of the human race, the system of manly virtue which makes heroic acts in conflict its epitome has crumbled. Human beings no longer should die for states or for production: the protection of life is their highest obligation. It is necessary to *rediscover* that the very wellspring of life is the home (1963: 133; emphasis in original).

This call by Ōkuma to 'change men to be like women' was one that pre-empted the advocacy in the Japanese Women's Lib movement at the turn of the 1970s for 'not changing women to be like men, but changing men to be like women.'

Chizuko Ueno, who brought together the whole picture of the housewife debates, sees historical constraints and transience in the way that both the first and second housewife debates lacked a perspective which interrogated the sexual division of labour itself. They did not ask why women alone had to do unpaid housework as 'housewives,' and shoulder the burden of raising children. Ueno points out that Ayako Ishigaki's 'On the second occupation of being a housewife,' which touched off the first housewife debate, was 'merely recommending having a "first occupation" in addition to trivialised and labour-saving housework,' and the second housewife debate 'ended up being an interchange of academic terminology from economics (especially Marx) from first to last, having neither cut into the ideology of the sexual division of labour, nor touched upon the grounds for changing housewives into workers' (Ueno 1982: 235–239).

There, the feminist perspective which aims to resolve the sexual division of labour and establish a new norm of 'men and women sharing domestic work' instead is weak. By contrast, Ōkuma's theory of 'changing men to be like women,' which was deduced from economic criticism and a shift in his view of the state, embryonically incorporated a perspective that could interact with feminism.

The cave-in of the 'annihilation of the public for the sake of the private'

Ōkuma's theory of 'changing men to be like women' invited all kinds of repercussions, and stirred up the so-called home debate (*katei ronsō*). Taking a firm critical stand against Ōkuma, Yūji Aida wrote 'Doubts towards the family-as-absolute theory' (1963), and Takeshi Muramatsu penned 'Rejecting a womanish age' (1963). These had a common theme in that both superimposed the 'man–woman' relationship onto the traditional 'public–private' relationship, and viewed Japan's post-war as the age of female-culture-centrism, family-as-almighty-ism, and the principle of prioritising private life with concern. In rebuttal of Ōkuma's argument for switching from 'sacrificing the self for the public good' to 'sacrificing the public for the private good,' they advocated the restoration and reinforcement of the pre-war model of 'sacrificing the self for the public good (*messhi bōkō*)' (Kano 1995).

It is not fitting, however, to see the argument they expounded for 'sacrificing the self for the public good' as meaning a back-to-the-prewar rebound. Considering the then-current social reality, a change in people's consciousness from 'self-sacrifice for the public good' to 'public sacrifice for the private good' was already in rapid progress. In this period, when the Japanese economy had started to gather steam under the income-doubling policy and the boom that accompanied the Tokyo Olympics, the principle of prioritising private life and 'my-home-ism,' which focused all of their interest upon fulfilment in private life in the family unit, had begun to spread as a trend of the times. The age had transitioned from a political season where 'independence' and 'democracy' were able to become symbols that moved people, to an economic season where the wish for a rise in their standard of living took root in people's consciousness.

The home, which had lost its connection with the local community, became a space for the satisfaction and consumption of the desires constructed by the market and mass media. In order to fulfil the urge to consume in the space of their private life, husbands were expected to show even greater devotion by enterprises in the public domain, which had become the economic means, while wives were required to create the comfortable home which would support their husbands from the inside. Loyalty and spontaneous subordination were demanded of families not only so that they could maintain an affluent home, but also for the enlargement and development of the enterprises that were its prerequisites, as well as economic income and total output as a whole. This was something that meant the formation of a new relationship between the family (private) and business/government (public), and the emergence and expansion of a new form of 'self-sacrifice for the public good' (which was also 'public sacrifice for the private good' in a new guise).

Taking 'public sacrifice for the private good' as the antithesis to wartime nationalism, Ōkuma pinned his hopes on the potential for growth of a spirit that treasured privacy in private life, and of autonomy for each individual. There is no doubt that this had a certain measure of validity as a transient ideology contraposed to state evil. The 'public sacrifice for the private good' argument did not, however, did not hold 'my-home-ism' in check. This was because, though the logic for the justification of 'serving the country' had crumbled and people had been freed from state control, the liberation of private desires came to be single-mindedly pursued instead, without the emergence of any aspirations towards the fulfilment of private life as a space in which privacy and autonomy were valued, or the establishment of a new 'publicness (*kōkyōsei*)' (a collective domain supported by responsible citizens).

In contrast to the negative and pessimistic aspects inherent in these 'changing men to be like women' and 'public sacrifice for the private good' discourses of Ōkuma's, his *seikatsusha* theories ought to have included a keen posing of issues to make people aware of privatised lifestyle conditions and overcome them.

Ōkuma's 'changing men to be like women' did not merely mean the return of men to the home, which had become the site of consumption. One could view this as something aimed at 'transforming men into *seikatsusha*' by rescuing them from specialising in production in their professional lives, and making them change their attitude from consumer to *seikatsusha*. The same applies as regards his idea of 'public sacrifice for the private good.' This is not something that gave a nod to people's tendency to lose concern for the public domain and increasingly place value only upon the private domain. It was supposed to be something that called for values which emphasised private life, aiming at the reconstruction of the private domain—especially the realm of the family, which had turned into a 'unit of consumption'—from the perspective of a 'unit of production' of human life.

Ōkuma's argument for 'changing men to be like women' and 'public sacrifice for the private good'—in other words, his family discourse—was something that had meaning only after having been supplemented and integrated by another *seikatsusha* discourse. Doubts remain, however, as to the extent to which Ōkuma at that time had an eye to that integration. This is because his advocacy of 'changing men to be like women' and 'transforming men into *seikatsusha*,' which existed as germs of thought, ended almost without any deep exploration as what might be the necessary realistic conditions for men to turn themselves into *seikatsusha*.

Why was that? One reason can probably be sought in Ōkuma's own eye, which saw 'the family' and 'the home' as absolute. As I shall later elaborate, due to his deeming the essence of the state to be evil, which stemmed from remorse over his own errors during the war; his zeal for finding the bearers of new values to replace those of the state in the home and family; and his over-idealisation of the family and home, Ōkuma overlooked the hidden aspects of the family—its self-protectiveness and family egotism that willingly tied and subordinated themselves to business and the state, if it meant enlarging the family's share of the pie.

'There is no wealth but life'

Ōkuma's economics was full of an originality that exceeded the margins of the traditional cognisance of economics. One might find the key to his uniqueness and originality in his literary interests, nurtured since his middle-school days, and his poetic intuition as a poet, for one, and in the turn in his view of the state, brought about by his experience of 'war and defeat' as an opinion-leader under the wartime regime, for another.

Ōkuma was born in 1893 in the city of Yonezawa in Yamagata Prefecture, and the curtain fell on his life in 1977 at the age of eighty-four. He lost his father at thirteen and was raised by a literature-loving mother. When in his fifth year at middle school, he loved reading the *tanka* poetry of Takuboku Ishikawa, and, under that influence, Ōkuma joined the journal *Seikatsu to geijutsu* (Life and art), presided over by Aika (Zenmaro) Toki, and began to compose *tanka* poems himself. After graduating from Yonezawa Middle School, he entered Tokyo Commercial College (forerunner of the present-day Hitotsubashi University), but was unable to interest himself in the school's subjects. He joined the editorial committee of the alumni association's magazine, and just managed to retain his connection with the world called school through composing *tanka*.

Leaving the Higher Commercial School, Ōkuma was employed in a flour-milling company, but soon quit and immersed himself in planning and writing a full-length novel, with the idea of pursuing literature. While doing so, he also was absorbed in reading the works of John Ruskin, William Morris, Tolstoy, Schopenhauer and the like. However, the long novel that he had inclined his enthusiasm to penning, to the extent of quitting his company job, remained unfinished. He was 'unclear' as to 'what had been the impetus for the cooling of [his] literary passion,' but spurred by the idea that he 'wanted to do something scientific,' he returned to his alma mater and studied economics anew under Tokuzō Fukuda. Four years had passed since his graduation (Oketani 1994: 20).

The two volumes, the famed economist Hajime Kawakami's *Binbō monogatari* (The tale of poverty) and Ruskin's *Unto This Last*, are said to have exerted the greatest influence upon Ōkuma's choice of course. He was particularly deeply struck by the quote: 'There is no wealth but life,' in Kawakami's preface to *Unto This Last*. There is nothing apart from life that counts as wealth—led by these words, Ōkuma completed a dissertation entitled: 'A comparative study of Carlisle, Ruskin and Morris' in Tokyo Higher Commercial School's postgraduate division. That single quote from Ruskin's book is what formed the key concept in Ōkuma's economics, and until his end at eighty-four, Ōkuma was never to deviate from it (Tsurumi 1993: 18).

His having thus followed a roundabout course for an aspiring economist—approaching economics from the outside world of *tanka* poetry and literature to which he inclined his enthusiasm in his boyhood years, and the artistic criticism and critiques of civilisation by Ruskin and Morris that he liked to read throughout his youth—comprises one feature of Ōkuma's economics. Moreover, the fact that both Ruskin and Morris were not specialist economists, but superb social thinkers, and studying them was not so much a direct path to economics research, but closer to a by-road, is an important point.

On the subject of his connection with literature, it is known that through poetry and *tanka*, Ōkuma had friendly relations with Takiji Kobayashi (1903–33), author of *Kani kōsen* (The cannery boat). In 1921, in the spring of the year that Takiji Kobayashi entered Otaru Higher Commercial School, Ōkuma took up the post of newly-appointed teacher in charge of economic theory. It was when he was twenty-eight. Ōkuma recalls the Kobayashi of around that time as being a literary youth who liked poetry and *tanka*, was 'neat and unpretentious, with a cheerful air, often speaking with his white teeth bared in a smile' (Ōkuma 1977: 215). One year later than Kobayashi, the writer Sei Itō entered Otaru Higher Commercial School. Itō writes of being jealous of Kobayashi, who spoke in familiar terms with Ōkuma, but Ōkuma did have a strange charm that attracted young men aged around twenty. The critic Hideaki Oketani writes that this was a charm generated not so much from Ōkuma's deep academic knowledge and broad education, but rather from 'the experience of having done up the buttons of his life wrongly, and taken a circuitous route,' such as his having suddenly announced that he wanted to 'become a monk,' saddening his mother, and his having experienced deep frustration in his literary aspirations (Oketani 1994:17).

The glow in the windows of little houses

Ōkuma's interest and ideas vis-à-vis 'the house' as the site of human reproduction dates back to the pre-war period. His original idea is hard to understand in the absence of his credentials as a poet. It was in the preface to his book published in 1938, *Keizai honshitsu ron* (Theories of the essence of economics) (Second edition), that Ōkuma first took up 'the house,' arguing the necessity for research on 'the house' which was 'the organ of human production (birth, cultivation and education).' Ōkuma had grasped his idea of 'the house' even earlier, during his teaching days at Takaoka Higher Commercial School. He records the moment he hatched the idea as follows. It is a little long, but let me cite it:

> Something that happened one autumn evening I will never forget as long as I live. When I was walking alone along a country road in that area of Takaoka called Nakagawa, with the intention of taking a stroll, there was a dark grove of trees on one side, while on the other, the bright windows of little farmhouses were dotted at distant intervals along the road. As a landscape, there was probably nothing special about it. It was the sort of ordinary road that a person would pass along without anything to give his mind pause, but something unexpectedly happened to me on that very spot that I would find hard to forget for the rest of my life, namely, that on that spot on the road at twilight, I realised 'the meaning of a house.' It is mysterious, should I say, how the image in my field of vision in that instant still remains in my mind's eye, like a picture set in a frame. During my lifetime I have had several similar experiences, but this was one of the most significant...
>
> The first time I thought I had really seen 'the house' that humans inhabit was that moment when I was walking down that single, absolutely deserted, silent road in the twilight. What was on the other side of those silent paper windows with their bright electric lights? *It was what is called family life: meaning that there the life of human beings was born, it was nurtured, and it died.* The human lifestyle, consisting of eating and working, working and eating, and going to sleep—what one ought to call the units of that lifestyle—the glow in the windows of the little houses along the road was exactly that. It was as if at that moment I had come from a world belonging to a different star, had alighted for the first time upon Earth, and had discovered the nests of humans. I must add that I was still unmarried at the time, and was living alone (1993: 70–71; emphasis added).

Ōkuma's words, such as 'the dark grove of trees in the autumn twilight,' 'the glow in the windows of the little houses,' and 'the life of human beings was born, it was nurtured, and it died,' and the idea of his theory of human reproduction and family theory which was spawned and expanded from that experience, can only be understood on the premise of Ōkuma's disposition and poetic intuition as a poet. Ōkuma says that it is strange in terms of 'common sense' that economics should drive out not only 'production' but also 'lifestyle' from the home, as the site where the cycle of 'eating in order to work, eating and giving birth, with those that are born working in order to eat' is lived out. For him, it was precisely the common sense that was derived from human's poetic intuition and life-intuition that had a more certain persuasiveness.

State evil and the ideal of a home

Ōkuma's post-war started from severe condemnation of his own war responsibility for having played the role of an ideologue under the wartime regime in the state's system of all-out war.

In 1914, when Ōkuma was spending his youth at the age of twenty-two, he harboured cordial sentiments towards socialism, as can be glimpsed from his investment of feelings for socialism in a poem: 'From what I hear/it is as if/all and everything/of their doctrine/already lies hid within us.'

According to the politicist Sannosuke Matsumoto, such a distrust of the capitalist order which Ōkuma had harboured since his youth had turned him not towards socialism but towards a state highly geared to national defence and a state regime for all-out war, in the form of his growing proximity to policy studies and state science (*kokkagaku*). 1937 was around the time of Japan's plunge into war with China; and in 1941, Ōkuma wrote his *Kokkagaku e no michi* (The path to the science of state), recommending the reinforcement of state functions for the fair distribution of resources and efficiency, and expounding the necessity for a total-war discourse to build a state regime highly oriented to national defence. Moreover, the next year, when the Dai Nippon genron hōkoku-kai (Great Japan press patriotic association) (president, Sōhō Tokutomi) was founded as a national policy body of journalists, Ōkuma willingly assumed the post of director. Why did he choose such a course? Sannosuke Matsumoto conjectures that for Ōkuma, who had continued to have socialist sympathies, 'the idea of a state total-war regime perhaps presented as a means for overcoming capitalism in place of the lost pathway of socialist revolution' (Matsumoto 1994: 10).

In 1947, not long after the war's end, Ōkuma published his reflections in the form of 'confessions,' in a book entitled: *Senchū sengo no seishinshi* (A spiritual history of wartime and the postwar) (1979). It was a severe condemnation vis-à-vis his own errors of historical recognition in the war period, and simultaneously also an incisive question as to with what kind of awareness he had been caught up in the nationalistic tone under the wartime regime. Apart from Ōkuma, there was only a tiny handful of intellectuals who made a fresh start after the war without omitting the procedure of summing up their wartime selves.

In this manner, Ōkuma set self-confession as the starting-point of his expressive activities, and, having himself corrected the mistakes he made during the war, penned *Kokka aku* (State evil). Further, in a quest for a principle of the home as something that could carry an opposing doctrine to that evil, he wrote *Katei ron* (On the home).

His new view of the state is expressed in his concise definition of the state as the sole legalised control apparatus that is outside the self (1957: 234). If they were to repudiate the state, the existence of a new group would be necessary for individuals who had severed their connection with the state. For Ōkuma, that group would be none other than the family. Behind Ōkuma's family discourse were hidden his own experiences of 'war and defeat.'

Emphasis on empirical knowledge

The impact of his 'war and defeat' experiences did not only bring about the turn in his view of the state. It also had a radical influence upon his academic methodology. In other words, his methodology was radical in the sense that he did not believe things that had not undergone a process of verification by means of his own experience.

Strictly speaking, his kind of scholarly methodology perhaps should be said to have continuity with the war years. This is because even during the war, Ōkuma adopted a way of thinking that involved 'not grasping the clue to speculation from reading books, but seizing a clue to abstract or fundamental thinking from gazing at the reality of Japan in the war period, and at the wartime lifestyle itself' (1993: 155). He gives more weight to 'empirical knowledge' learned from reality rather than to 'conceptual knowledge' gained from books. That was where his methodological characteristic, which had continued since the war period, lay. It would probably be more appropriate to deem Ōkuma's own experience of frustration due to Japan's defeat as having fulfilled the role of even more stringently tempering his methodology. Ōkuma writes as follows:

> What I think I have newly learned about politics and the state is not something due to words, but to experience…Having got to know something by experiencing it is almost like having the thought that one's humanity has changed by that knowledge' (1979: 500–501).

One continually shapes one's thought by probing the past and experiences within oneself, and by interrogating the meaning which it has for one. Ōkuma, who emphasises the importance of that method, argues that the very common sense born from human beings' life-intuition is 'the real thing.' 'I would like us to return the word "consumer" to economics, and adopt a new awareness that we are *seikatsusha* in everyday life'— as a clear-cut oppositional notion to that of the consumer, the '*seikatsusha*' concept, too, was none other than something generated from Ōkuma's kind of academic methodology.

Ōkuma's *seikatsusha* theory began as a criticism of economics that had driven 'lifestyle,' which is the human business of sustaining life, out of 'production,' and locked it away in 'consumption.' It was in the age of rapid economic growth, when no doubts were ever cast upon the industrialist values of mass production and consumption, that Ōkuma endeavoured from that position of economic criticism to seek the greatest value in the reproduction of human life and find the figure of the *seikatsusha* within the behavioural principles of people who were trying to expand their autonomous domain of living. That was also an age in which the set of values that prioritised economics began to put down roots in people's consciousness. The times were not on Ōkuma's side, and no serious attempts to accept, inherit and develop his problem-presentation made their appearance.

Now that more than a quarter-century has passed, Ōkuma's *seikatsusha* discourse has come to have a much more compelling significance. Amid an overflowing abundance of material things, why is it that people cannot embrace a true feeling of affluence? The value of goods lies not in the exchange value that the goods have in themselves, but on the side of the abilities and values of the people who appraise, enjoy and fully utilise them, does it not? In an atmosphere where the inner truth of people's lifestyle is under question, Ōkuma's *seikatsusha* theory seems now to have begun to have new life.

The malaise of soft individualism: Masakazu Yamazaki and Bellah

The new middle mass

From the late 1970s into the 1980s, discourses on consumer society from a variety of angles mounted the critical rostrum. Debate involving numerous disputants was unfolded, from a problem-concern towards the qualitative transformations in consumer society and the general public, on the one hand, and a crisis-consciousness that the mass market of the period of high economic growth was no longer viable, on the other. Moreover, the figure of the *seikatsusha* began to appear within those consumer-society discourses.

Yasusuke Murakami's *Shin chūkan taishū no jidai* (The age of the new middle mass) (1984), Masakazu Yamazaki's *Yawarakai kojinshugi no jidai* (The age of soft individualism) (1984) and Hakuhōdō seikatsu sōgō kenkyūjo (ed.) *'Bunshū' no tanjō* (The birth of the 'segmented masses') (1985) can be seen as the three volumes that typify the consumer-society theories of these times.

If one looks at the results of public-opinion polls, it will be seen that middle-class consciousness, in which people positioned their own life circumstances as being 'in the middle,' began to permeate rapidly among the Japanese during the high-growth period. From the mid-1960s, the ratio of people with 'middle of the middle' consciousness increased from thirty-seven percent in 1957, to fifty percent in 1964, fifty-seven percent in 1970, and fifty-nine percent in 1977. Furthermore, in 1970, with the addition of 'upper middle' and 'lower middle' to this, the ratio of people with 'middle' consciousness actually reached ninety percent, and the phrase '*ichioku sōchūryūka* (hundred-million-all-turned-middle-class)' society began to be voiced (Sōrifu). In the background, in addition to the equalisation of income, assets and consumption expenditure, there was the homogenisation of lifestyles due to informatisation and the transport revolution.

Murakami takes up this 'whole-populace-has-turned-middle-class' situation, arguing that Japanese people's middle-class consciousness, unlike that of the Western middle class of former times, is not a positive self-definition built on a firm life-base, but, in the sense that they are not upper-class, yet will not be short of tomorrow's crust, either, is nothing more than a 'middling condition' in which they place themselves. He says that it is the expression of a negative self-definition that arose as the result of the melting of a 'one-dimensional measure of class.' Moreover, he proposed a new concept called the 'new middle mass (*shin chūkan kaikyū*),' for though they were 'the masses' in terms of being a 'prodigious number' of people situated in 'the middle' of Japanese society, even so, they were differentiated from the old and new 'middle classes (*chūryū kaikyū*)' in that they were 'not "the masses" as lower-ranking persons or followers, in contrast to the elite as higher-ranking persons or leaders' (Murakami 1984: 194).

Murakami's 'new middle mass' theory had great significance as something that offered a new label to the enormous stratum of people whom it had become impossible to apprehend with a one-dimensional yardstick. Murakami's assertion, which had given the label of 'new middle mass' to the people who were both the beneficiaries of the 'affluent' society and the subjects of consumption, went on to play a role in giving direction to subsequent consumer-society discourses.

Being somebody

Masakazu Yamazaki understands Murakami's so-called 'new middle mass' to be a 'mass society with visible faces.' Yamazaki sees the impending demise of 'three centuries of the industrial age' which 'had a hard, militant production setup on the one hand, and a vast mass society on the other, where the face of one's neighbour was not visible, and where one seldom discovered the human group that ought to have been in the middle.' Yamazaki's assertion was that the transition from 'mass society where faces are invisible' to 'mass society where faces are visible' was a huge shift in terms of the history of civilisation, from a production-dominant society (industrialised society) to one centred on consumption (de-industrialised society); and that the very shift in value-consciousness starting to occur along with that transition was the important thing.

Yamazaki interprets that shift as being a transition from a goal-achievement type of society in which 'the meaning of life' is given by the state, to a goal-exploration type of society where individuals grope for it in a self-aware manner—in other words, he sees it as a change in people's way of being, from that of a 'nobody' who, while being ubiquitously respected, is only treated ubiquitously, to that of a 'somebody' who has individuality in every case. There, people convert themselves from beings that let the greater part of their personality belong to families, schools or enterprises, to beings that seek 'social intercourse' (networks of human relationships) for various kinds of enjoyment in itself, and perform freely there.

Let me cite some examples. In a society where production is dominant, leisure activity meant everyone heading off to play golf. In that context, golf automatically also was business; and so in that sense it was goal-oriented behaviour. That is an abnormal situation, an expression not of affluence, but only of poverty. By contrast, in a consumption-dominant society, leisure activities become determinedly individualised and diversified. People only know in advance that they want 'something fun to do,' but do not know what it is. It is the moment when they discover specific activities and others with similar tastes able to satisfy them together that people realise the content of their own desires and confirm themselves, and in that sense their actions are goal-explorative. Self-exploratory pursuits through all kinds of endeavours and dialogue with others, in contrast to avid, self-aggrandising pastimes such as symbolised by golf—it was within such behavioural principles that Yamazaki recognised the characteristics of a 'somebody.'

The dreams that consumption dreams

Yamazaki sought to see, within this 'person who was somebody,' the germ of a 'soft' individualism based on the de-industrialisation of Japanese society. 'Soft' individualism is used here to mean an 'ego with a more reserved self-assertiveness,' in contrast to traditional Western 'hard' individualism that severely limits the self, and is characterised by goal-orientation, competition and rigid beliefs—in other words, the 'self-assertion of a hard and inflexible ego.' While 'hard' individuals in modern individualism are self-centred, self-reliant and turn other people into instruments, 'soft' individuals are not assertive towards others, but, in the sense that they seek others' empathy, and try mutually to confirm satisfaction along with others, they are explained as being even more 'individualistic' than 'hard' individuals.

One may probably assume that behind such claims there is a crisis-consciousness vis-à-vis individualism in Western advanced countries having 'gone too far,' and an expectation towards an 'alternative' individualism that differs from the former, as a new way of existence for ethics in Japan's consumption-dominant society that is now in the process of becoming reality.

What is important in this claim of Yamazaki's in its connection with *seikatsusha* theory is the point that he has contraposed the 'logic of consumption' to the 'logic of production,' and foreseen the advent of an age in which the logic of consumption in a positive sense will lead the logic of production. What is brought about by this turn of logic is release from the spell of the 'doctrine of efficiency' that has bolstered industrialisation. In a different way from its general definition in economics, Yamazaki defines consumption as: 'action which, while making the consumption (*shōmō*) and regeneration of goods its provisional objective, actually makes the very consumption of fruitful time its true objective.' As for its concrete substance, he explains as follows in his *Yawarakai kojin-shugi no jidai* (The age of soft individualism):

> I think that if everyone thought earnestly about consumption in its real sense, their way of living would change. What I mean is, consumption and production are always two sides of the same coin, but they have one fundamental difference. *In the case of production*, the important tasks *are to come out with conclusions swiftly, and reach goals swiftly. In the case of consumption*, it is important *to stretch the process out for as long as possible.* I grew up in times of poverty, and so when I was a child, if I were given a fried egg, I would eat it starting from the white. I enjoyed delaying the eating of the yolk until even a bit later, you see? And so, if people really treasure the thing called consumption and step away from the logic of production, a society that values the process a little more might come into being (Yamazaki 1984: 30–31; emphasis added).

Rather than single-mindedly racing ahead and aiming for the quantitative maximisation of satisfaction, the child here is trying to draw out the saturation of his satisfaction, and lengthen the pleasant time that he can savour during that process. In other words, he knows the finite nature of material desires, and is trying to seek spiritual satisfaction. If we suppose that what lies at the bottom of the logic of consumption is the drawing out and enjoying of the process of consumption, then consumption will become something radical, namely that while seeking meaning in consuming things, one simultaneously finds meaning in consuming as little as possible.

Additionally, when Yamazaki positions the behaviour of consumers demanding goods as a process of self-exploration in which they try to express themselves through the consumption of goods, and a self-recognition activity that differs from the avid, self-aggrandising pursuits of former times, consumers in that context are assumed not simply to be beings that satisfy 'constructed' desires, but multi-faceted beings who act freely in order to discover their own desires, and beings who savour the enjoyment of consumption as social intercourse in which they mutually confirm their satisfaction with others.

Yamazaki has not used the words 'lifestyle logic' or '*seikatsusha*.' When he talks about 'people who really treasure the thing called consumption and step away from the logic of production,' though, those 'people' are infinitely close in meaning to '*seikatsusha*' who explore their own 'meaning of life,' free from an attitude that places central value upon goods and quantities.

The *otaku*-fication phenomenon

Yamazaki's way of thinking attempted to see, in the birth of 'soft individualism' due to the progress of de-industrialisation, people who 'treasured the act of consumption in its real sense' in a non-contradictory and harmonious manner. When viewed from the lifestyle realities of people in the 1980s, however, one cannot evade the suspicion that his way of thinking was too optimistic in terms of a view of humanity. This is because people had not yet been sufficiently refined to get the knack of 'soft individualism.'

About the same time that *The age of soft individualism* was published, R.N. Bellah's *Habits of the Heart* (1985) was attracting controversy. An individualistic set of values that sought individual freedom and independence, belonging to people who had been liberated from the existing authoritarian order, had come to take deep root in American society, which had been shaped by immigrants.

Bellah says that since America's founding, four forms of individualism have existed. These four are: 1 biblical individualism, which has its foundations in Protestantism (a puritan ethos); 2 republican individualism, which is backed by a sense of civic responsibility;

3 utilitarian individualism, which pursues freedom to pursue personal advantage and desires; and 4 expressive individualism, which places value upon the expression of individuals' inner sensibility and preference.

Bellah points out that while values made up of the 'Three C's'—cash, convenience and consumerism—are permeating the life-world of middle-class people in contemporary America, the tradition of individualism that bases itself on a puritanical ethos and civic responsibility is rapidly declining, and utilitarian individualism and expressive individualism are becoming dominant instead (1985: 158). At the same time, he fears that the 'malaise' that constitutes immersion in private interests and concerns, the turning of human relationships into instruments, and indifference towards politics and public facilities, has begun to advance; and, as something that would curtail that advance, he calls for the revival of an individualism accompanied by definite moral and public concerns and practices.

What Bellah especially marked as a target for criticism was 'excessive' expressive individualism. It does not only breed narcissistic interpersonal relationships connected solely by the medium of similarity of mutual lifestyles and the feelings underlying their choice. Bellah says that the real problem is people's increasing withdrawal from the public sphere, and their shutting themselves away in the narrow world of expression of their own interests and sensitivities.

According to the religious scholar Susumu Shimazono, who translated Bellah's work into Japanese, Yamazaki's 'soft individualism' is precisely the Japanese version of what Bellah calls expressive individualism. Yamazaki emphasised the positive side of 'soft individualism' which 'always reserves itself as a flexible and unrestricted presence,' and 'places value on more pliable aesthetic taste and open self-expression,' and he gave it high praise as an 'individualism for mature times.' By contrast, Bellah stressed the 'malaise' aspect that expressive individualism in a mature society brings about. Moreover, the sort of individualism which had begun to be widely shared in Japanese society since the mid-1980s probably needs to be seen as belonging to the 'malaise' side that Bellah indicates.

By the 1980s, the 'my-home-ism' of the 1960s, which had been a move towards the privatisation of lifestyles where concern was concentrated upon the family, was being further transformed into a set of values that prioritised individualistic private life, away from the family and towards the individual as a unit. On the other hand, amid a lifestyle-conservatism that took 'affluence' as a given, there was spread of the phenomenon of '*otaku*-fication' in which individuals shut themselves into a world of 'me' and 'my buddies' where they could only have communion in a world of hobbies and preferences. Desires were exclusively directed at 'me' and 'my buddies,' and, in concert, other-oriented, social interests were starting to stall.

People who pursued the expression of their own desires and feelings were beginning to turn not in the direction of what Yamazaki calls 'treasur[ing] the act of consumption in its real sense,' but rather towards single-mindedly locking themselves within their own consumption and leisure intentions, and competing with others for boundless differentiation.

The signification of goods

The authors of *'Bunshū' no tanjō* (The birth of the 'segmented masses'), published at almost the same time as Yamazaki's volume, who stirred up a huge debate over the qualitative change in the masses, gave a positive appraisal to people seeking such subtle differentiation from others. They saw that the conventional homogeneous mass-consumption society was collapsing, and that individual groups (lifestyle groups) based on diverse values were emerging in their stead.

> Now, people are starting to live in a way faithful to their own sensibilities, tastes and likes and dislikes. Having passed through the age of the masses when they aimed for an average livelihood and aspired to be shoulder-to-shoulder with everyone else, people are again beginning to aspire to a fragmented (*barabara*) way of life and living. Unlike the 'fragmentedness' of the immediate post-war, the present-day 'fragmentedness' is not one in which people cannot gather as a mass because of poverty. It is that they venture 'not to gather' (1985: 14).

The masses, hitherto considered to be characterised by 'uniformity,' were becoming more and more segmentalised and divided on an axis of 'differentiation.' The authors used the term *'bunshū* (segmented masses),' in the sense of 'masses that were segmentalised,' to describe the situation in which people disassembled into ideal reference groups of which they also wished to be members, or into the lifestyle of those groups. The distinguishing feature of 'the segmented masses,' in contrast to 'the masses,' can be found in the differentiation of their lifestyles and the difficulty of manipulating them. By way of example, people's interest is not in merely 'having' a car, but is shifting to 'what kind of' car would express their sensitivity and values, and suit their lifestyle. Whether it is a matter of a car of a certain make, or a big-name designer jacket, people buy a certain specific item because they wish to flaunt a lifestyle that is 'just a bit different' from that of others. In other words, people do not merely consume a particular commodity, but have begun to consume a lifestyle appropriate to that commodity.

In this kind of theoretical development by the authors there is a strong awareness of the work of Jean Baudrillard, who argued that with the transition from a mass consumer society to a 'coded' consumer society as a backdrop, the consumption of commodities lies not in the manifestation of the concrete serviceability and utility value that a commodity brings to bear, but in the manifestation of the sign value that illustrates the social position and spending power of the stratum that consumes the commodity (Baudrillard 1970 [1998]; 1972 [1981]).

When the provision of goods and services reaches a certain level, consumer society reaches a deadlock. It is coded commodities that break through that deadlock. For instance, if cars were to become commodities that anyone could afford, then, unless desire for social position took the place of desire for a car, and competition for rank changed into coded consumption in which people vied with each other over subtle differences between cars, then there would be little hope of an expansion in consumption. In this manner, says Baudrillard, consumption appears to homogenise society as a whole, but actually goes on to create a system of subtle disparities within society.

Baudrillard endeavours to give the contemporary society we inhabit a 'critical' reinterpretation as a coded consumer society. A society where those commodities that have become accessible to anyone now start to function as differentiating signs does not necessarily mean a 'liberated' society for people. The diversification of choice of consumption based on people's 'desire for difference' does not indicate 'spending power liberated by an affluent society,' but merely means 'a productive force required by the functioning of the system itself, by its process of reproduction and survival' (Baudrillard 1972 [1981: 83]; emphasis in original). Baudrillard points out that the mechanism of social differentiation alone penetrates the ego through people's absolutely insatiable desire for commodities.

The *seikatsusha* in the marketers' sights

In contrast to Baudrillard, the authors of *The birth of the 'segmented masses'* unrestrainedly praise people who seek differentiation through a desire for commodities, both as the 'segmented masses' and as the target of strategy, seen from the side of marketers.

Out of all generations, it is among young people that segmentation of the masses is most advanced. If one attempts to divide this into the two axes of attitude in terms of contact with information, and orientation, that is, whether they are present-oriented or future-oriented, their lifestyle can be divided into the four categories of: 1 the fashion-follower type (follower young); 2 the dissatisfied-with-present-circumstances type (powerless young); 3 the fashion-leader type (antenna young); and 4 the future-investment type (future young) (Hakuhōdō 1985: 193). Consumption patterns responding to those four types are envisioned, namely: the 'fashion-follower type' aspires to major brands; the 'dissatisfied-with-present-circumstances type' indulges in compulsive purchasing; the 'fashion-leader type' is oriented to minor brands; and the 'future-investment type' spends in a calculated manner according to their future plans. By arguing that the important thing for those on the selling end is to discover lifestyle concepts that such diversification of people's consumption patterns has brought about, the authors are endeavouring to offer a clue to vendors for approaching consumption behaviour that has become impossible to see.

The age called the present is not an age of mass production and mass consumption, as it once was. It is an age of high-mix, low-volume manufacturing premised on diversified and differentiated segmented masses. The 'consumer' group from the mass age, which was understood by simple indices such as sex, age, income and life-stage, is diverging into a '*seikatsusha*' group in the age of segmented masses, whose awareness, values and lifestyles differ (Hakuhōdō 1985: 195).

The authors use *'seikatsusha'* to refer to people living in such an age of 'segmented masses,' in order to 'differentiate' them from consumers in the age of mass-consumption, and positively define them as people who 'have established their own sensibilities and set of values', and 'can choose information themselves' (Hakuhōdō 1985: 35). For the record, since *The birth of the 'segmented masses,'* this means that the term *'seikatsusha,'* rather than consumer, will become fixed as a keyword among market research practicians and researchers (in Dentsū sōken (ed.) 1990, for example).

The aim of *The birth of the 'segmented masses,'* in 'circumstances where the uniform masses had vanished, and the market had become hard to discern'—in other words, in a situation where people had become difficult to manipulate—was to explain how to grasp the kind of *'seikatsusha'* that the segmented masses wanted to be, and the lifestyle that they were made to think existed, and to develop a marketing strategy to match their desires. The *seikatsusha* in that context is only ever understood as the 'object' of marketing strategy: in other words, as the target of sales. The characteristic of the *'seikatsusha'* in the age of the segmented masses, in comparison with the 'consumer' in the age of mass consumption, can be summed up as in Table 3.2.

Differentiation and autonomy

The *'seikatsusha'* apprehended by marketers, who, as the segmented masses, consume specific brands in tune with their own lifestyles from among a wide variety of goods, differ from those 'unique' people who, as Masakazu Yamazaki says, 'think...about consumption in its real sense,' and 'have cast off uniformity.' The latter people want to be unique, but, while being strongly aware of the differences

Table 3.2: Comparison of consumer and seikatsusha (2)

	Consumer in an age of consumption by 'undifferentiated masses'	*Seikatsusha* in an age of consumption by 'segmented masses'
1	Homogenisation of lifestyle	Diversification of lifestyle
2	Easy to manipulate	Difficult to manipulate
3	'Target' of min-max (maximum production of minimum variety of goods)	'Target' of max-min (minimum production of maximum variety of goods)

between them and others, ultimately are tied to a mediocre lifestyle through marketing strategy. The relationship there between goods and '*seikatsusha*' is not the process of individual self-exploration such as Yamazaki outlines, either: if the strategy is clever, then this will be nothing more than a consumption process by the passive segmented masses who are easily 'taken for a ride' and open their wallets. Even if one does try to substitute '*seikatsusha*' for consumer, it will be hard to find a positive reason for that substitution.

The developer of the 'new middle mass' theory, Yasusuke Murakami, problematises 'diversification and autonomy' in his 1985 article: 'Yuragi no naka no taishū shakai (Mass society in fluctuation).' According to Murakami, even if people's 'desire for difference' comes into operation, differences in behaviour, including consumption, become greater, and the breadth of behaviour grows wider and more diverse, that does not necessarily mean autonomy. Murakami argues that autonomy is preserving an unwavering consistency to the bitter end, under whatever conditions. The judgement as to whether a person's behaviour is autonomous depends upon whether she or he has been able to preserve her or his intrinsic consistency without bowing to pressure from others. Rather, to vie for subtle differences in lifestyle and to have consumption patterns being endlessly differentiated represents a degeneration of autonomy, and a regression towards a mass-consumption society. From the perspective of whether people maintained an autonomous pattern of judgement that controlled desires and interests in this way, Murakami pointed out the problem situation inherent in differentiation in an age of the segmented masses, and critically questioned it.

At its base, this questioning by Murakami has something that resonates with the problem-presentation of Ōkuma's *seikatsusha* discourse (namely, placing the criteria for discriminating between lifestyle 'needs' and 'wants' in one's own hands).

The 'public/private' life-culture strategy

A quest for a way of marketing to offset the age of the segmented masses was unfolded throughout the 1980s as companies' 'life-culture' strategy, in the form of the establishment by enterprises of life-culture research institutes and their life-culture proposals. It was that 'life' and 'culture' as a lifestyle had made their appearance as a new strategic position.

It was not only private enterprise: government, too, went on to fulfil a role of leading, rather than supporting, the creation of a mood of 'abundant life-culture.' The 'Seikatsu bunka to sangyō o kangaeru kondankai,' a colloquium of business people set up to think about life-culture and industry whose inauguration was led by the then Ministry of International Trade and Industry (MITI) in 1985, developed into a 'life-culture forum' involving the same members, and expanded to advocacy of a 'life-culture renaissance' aimed to design the metamorphosis of existing lifestyle-related industries into the type of industry that made 'life-culture' proposals, glued to the improvement of 'lifestyle quality.' What MITI was trying to advocate by the words 'life-culture' is clear from MITI's conception for building a basis for life-culture creation:

> In order to aim for the honing of people's insights as to life-culture, and the creation of a more abundant life-culture, it will be important to build an environment such as will endeavour to diversify the channels by which *a wide array of life-culture 'proposals' from the industry side* and consumers' diverse 'choices' are realised, by such means as introducing superior examples of life-culture from Japan and overseas, and making near-future life-culture proposals that exploit lifestyle technologies (MITI 1990: 47; emphasis added).

While this also applies in the case of enterprise, here, too, there is no clear-cut definition of what 'life-culture' means. From the entire text, it can be inferred that the expression 'life-culture,' which began to move independently without that definition, had until then been regarded as a means for the sake of economics and production, and is being used as a concept that gives the new cultural values of 'leeway and abundance' to 'everyday life,' which had not been afforded a rightful position. A lifestyle that brings about a sense of 'leeway and abundance,' might one say?

The characteristics of the temporal situation called the present are expressed in how lifestyle and culture, and life-culture, as well, become a strategic position in this way. The days when 'even if you are clothed in rags, your heart will be [clad] in brocade' are now in the distant past. Just as in the saying: 'Once food and clothing are adequate, one will learn good manners,' after economic fulfilment, the next object of desire will be the 'cultural' aspect of 'lifestyle.' It is the industrial world that eagerly 'proposes' such life-culture, however, and *seikatsusha* are mostly placed on the side of making passive choices.

The life-culture discourse here stands on the same foundation as the 'cunning consumer' discourse which appeared in a form led by government in the mass-consumption age of the 1970s. 'Cunning consumers' referred to people who chose goods from a varied menu according to their own 'purchasing criteria,' not being led astray by the 'sales points' hammered out by those on the production and merchandising side. They are consumers who, by cleverly selecting goods they themselves desire from the menu that is offered, have the power indirectly to reduce and expel undesired goods. Nonetheless, even they cannot do such things as make goods that are not on the existing menu appear in the market, nor recall to the market goods that once were present but which vanished because they were unprofitable. What they possess is nothing more than consumer sovereignty in the 'weak' sense (Nakamura 1992: 62). Hidden there was a 'sham' which, while stressing that 'the consumer is king,' never says that 'the producer is king.'

It is the same in the case of life-culture. It does not mean that people, as life-subjects, test all kinds of cultural expression, based on the lifestyle values they have internalised. Basically, the subjects that create life-culture are enterprises, and *seikatsusha* are positioned as beings that respond to proposed lifestyles which have a feeling of 'leeway and abundance.' Consumers merely choose a culture in accordance with a pattern of lifestyle values that businesses create: a Japanese-style room with a *tokonoma* alcove and hanging scroll, or else a Western-style room with a lounge suite and oil painting. One might term that a soft, loose form of lifestyle and culture control.

There is probably no need to reiterate that the business- and government-led form of life-culture and the *seikatsusha* who were its bearers differ from the common people's self-styled life-culture that Kiyoshi Miki and Itaru Nii advocated in a form contraposed to the lifestyle framed by the state, and different again from the autonomous *seikatsusha* who grasped that culture in their own hands, as Nobuyuki Ōkuma points out.

4 From 'theory' to the 'activism' stage

The strength of the 'weak' individual: the Beheiren experiment

The demon that prosperity spawned

Upon the scene there now came people who, drawing a distinct line between themselves and the aforementioned theories of the *seikatsusha* as a discourse, were searching for a way of living approaching that of '*seikatsusha*' as everyday practice. These were the Beheiren (Citizens' Federation for Peace in Vietnam) and the Seikatsu Kurabu Seikyō (Seikatsu Club Consumer Co-operatives, or SCCC).

Beheiren was a movement inaugurated in 1965 with the following objectives: 1 peace in Vietnam; 2 that Vietnam be in the hands of the Vietnamese; and 3 that the Japanese government not cooperate in the war. It was disbanded in 1974 along with the conclusion of the Vietnam War. Beiheiren members, who lay the foundation for various kinds of subsequent citizens' activism, not infrequently referred to themselves within their movement simultaneously as 'citizens (*shimin*)' and '*seikatsusha*' or '*seikatsujin* (*seikatsu* people).'

Seikatsu Club, on the other hand, which started up in one corner of Tokyo's Setagaya Ward in 1965 (becoming a consumer cooperative in 1968) from one young person's wish to 'create a movement rooted in the local community, not adhering to established political parties or labour movements,' is a *seikatsusha* movement triggered by rejection of the consumer movement. This can be seen as putting into everyday practice Nobuyuki Ōkuma's exhortation that 'we quit being consumers and become *seikatsusha*.'

Incidentally, apart from Seikatsu Club, are also some other movements that have rejected being 'consumers.' Examples of these include the 'Daichi o mamoru kai (Association to Preserve the

Earth)' started up in 1975 under the activist banner of 'questioning the ways of everyday life and society without reference to the old boundaries of consumer or producer.' Here, however, I will discuss Seikatsu Club, which is by far the leader in terms of the influence of its activism and its interesting qualities.

Both Beheiren and Seikatsu Club Consumer Cooperatives are situated as part of Japan's 'new social movements' arising in the late 1960s and becoming well-established in the 1970s. The emergence of 'new social movements' is a phenomenon shared by advanced industrial societies. These began with the student movements of the 1960s, the matrix for the rise of a variety of movements encompassing minority civil rights movements, feminist and ecological movements and the peace movement.

These movements had diverse objects, goals and means of achievement, but their common elements were their criticism of the framework of highly industrialised societies supported by economic growthism and the contestation of values that aimed to promote the latter. In other words, their reflection upon the 'Materialist' values pursued by advanced industrialised societies and their shift towards 'Post-Materialist' values comprised a unique set of value priorities that led to new social movements. In that sense, these movements could be said to have been spawned from the midst of 'affluence,' and, moreover, to be aiming for a confrontation with such 'affluence.' Inglehart's book, *The Silent Revolution*, calls these values 'social and self-actualisation needs': 'Beautiful cities/Nature; Ideas count; Free Speech; Less impersonal society; More say on job, community; More say in government' (1977: 42).

Challenging the obvious

The newness of 'new social movements' does not simply derive from the temporal freshness of their rise as movements. Their novelty lies in that they draw a clear line of demarcation between themselves and orthodox social movements in the following three points: 1 the subjects of the movement are neither a social class nor workers, but people situated on the margins of highly industrialised society, such as minorities, youth and women; 2 the issue in dispute is not a question of the point of production such as is typically seen in the labour movement, but has been laid amid the problems involved in the totality of living life, such as the environment, human rights, or peace, and there, the key words are 'identity,' 'self-management,' 'self-determination,' and so on; 3 the movement's method of formation is not a hierarchical type of organisation governed by a handful of people in leadership positions, but an interpersonal network kind of organisation where each person takes as much action as she or he can responsibly handle.

Apart from Beheiren and Seikatsu Club Lifestyle Co-operatives, all kinds of residents' campaigns, anti-pollution and anti-nuclear-power-generation movements, the feminist movement, and so on, could be cited as other concrete examples of these movements which, as if in response to the 'new social movements' in advanced countries, had also made their appearance in Japan, which had become an 'affluent society.' The 'affluent society' that high economic growth had created made people's interest focus upon private life, but conversely it made people sensitive to 'personal' rights and spawned resistance to powers that attempted to violate those rights. In Japan's case, especially, the destruction and pollution of areas which the advance of industrial development had brought about went on to induce spontaneous residents' campaigns rooted in the life of the community. Takeshi Ebisaka, a participant in the Beheiren movement, recalls as follows the atmosphere of the times in the mid-1960s, when 'all kinds of movements appeared in droves.'

> One thing that can be said is that it felt like the sort of age when, in short, we thought we had to change this rotten society, and could have the hope that we could change it. Of course, in human history there have been numerous times like that. In about ninety-nine out of a hundred cases they have not gone well and have just been swept away, but at least—how should I put it—I did see that kind of thing, or rather, I was able to have such hopes, though in retrospect it might have been an illusion, but anyway, I feel sure that they were those kinds of times (Ebisaka 1994: 61).

Bar a few exceptions, what the majority of such movements aimed for was not merely to raise objections to state-led development or progress.

The set of values that had supported rapid growth and mass consumption had taken firm root amid an urban-type lifestyle and day-to-day-ness that boasted of quantity without questioning quality of life. The 'new social movements' which sought to reinterrogate these from their very foundations demanded of each of their participants that they question and reform their own lifestyle and ordinariness. If we are to call doubts and criticism towards dominant culture and the existing lifestyle and day-to-day-ness based on it 'alternative culture (*taikō bunka*),' then these movements which offered counter-proposals were alternative culture movements, and the movement participants had a commonality in that they called themselves 'citizens (*shimin*)' or '*seikatsusha*.'

Enter the citizen

On 24 April 1965, under the slogan 'Peace in Vietnam!' about 1500 people gathered in Tokyo's Shimizudani Park. They were individuals who did not belong to any political party or labour union, or to any particular group: people who thought of themselves as 'citizens.' At this point, the day's 'rallying cry' already clearly indicated Beheiren's subsequent campaign style.

> We are ordinary citizens. By ordinary citizens we mean that we have company employees, primary-school teachers, carpenters, female innkeepers, newspaper reporters, florists, men who write novels, boys who are studying English—in short, we have you who are reading this pamphlet, and what we want to say is only one thing: 'Peace in Vietnam!' ('Shiryō' 1965 [1974a]: 6).

I wonder how the movement participants would have replied if they were asked: 'Who do you mean by "citizens"?' Most answers probably would have been something like: 'Individuals who go on choosing their actions voluntarily,' or 'Me: someone who is participating responsibly and voluntarily.' They were not doing it because they were told to by somebody: they decided for themselves, and voluntarily chose their actions. That definition of a citizen was sufficient for Beheiren, which upheld the slogan of being an open group that anybody could enter. Beheiren's three rules were: 1 the person who proposes something does it; 2 do not find fault with the things that other people do (if you have the time to complain, take action yourself); and 3 do whatever you want. Moreover, if two people gathered together, they could call themselves Beheiren. For the record, 'Beheiren had neither members nor membership fees, to the very last' (Yoshikawa 1994: 94).

The word '*shimin* (citizen),' which is contraposed to '*kokumin* (national),' is a translated term originally arising in Western society. The '*shimin*' in this case refers not to members of a community that submerges individual lifestyles in an undifferentiated form, but to individuals who aim to maintain a set distance between themselves and the community, and to create as autonomous a relationship as possible. In reality, however, before we are 'citizens,' we are born 'nationals.' People's lifestyles have the dual aspects of simultaneously being lifestyles as 'nationals,' which indicate belonging to a state (as taxpayers and beneficiaries of the state's various policies) and lifestyles as 'citizens,' and those lifestyles are carried on in a form that fastens the two disjointed relationships together.

For Beheiren, 'citizens' were people who put distance between themselves and the state, which included vigilance and criticism vis-à-vis the shape of the state and political power, and who clearly asserted that sovereignty lay not in the state but in the individual as a citizen. In that sense, the emergence of Beheiren, a self-proclaimed citizens' group, was one which demonstrated that the idea of the 'citizen,' which had its origins in the West, had begun to send out shoots and put down roots at long last in Japan, as well.

This self-definition as citizens was also used as something to signify that the subjects of the movement were neither a 'class,' nor workers or students. In conventional types of political movements, under the slogan of an 'alliance of workers, students and citizens,' the rallying-cry had always been couched in the order of 'all you workers, students and citizens.' That illustrated the order in which they were expected to be the bearers of the movement, and also meant that people who were neither workers nor students were citizens. In short, 'citizens' in that context were nothing more than the 'residuum' from workers and students. In that aspect, too, Beheiren differed markedly. If to act according to one's will were the requisite condition for being a citizen, then first there would be the citizen. Workers and students also could become citizens.

By making a definition in this way, Beheiren was able to draw a line of demarcation between itself and conventional labour movements or any movement espousing a political ideology, and disassociate itself from them. Its having freed itself from political ideology on the one hand enabled its 'persistence,' in that people continued to campaign in a form not divorced from their everyday way of life, while it went on to establish a unique movement style in which individuals with the will to participate took action to the extent over which they could shoulder responsibility, on the other. The nonaligned citizens who took part in the Beheiren movement without becoming enmeshed in political parties, labour unions or religious groups made their appearance under such a definition of the citizen.

Beheiren's principles as a citizens' movement—that it was open to everybody; people were free to join or leave; and what was emphasised was individuals' self-motivation and creativity, so personal responsibility was heavy for that very reason—came to be adopted by various different kinds of later 'new social movements' concerned with the environment, pollution and human-rights issues.

Ideas from the life-site

Beheiren participants also called themselves '*seikatsusha*' at the same time as 'citizens.' The *seikatsusha* in that context primarily meant that the bearers of the movement were not career politicians or peace-movement specialists, but people who were political amateurs, who were 'not feeding themselves through this movement.' In other words, the term did not indicate people who governed their actions by some concept or ideology, but people who had their own life-site—people who carried 'the weight of daily life,' meaning those who, in order to earn their living, could only participate in action on a part-time basis, but still wanted to participate fully in terms of their 'aspiration.' The word '*seikatsusha*' was used to emphasise that point. The '*seikatsusha*' here could be said to be a notion that connects with the stream of Itaru Nii's '*shiseijin* (common people)' and '*atarimae no hitobito* (ordinary people).' Rokurō Hidaka observes:

> Assuming for argument's sake that we call [Beheiren] a citizen's movement, the ones who will bear its burden, those 'citizens,' will be <u>seikatsusha</u> who do not make politics their profession. If we suppose that there are two forms of political participation—full-time and part-time—then <u>seikatsusha</u> naturally will not be able to be twenty-four-hour activists. They will only be able to devote a certain scant time out of every week. But on the assumption that there is something like a person's strength of internal motivation when taking part, or what in old-fashioned terms was called '*kokorozashi* (intentions),' then among

citizens there will be people who are striving to have full intentions (Hidaka 1968 [1974a]: 379; emphasis added).

Yōtarō Konaka remarks:

> A 'citizen's movement' (though the term is a strange one) refers precisely to a movement in which people going about their daily business in their livelihood loosen themselves to a certain extent from it; and bakers and hunters and fishmongers and salarymen and university professors all stop doing the things in their occupations, each returning to being a 'hand-made person.' It therefore is not a spatial gathering of people, but a temporal gathering...The hours when humans who usually are up to their necks in the mud of day-to-dayness free themselves from it and fight are what comprises a citizen's movement (Konaka 1968 [1974a]: 484).

Seen from the perspective of movements by people to which 'the weight of daily life' does not adhere, any movement by *seikatsusha* who do 'go about their daily business' carrying such a weight will be a slow and halting one. While there were many movements that rushed in the direction of the former, Beheiren, with its 'weight of daily life' still attached, considered things at the tempo of everyday living, and wagered on the possibility of continuing its campaign. So-called *rōnin* (high school graduates who had failed to gain admittance to university and were preparing to re-sit the entrance examinations) formed a '*rōnin* league' and joined demonstrations in their spare time between studying for their next examinations. Young people cut back on what they spent on coffee during dates, putting the money towards fund-raising campaigns to buy things to send to Vietnam. Salarymen put aside at least one day a month to work for solidarity with the people of Vietnam. It was due to its self-definition as a *seikatsusha* movement that Beheiren endeavoured always to use everyday language in the naming of its gatherings, the addresses made there, and the calls in its pamphlets, too.

Beheiren also referred to people with a life-site, that is, '*seikatsusha*,' by using the words '*futsū no hito* (ordinary people)' and '*tada no hito* (common people).' The lives of 'ordinary people' involved working to make their own livelihood, supporting their families, loving people, and having fun. When Beheiren said: '[Bring] peace to Vietnam, as ordinary people!' the Vietnam to which it referred was not an abstract state. It meant a site where 'ordinary people' like themselves were living their lives—working to make their own livelihood, supporting their families, loving people, and having fun.

Beheiren's expression, 'ordinary people,' ignited the imagination of the movement participants, who were certainly *seikatsusha*. If there were anything unfairly jeopardising the livelihood of 'ordinary people' like themselves, they were determined to confront it as a shared problem that transcended differences in nationality and ethnicity. A common principle, a common awareness that overcame national and ethnic differences, functioned there. The 'site' in that life-site was always dynamic and open to the outside. That perspective further reflects the lifestyle of Japanese people from beyond, across national boundaries. The '*seikatsusha*,' being the possessor of such a site, was an important keyword in putting the Beheiren movement together.

The viewpoint of a 'hard death'

Secondly, *seikatsusha* signified the 'attitude' of citizens towards the topic of the movement. To borrow an expression from one of the facilitators, Makoto Oda, Beheiren was a movement 'paid for out of the pockets' of its participants, but before being 'paid for out of [anyone's] pockets,' more than anything it had the premise that the Vietnam War was not somebody else's problem, but their very own 'piercing' issue ('"Mi ni shimiru" koto ni "mizeni o kiru" koto' 1970 [1974b]: 356). Given that it was a 'piercing' issue, it was a topic that members had no choice but to face by 'paying out of their own pockets.' Their being able to make the topic of the movement their own problem, as one that was 'piercing,' was a prerequisite for being *seikatsusha*. To borrow Makoto Oda's words again, one could call it the co-ownership of the perspective of a hard death.

> The thing that thrust the deaths of Vietnamese people into my world was the connection—or rather entanglement—of the dead with the living. When I tried to gaze at the world from the vantage point of the dead of Vietnam, what I could see, whether I liked it or not, was the figure of the multitude of the living who had power; and the living from Japan numbered among them, along with those from the United States. In other words, I myself was included.
>
> Moreover, why are the living able to be so? It goes without saying that it is because they are alive, but the business of human life gives

shape to people's livelihoods. In other words, because humans are leading their lives, and making their livelihood, that makes them the living. No, I need to add one thing more: they build all kinds of mechanisms in order to make their living, and having created those mechanisms, they set them in motion, and their livelihoods become viable at that point—that is why they are the living. *What I came to see was that that very mechanism was producing the dead. So, our very livelihoods, which are entangled in that process, are also producing the dead*, nothing less (Oda 1971 [1974c]: 518).

For Oda, taking the vantage point of 'the dead' meant understanding, through ('piercing') 'sympathy,' that the agony which specific people were physically suffering was a problem for which he himself was responsible, produced by the very 'mechanisms' that were making his own livelihood viable as one of 'the living.' It also meant turning that sympathy into an opportunity for 'action' (paid for out of his own pockets) to confront those 'mechanisms.'

Here, 'sympathy (*kyōkan*)' indicates the operation of sentiments not limited to mere emotional fusion with the other, but based on mutuality and equality—namely, on 'another self.' Kōhei Hanasaki uses '*kyōkan*' to mean the feeling of 'caring (*yasashisa*)' by which one apprehends the socially isolated individual's manner of existence in terms of the latter's connection with the situation in which one has been placed (1981: 12).

In the process of campaigning, the various Beheiren participants came to see themselves as Japanese attackers who were benefiting by making Vietnamese people into victims (sufferers). At the core of the Beheiren movement, there lay a question of identity, mediated by the people of Vietnam: 'Who am I?' When movement participants said, 'as *seikatsusha*,' *seikatsusha* in that context was none other than a name for people who employed such a way of confronting the topic.

The weight of 'just anybody'

If one traces the meaning that Beheiren invested in the words 'citizen' and '*seikatsusha*,' one will appreciate how consistently this was a movement premised on the 'weak individual.' One youth who took part in Beheiren's regular demonstrations, for example, has spoken as follows:

> To start with, the very fact that I, the person in charge, arrived at the venue five minutes late illustrated the lack of order in that day's demonstration…I apologise to my fellow demonstrators, but no matter how many times I go to a demonstration, all the time I am walking in the demonstration *I am so embarrassed that I cannot see what is straight in front of me.* It is because my face has to reflect a role of a sense of justice, which is out of character for me, but if I do not put up with this embarrassment and demonstrate, my whole life will become something even more embarrassing (Yoshizaki 1970 [1974b]: 241; emphasis added).

Here, there is no figure of a strong individual with a lucid will to oppose the war, or of a strong individual who was going to sever himself from a Japanese state which supported the American government. All there was a weak individual who, while bearing his embarrassment, still braced himself and took part in the demonstrations.

Beheiren did not tell the 'just anybodys' and 'ordinary people' who comprised its campaign participants to put all their heart into the country called Vietnam. The movement emphasised modest convictions towards Vietnam, as evidenced by their abovementioned calls to 'devote one day a month for Vietnam!' or to 'cut back on coffee while on dates, and donate the money!' Strong though it might be at the beginning, individual initiative will later weaken and fade. Individuals' sense of responsibility, also, tends to become less acute as a movement drags on. For Beheiren—which had absolutely no organisational pedigree worthy of the name, naturally, nor any stipulation of clear-cut rights and obligations, but made the spontaneity of individual participation its sole principle—the very motivation of people who committed themselves to 'one day a month' or 'donating what they would have spent on coffee' had great significance.

According to Makoto Oda, the standpoint of being 'just anybody' meant a 'weak individual' who prioritised 'human convenience,' in other words, private interest. This was not the 'strong individual' that Hisao Ōtsuka once described as the human model for civil society, one with self-discipline on top of an asceticism that discarded everyday life and rejected the mundane. Neither was it a Robinson Crusoe-like individual who carved out paths all alone on a trackless desert island. It was the quite helpless-looking features of 'one individual comprising the masses (*hitori no taishū*).' The *seikatsusha* who was 'just anybody,' an 'ordinary person,' temporarily broke free from the everyday, scraped together a humble monetary contribution from the household budget, had occasion to do labour service for the sake of the Vietnamese people, and carried out self-verification of anti-war commitment—that is where Beheiren tried to invest the feeling of the weak individual.

An unfinished task

There were, of course, all kinds of problems in a movement composed of weak individuals. When, for example, a movement based only upon individual motivation and responsibility reached a certain 'critical mass,' how would it solve the inevitably-arising contradictions between spontaneity and 'management' = organisation? Beheiren was not entirely free from such contradictions. There was no dearth of trouble on the operational front (Oda 1969: 241).

Nevertheless, Beheiren's activism involving those 'weak individuals' expanded into a diverse and unique movement, including all-night teach-ins, anti-war advertisements in *The New York Times*, aid for deserters from the American military, and the organisation of anti-war campaigns by American soldiers inside military bases. When one looks back at that Beheiren movement from today's perspective, how will it appear? Takeshi Ebisaka, who had taken part in activities Beheiren to help American army deserters, spoke as follows at a gathering held in 1994 on the occasion of the first visit to Japan in twenty-five years by one of the then-deserters:

> One of the things that these twenty-five years of history have taught us is that when we say 'individuals,' there are weak individuals involved. That is, there are all kinds of 'weak individuals,' weak by virtue of nationality, age, sex, or physical or mental condition...It being difficult for them to become strong individuals probably means that their civic awareness will be lost, and this in turn will tie to the atrophy of the civic movements themselves. Even considering my own case, in the old days I used to buy every issue of the magazine called *Sekai* (The world) [a general magazine of high quality]. Lately, I have only been buying it about once a year. But I do buy every issue of *Pia* [an entertainment magazine]. (Laughs) So we have to start from there and build a new image of the individual, a new image of the citizen (1994: 66–67).

The Beheiren movement was one that started off from the weak individual and sought to explore a new image of the citizen, and a new image of the *seikatsusha* (Tsurumi 1994: 142). There, while dwelling upon human weakness, vagueness, unsteadiness and brittleness, one can start to see a commonality with the methodology of the Shisō no kagaku kenkyūkai (Institute for the science of thought), which endeavoured to capture the ideological and dynamic potential of 'the people.'

As long as civil society comprises a conglomeration of weak individuals' lives, there must be a course premised upon those weak individuals that searches for the image of the *seikatsusha*. The question of what kind of thing that *seikatsusha* image can be still remains as an 'unfinished' task: as 'homework' left to do.

Women who transformed their ways of living: Seikatsu Club's *seikatsusha* movement

From 300 bottles of milk

In May 1965, just a few days after the launch of Beheiren, the Seikatsu Club movement was born in one corner of Tokyo's Setagaya Ward.

Seikatsu Club co-operatives (Seikatsu kurabu seikyō), which as of 1996 had grown to incorporate 230 thousand member households over Tokyo, Hokkaido and ten prefectures in Japan, began from the call to housewives: 'Let's join a Seikatsu Club to drink milk cheaply!' from a group of young activists (Kunio Iwane and his companions) who, from their experience of the 1960s Ampo (US–Japan Security Treaty) struggle, hoped for the creation of a citizens' movement rooted in the local community, one that differed from existing political parties and unions. At the time of its launch, its members numbered 200, and the milk it handled amounted to a mere 300 bottles.

Later, the range of goods it handled gradually spread to other things besides milk, and its membership grew. At the same time, a stable management base became necessary. Simultaneously, there was increasing desire to gain social recognition as an organisation, and in 1968, Seikatsu Club made a fresh start as a lifestyle co-operative.

Seen from the momentum for this emergence of Seikatsu Club, whose instigators were young activists, it might seem that the housewives who were inspired by that call were passive beings.

That is not so, however. In 1960s Japanese society, a spontaneous ember had already been smouldering among housewives with no experience hitherto of participation in activism. It went on to involve them in the movement, and the young activists' call merely played the role of setting it ablaze.

Just as criticism towards industrial development had emerged from among the fishing and agrarian populace when they were driven to the periphery of rapid economic growth and faced the crisis of destruction of their own livelihood-base, the ones to respond sensitively to changes both in the safety of the things they were eating every day and in their own life-base and quotidian life-environment were not the bearers of industrialisation, that is, men on the side of making the goods, but housewives placed on their periphery. Moreover, as previously noted, they, as full-time housewives, had also been excluded from the communal and civic sphere, as well as the sphere of employment, and the arena where they could engage with public issues as citizens was narrowly limited to such things at the PTA. This gave rise to housewives having intense feelings of entrapment.

In such circumstances, the 'conscious' encounter between young activists—whose aim was a movement that would reorganise, from a co-operative perspective, the local lifestyle in which privatisation had advanced and people had become mutually isolated—and housewives who sought food safety and desired an escape from their feeling of entrapment, gave rise to a unique co-operative movement discourse that made the housewives who were 'full-time residents' of the local community its protagonists. This suggests that, at least for the young activists (full-time staff), the ultimate objective of Seikatsu Club from its very inauguration was not placed in the very creation of a lifestyle co-operative for obtaining 'better things, more cheaply,' but in the formation of a 'movement' that would go on remaking everyday lifestyles anew.

It was into the 1980s that the word *seikatsusha* began to appear frequently in the daily conversation of Club members. It was on 1 October 1979 that '*seikatsusha*' made its first appearance in Seikatsu Club's in-house magazine, *Seikatsu to jichi* (Life and autonomy), in a title calling for: 'Reflection of our live voices as *seikatsusha*!' The fact that this word *seikatsusha* made its appearance along with the word 'alternative' is important.

The term 'alternative' was initially used in a 1975 report entitled 'What now?' submitted to a Special Session of the United Nations by the Swedish Dag Hammarskjöld Foundation. It means another view of development in relation to the Third World (a spontaneous, and therefore pluralistic, view based on the energy and resources of members of its society) which 'overturns' the direct (in other words, one that is one-dimensionally penetrated by the logic of capital) development view which made the modern West its ideal type. 'Alternative' in the Seikatsu Club is heir to that of the Hammarskjöld Foundation in its having been employed with the incorporation both of subjectivity: 'not to live as we have up till now' and 'let us change our way of living'; and of resistance towards the prevailing values of contemporary society = the historical view of forces of production, and the lifestyle based on it. *Seikatsusha* emerged as the people who aspire to an alternative way of living.

However, the point of origin of the '*seikatsusha*' concept in the Seikatsu Club does not lie there. This is because a quest for a '*seikatsusha*' concept had already begun within the 'pre-ordered collective purchase by *han* (a small group of households)' movement which had been developed since the Club's launch, in their question vis-à-vis their own activities, namely, 'What does "pre-ordered collective purchase" mean?' and in their search for the answer to that question. The word *seikatsusha* had also started to be used to sum up and give meaning to their activities so far. The quest for that '*seikatsusha*' concept then was widened from collective purchase activities to the deputy movement (a campaign to send representatives to local assemblies) and workers' collective activities (ones that created new ways of working on a self-managed model).

Here, let us pursue the following three streams within the Seikatsu Club's practices, namely:
1. the lineage from 'consumer' to '*seikatsusha*' (collective purchase activities);
2. the lineage from 'national' to '*seikatsusha*' politics (the deputy movement);
3. the lineage from 'consumer' to 'producing *seikatsusha*' (workers' collective activities)

and look at the process of discovering the '*seikatsusha*' in the Seikatsu Club.

Reinterpreting day-to-day-ness

One housewife who joined Seikatsu Club (Tokyo)'s *han*-by-*han* pre-ordered joint purchase activities recounts her own later transformation as follows:

> Though I joined the Seikatsu Club on the word that they would deliver safe food and heavy things, when I then realised that it had been a ridiculous misapprehension, I was disappointed. The first year, it was a bolt out of the blue, you might say, because though we were spared the deliveries, members were made to do everything from unloading to transportation. The full-time staff would always say, with a hint of sarcasm: 'This is a movement. The subject in the movement is you yourself.' On top of that, the meat that came as raw material would be in one-kilogramme lumps, fat and all, the fish would be whole, with head and innards intact, and the vegetables would be in great big bunches with the mud still attached. Up until then, it had been natural to buy sliced and packaged meat all of one cut, and vegetables that were washed clean and in small bunches, as well, so now it was stupid how much time and effort it took to cook them. Though we couldn't eat up such huge quantities raw, it was idiotic the way we could not buy only the small amount we wanted. And then it was so much trouble and so complicated to co-ordinate my order in the *han* with that of neighbours, and divide up the stuff among us. I had nothing but complaints.
>
> That being said, it would have been aggravating to quit immediately after having paid the subscription, and I would be sorry to the other members if my leaving meant the *han* would become unviable. As I had not started off with such a lot of motivation, I kept on hesitating for four years, thinking I'd quit soon, and that I'd definitely leave. But then, when I came to my senses, I was eating vegetables in season. And the series of processes, from washing off the mud, peeling them, and even eating up all the various kinds of leaves attached to the green vegetables, the large and the small, and pickling those I could not finish eating raw, had become commonsense to me. With something like pork, the once unheard-of nonsense of buying a whole pig and dividing up amongst everyone all of the parts, from belly to fillet, has now become commonsense. Inside me, there had been a turnabout in the meaning of pork and vegetables (Oral transcript).

This housewife's words graphically describe within which of the day-to-day practices of the Seikatsu Club the *seikatsusha* was discovered. Leaving until later my discussion of the *han* pre-ordered joint purchase method, which is one characteristic of Seikatsu Club, here allow me to add a little explanation of another characteristic, namely, 'concentration on one item (*tanpin kesshū*).' Seikatsu Club started off as a lifestyle co-operative with 'better things, more cheaply' as its slogan, but soon, ironically enough, it was realised that 'good things, by rights, are not cheap.'

> If really good things were cheap, then there would be some hitch somewhere. For example, there is the possibility that someone has beaten the producer down on price, or something. If we do not guarantee the producer at least the cost of reproduction, then the producer will probably go bankrupt and no incentive to try to produce good things will arise (Seikatsu kurabu seikyō Kanagawa 1981: 81).

How, then, is it possible to obtain safe goods for a fair price? The conclusion that was drawn amid continued groping in the dark was to find producers who 'want to grow and ship things that they themselves and their families could eat,' and to introduce a new purchasing method called 'concentration on one item' in solidarity with those producers. If there are good products that have a reliable pedigree, then let us buy them together. If we do so, then, as we can systematically pre-order at least a certain quantity of each item, we can guarantee the producers systematic production, and, conversely, we can have a strong voice vis-à-vis the producers. Also, by combining the purchase within a specific locality, the efficiency of shipping also improves. This is what the method involves.

Seen from a different angle, this is an attempt to establish initiative from the consumption end in an age dominated by the mass-production system, and, at the same time, it runs counter to the direction in which a high-consumption society that responds to the diverse needs of consumers by offering an 'assortment of products' is heading.

This 'concentration on one item' method made possible the kind of daily practices that led each member to query the very manner of living that they had considered natural and self-evident until then, and turn into '*seikatsusha*.' For housewives, vegetables stopped being cleanly-washed and packaged commodities lined up in supermarkets. Vegetables were now things with clearly-known origins, even down the safety of their fertiliser and the quality of their soil; and, as such, were things with a high utility value close to that of 'life' itself; things that were produced from within a 'mutually-dependent' relationship with the producers of locally-grown vegetables; things that were bought by the field-full and eaten in order to guarantee the producer's sustained production; and things that, by continuing to be eaten, reliably promoted the rehabilitation of the soil on local farming land. This series of 'reinterpretations (*yomikae*)' arose within those women.

This was also a process of taking the things that were arrayed in shops as 'commodities' and reinterpreting them as 'consumption materials (*shōhizai*)' (safe goods whose origins were known) that they use for their own sakes (Yamazaki 1988: 220).

'Reinterpretation' was not only carried out in the case of foodstuffs such as vegetables and meat. It later gave rise to the question of what constitutes detergent that does not harm the environment. Activities that relativised the existing order and values began to display a diverse spread, starting firstly from a campaign to remove synthetic detergent from the list of items for joint purchase, and extending to the environment, recycling, and anti-nuclear campaigns. Through their participation in such activities, members recognised that they were part of the environment, and that the consumption they undertook always took place within the environment in which they themselves were included, and they took on the responsibility that arose from that and began to live with awareness.

Furthermore, the 'reinterpretation' process breeds recognition towards more public values which dictate that one has to keep changing the shape of production, distribution and disposal, and the state of the local community and environment—a recognition that transcends private values which say that it would be sufficient for one and one's family merely to obtain safe, high-quality goods for themselves.

This is indicated, for example, in the following remarks from a member:

> Having stopped using synthetic detergent and started using powdered natural soap for the personal reason that my hands were getting severely chapped, I found out that using soap was not just something

personal, but was a movement that urged us to question the quality of the civilisation in this society where we live (Oral transcript).

In this way, housewives who had initially joined Seikatsu Club seeking safe food for themselves and their families started along the path from 'consumers' to '*seikatsusha*.' At the same time, it was also a process in which Seikatsu Club made joint purchasing its economic base, and unfolded all kinds of social movements on top of the various local resources which it obtained from that base.

The essence of consumption

In 1973, Seikatsu Club issued one answer to the question, 'What does joint purchasing mean?' about its own activities over some seven years:

> It refers to workers (housewives) subjectively thinking about and closing in on the essence of consumption, in regard to the consumption goods that they are about to purchase themselves. It is for that reason that [they] establish a co-operative space, make rules and engage in activities (Seikatsu Club 1973, 15 April).

In this passage, the word '*shōhizai* (consumption materials)' is used in place of '*shōhin*,' the usual term for commercial goods. The word *shōhizai*, newly coined by Seikatsu Club, is imbued with the desire that '[joint purchasing] be an activity which, while being within this commodified society, does not pursue the latter, but subjectively creates [members'] own lifestyles.'

In the case of commercial goods, their utility value is not something that the user (consumer) decides, but if producers and vendors decide they are 'useful,' then their utility value will arise from that. The term 'commercial goods' has a value added to it which differs from the original form it was supposed to have. Seikatsu Club members deliberately use the word 'consumption materials' because they negatively apprehend the true nature of such commercial goods and want to stop being passive consumers who merely accept the utility value of the commercial goods determined by producers and vendors. Their choice to spell '*zai*' with a character meaning 'materials' rather than 'goods' was also for the purpose of repudiating the exchange value inherent in the character for 'goods,' and emphasising the 'materials' aspect, as in 'life materials (*seikatsu shizai*)—in other words, their value as raw materials to which the attachment of 'added value' in the form of colouring agents or preservatives was not allowed (Iwane 1974).

Such a way of thinking connects with that of Nobuyuki Ōkuma, who deems *seikatsusha* to be 'those who are aware that the basis of a lifestyle is human beings' self-production (the reproduction of life).'

In this way, one can learn that momentum for the birth of the notion of *seikatsusha* was encased within the very discovery of the 'consumption materials' concept as an answer to the question, 'What does joint purchasing mean?' Contained therein was a way of thinking that saw the placing into their own hands of the entire range of processes—judgments as to what to consume; decisions about what to produce; reorganisation of distribution that mediates consumption and production; and a growing awareness of the 'intra-environmental consumption' linking consumption and disposal—as none other than the process of becoming *seikatsusha*.

Me in the third person

> Every month, it is quite a lot of trouble to adjust the quantities of orders with the people in the *han*, and it is surprisingly bothersome to have to go and confront other people whether I like it or not when I go to collect money or to fetch things that have been delivered. As well, I used to be amazed at myself for doing something as stupid as being chosen by drawing lots or by 'rock-scissors-paper' games to serve as *han* leader or the duty person, even though I paid a subscription. I would think how nice it would be if only there were a Seikatsu Club shop nearby. I do feel a certain annoyance at the meaning of there being no stores and at the social obligations, but it is only around now that I have at last started to understand a little that there are other pleasures to it (Oral transcript).

It is not rare to hear such a voice from Seikatsu Club members. Seikatsu Club co-operatives as a general rule have no shop-fronts. The *han*-by-*han* pre-ordered joint-purchase system was a last resort born of the reality of small numbers of full-time staff and small operating funds, but that gave rise to a major feature which other lifestyle co-operatives lacked (recently, individual *han* for families with both adults working, and for singles, have been set up as part of Seikatsu Club Tokyo).

Under the *han* joint-purchase method, which does not depend on stop-fronts, one must work on the people living nearby and gather seven or eight associates in order to obtain the things one wants. *Han* members are neighbours whom one meets on a daily basis. The string of processes, from forming a *han*, to co-ordinating orders and dividing up the delivery, become the point of origin for building relationships and building communities through the medium of direct dialogue.

To a greater or lesser extent, this is accompanied by co-operative action that mutually accommodates relationships with others who have differing opinions from oneself on a daily basis. In some eyes, the series of processes—having briefing meetings about how to allocate each 'lot' of pre-ordered and purchased goods; dividing up the delivery; collecting the money and having *han* meetings—is bothersome and annoying. In other words, if one wishes to protect one's own and one's family's lifestyle, one must transcend the personal dimension that says it is sufficient just for oneself to obtain safe, good-quality products: one must co-operate with others, mutually contribute effort, and change the ways of production and distribution. And that is not all—in order to obtain the things one wants, it is also vital to have repeated dialogue with producers who by rights should be one's opponents in terms of interest.

Basically, if we are not socially mutually dependent, we will not be able to live one single day. When that dependent relationship is built through the medium of money and goods, however, we lose sight of the existence of others. 'Commodification' means the process in which goods are self-contained solely in a process of being bought and sold through the medium of money, and the social relationships behind them become invisible. Joint purchasing by *han* was an attempt to replace such 'unconscious dependency' with 'conscious co-operation'—in other words, it was a process of rediscovery, through conscious co-operative relationships with others, of the meaning of 'lifestyle,' one that could not be reduced to cash (Orito 1983: 51).

Becoming a '*seikatsusha*' meant venturing consciously to create dependent relationships in order to make visible the hidden relationships of dependency upon others. Seikatsu Club's having sought *seikatsusha* who would 'make and ship the things they also could eat' and deepening its connection with them was for the purpose of acknowledging the life-chain in which Club members themselves lived and let live, within a 'give-and-take' relationship that was something more than the mere exchange of goods for money.

The Beheiren movement always stressed the singular form of individuals, as in 'I will make decisions on my own behalf' or 'I will be responsible for my own actions.' By stating positively that 'I am I,' it tried to make sure that the citizen's movement was one that gave itself life rather than killing itself, and that it was a campaign which encouraged others to live rather than repressing them.

By contrast, the Seikatsu Club movement takes on multiple forms, such as its members being 'a lot of "mes"' or 'deciding their issues for themselves.' In those situations, there is a kind of philosophy that says that even if the point of departure is the first-person singular 'I,' things cannot end as 'I am I.' There is a perception of the existence of others who differ from 'me' there. One person's self-determination to 'decide her own matters for herself' will often conflict with another's self-determination. In order to 'decide things for oneself,' one must always fit the private significance of one's own experience together with others' experience, have these communicate with each other, and form some kind of consensus. Even if consensus is reached, it might come apart like the pages of a temporarily-bound notebook.

In other words, at the same time as changing the 'me' into the third person and relativising it, one must repeatedly extract the 'me in the third person' (Hanazaki 1981: 64) that connects the third-person-like other with 'me' by some common factor. At that point, people can for the first time 'decide their own matters for themselves.'

Therein lies Seikatsu Club's basic way of thinking, which says that if it were possible for me to 'make decisions on my own behalf,' or 'be responsible for my own actions,' this would be due to the realisation that I was supported by such a large number of people.

The selfishness within oneself

The emphasis upon co-operative action as an indispensable condition for becoming *'seikatsusha'* derives from Seikatsu Club's considerably pessimistic view of humanity that sees people as easily becoming self-enclosed beings who seek only to satisfy their private desires, or ones who readily become reliant upon others or upon systems, unless they consciously attempt to create relationships with others.

From the period of high economic growth onwards, people's appetites and concerns have been consistently oriented towards their homes, and, further, to their own lifestyles. The privatisation of lifestyles, while on the one hand allowing a civic awareness sensitive to quotidian interests to take root, also gives rise to such human psychological tendencies as excessive self-protectiveness and selfishness. That is what Seikatsu Club has experienced firsthand.

At the time of the first Oil Crisis in 1973, for instance, its members were assailed by a psychological panic, and the campaign for pursuit of consumption materials for which Seikatsu Club was supposed to have aimed was blown away in just half a year. Its members also rushed to buy up toilet paper, detergent and soy sauce. On the other hand, Seikatsu Club was inundated by people seeking to join in order to evade the goods shortage, and it became bloated. One member reminisces: 'At a time when we were sharing one bottle of soy sauce among three people, or sneezing as we divided up one bag of flour, when we went to take some cushions out of the closet to sit on at the member's house where *han* meetings were held, all the goods that had been shut away in there came tumbling out.'

Amid goods shortages and skyrocketing prices, '*hadaka no watashi no seikatsu* (my life, naked)' was unilaterally victorious, and Seikatsu Club's movement principles and accumulation of co-operative action were exposed as being almost powerless. The next year, 1974, was a 'year to remember' in the history of Seikatsu Club for having the greatest number of withdrawals of membership. Many people joined, and many left.

In comparison with consumer co-operatives that have shopfronts, Seikatsu Club 'boasts' an exceptionally high withdrawal rate both in times of emergency and in ordinary times. To take Tokyo in the late 1980s as an example, while there were about 12,000 people joining every year, withdrawals numbered nearly 10,000. About thirty percent of withdrawals were due to relocation, but the remaining seventy percent quit the club because they could not get used to the *han*-by-*han* pre-ordered joint purchasing system, which, in the eyes of consumers, did not address their natural demands for convenience, ease and abundant number of products (Yamasaki 1993: 233).

The reasons are various: 'I don't want to be the *han* leader or an office-bearer,' 'Associating with the neighbourhood people is a nuisance,' 'The *han* has disbanded,' 'I have started work,' 'With pre-ordered purchasing, I cannot get the things I want immediately,' and so on. The fact of such rampant turnover in itself is proof that Seikatsu Club is an autonomous and spontaneous organisation. That being said, it also shows that members who can turn the stress which almost unavoidably accompanies joint purchasing into a direction for requestioning their very demands as consumers, and discern the enjoyment in co-operation that goes back-to-back with the annoyance, are by no means in the majority.

One could also rephrase it as follows: amid the mechanics of *tatemae* and *honne*—people's public stance and private feelings—the pessimistic view of humanity which says that people seeking 'my life, naked' cannot easily trace a route to 'living together' is conversely making Seikatsu Club undertake its tireless attempts at subject-formation and gamble upon the ideological and conceptual value of emphasis on co-operative action.

'*Seikatsu*' is not something so simple that it can be grasped by such beautiful words as 'harmony' or 'co-existence.' In the Seikatsusha Club, words like '*seikatsusha*' and 'alternative' reputedly fly around, and ideas take the lead. It is possible, though, to see a directionality there which has a realistic grasp of the selfishness and passivity harboured by its members, and rather than rejecting these just for the sake of rejection, it conversely tries, through rejection, to turn them into a positive opportunity, and to gain vigour from that. Moreover, its view of humanity overlaps that of 'Science of thought's' image of 'the people' and Beheiren's 'weak individual.'

That is a contrasting direction to the one in which Masakazu Yamazaki cast romantic expectations towards people who take an optimistic view of humanity and search for 'raw meaning.'

Faces are visible in the local community

The space in which Seikatsu Club joint action is conducted is the domain of the local community and citizens. Its joint-purchasing activities, which progressively tackled issues extending from milk to pork, to beef, to vegetables, and on to detergent, finally ended up in the 'local community' where the members lived. The community—even while making private interests, namely 'me' and 'my family' the basis—is called the 'collective' domain in the sense that it is a space where people transcend 'the private' in building together a common foundation for their livelihood. Engaging with this domain is an extremely important condition in locating the '*seikatsusha*.' Being particular about locally-grown vegetables in joint-purchasing; or, in a workers' collective, building a work-space within the local community and trying to produce processed goods from local agricultural products; or striving to achieve participation in regional assemblies through the deputy movement —each one is a proposal aimed towards the formation of a small locally-autonomous society.

This has been indicated in fragmentary fashion by Itaru Nii as 'micro-community emphasis' or by Yasuko Mizoue as the *seikatsusha* living the reality of the farming village, but it is a new perspective that had never been fully developed as a *seikatsusha* discourse. Nobuyuki Ōkuma sought, in the site of private life comprising the home and family, the potential of the *seikatsusha* to attempt a value-shift from the product-centric to the life-centric. This home and family, however, as we have seen, had changed into a space for the satisfaction of overblown private desires. The existence of the local community encircling the home was not visible to Ōkuma.

In the case of Beheiren, participants in the movement were mutually connected by the single 'motivation' of 'Peace to Vietnam!' but there was the premise that each of them was living in a separate life space. According to Yōtarō Konaka, Beheiren set the foundation of its movement not in people's 'spatial assembly,' but in their 'temporal assembly.' For a time, they left their immediate life and became fighting 'street' citizens. By contrast, for members of Seikatsu Club's movement, the reality that they were settled in one place and were sharing a common experience of life-co-operation in that location gave a positive meaning to 'local community.'

The local community (*chiiki*) in that case is not the abstract one that can be understood by the words *gyōseiku* (administrative area) marked off by the public domain, or *chiiki shakai* (regional community). It is a life-space in which the spread and density of human relationships are guaranteed, where people can come and go on foot or by bicycle, on a daily basis. It could be called a 'biotope (*seikat-*

suken)' that represents the parameters of people's individual daily lifestyle behaviour, the basis of their everyday livelihood. Within the local community, people live with the concrete and shared challenges of eating, excreting, working, resting, sleeping, socialising, learning and playing. In that sense, the local community as a biotope could be called a space not inferior to the home in that its utility value for people to go on living is all the more clearly visible.

The advance of industrialisation and urbanisation has polarised people's basic life-space in two directions. At one extreme lie huge organisations such as government and business, comprising the public world, where people are relegated to an anonymous existence measured by efficiency and profitability. At the opposite pole is the closed, private space that is the home. There, people's interpersonal relationships are narrowed, and none of its pursuits, being private matters, sees the light of day. The local community, as an intermediate space where public and private interact, has hitherto receded far into the distance amid the advance of this kind of polarisation, and has been robbed of its basis for existence. P.L. Wachtel describes that shift as follows:

> In the preindustrial world the first question one was likely to ask a stranger in order to get a bead on him was, "Where are you from?" Now we are more likely to ask, "What do you do?" Place no longer gives us the same sense of a person, nor is it for many people the core of their sense of who they are (1983: 244).

The industrialisation of service has progressed in a variety of domains in community life, and even people's life-culture and assistance relationships have become commercialised, becoming the object of monetary exchange. This situation was what the sociologist J. Habermas (1987: 318–31) called the 'colonized lifeworld' which was incorporated in the 'politico-economic system.'

In the midst of such changes, people came to make mutual nonintervention and non-interference into the norm for everyday life, in exchange for the convenience of buying goods and services. The reproduction of the 'sticky' type of interpersonal relations once seen in agrarian regional communities, which made individual independence impossible, are neither to be desired, nor are desirable. I do not mean to suggest, though, that it is unconditionally desirable in terms of people's living environment for the 'dry' type of human relations typical of urban society to become dominant, either.

With such a community as its foundation, what the various campaigns of the Seikatsu Club have aimed to achieve, starting with joint purchasing activities by each *han*, was the creation of a 'communal' sphere that was neither public nor private, but was supported by direct, face-to-face dialogue between people—in other words, a 'warm and fuzzy' kind of interpersonal connection. One could describe this as building relationships and biotope networks that are something greater than regional bonds arising from 'coincidental decisions to live in a particular place,' and are based, rather, on 'empathy' between people who embrace common issues and share the same living situation.

Focus upon transformation of a community as this kind of life-space led to Seikatsu Club taking a further step away from joint-purchasing activities onto the path of participation in politics.

Politics: a tool for life

Over the sixteen years up to April 1995, the *dairinin* (deputy) movement, which was proposed in 1977 by the Seikatsu Club and actually started from the 1979 assembly elections in Tokyo's Nerima Ward, sent 117 deputies to local assemblies in nine prefectures all over Japan.

It was the capital's municipal- and ward assembly elections crowning the 1987 nationwide local elections that enabled the dazzling debut of 'hordes' of 'ordinary housewife' assembly members through the deputy movement to make a widespread impression. These elections had the following characteristics: firstly, the practical application of participatory politics in the form of the deputy movement opened the way for political participation as assembly members to women who hitherto had been said to 'go no further than voting,' and fulfilled a pioneering role in the age of 'women and politics.' Secondly, in contrast to the majority of other assembly members, who aimed to advance into the realm of central government by using their membership of local assemblies as a scaffold, these women placed great significance upon 'local' assemblies as an arena for political expression. Here, what 'local' meant was a 'site' where life issues came into existence, and a place for the ideological expression of the sovereignty of the *tōjisha*—the parties locked in confrontation with those issues.

Thirdly, as can be seen from the statement of one party, Yoshiko Fukushi, 'I get impatient with nothing but formal petitions (*seigan*) and appeals (*chinjō*). There is only one iron in my fire, and I have never thought of politics and everyday life as being separate things,' these women's political stance was not to interpret politics as 'interest politics' but as a life-tool with which citizens protect their own lives. In other words, this incorporated the intent to transform the concept of 'politics,' to see it as 'lively politics (connected to lives and livelihoods, as well as vigorous)' (Shinohara 1988: 90). Fourthly, as can also be appreciated from one woman's declaration that she did not enter the race with ambitions towards becoming a politician: 'Protesting all the while that I didn't want to do it, I went and ended up an assembly member,' the 'spirit' which imbued their electoral campaigns was brimming with 'light-heartedness,' meaning that they enjoyed the very process of campaigning.

Having such characteristics, what, I wonder, was the deputy movement seeking, and in what way did it develop?

'Joint purchasing' of assembly members with reliable origins

One housewife speaks as follows about the process of expansion into the deputy movement:

> The soap committee made a formal petition to the city council to use soap instead of synthetic detergent in the school lunch programme. On that occasion, too, the assembly members' response was to say that an appeal would have been acceptable, but that a formal petition was too impertinent. It was tabled with no deliberation whatsoever, and eventually was not adopted. It was my first occasion to peek into an assembly, and I started to feel ashamed when I asked myself if I had given my vote to such people, while I felt intense anger at the same time. I think it was the first time for me to have a sense of my own responsibility for politics. This kind of petitioning campaign later developed into deputy activities (Nakamura 1995: 135–136).

By means of joint purchasing, the Seikatsu Club has solved problems connected with individual consumption, as epitomised by food. However, all of the compelling issues in civic life—school lunches and education, rubbish and water, atmospheric pollution and the like—are managed as public systems through rates and taxes. Though the sovereign of those public systems ought to be the taxpayers, under the current system of indirect democracy (a system of representation), one suspects that politics might virtually be being conducted without taxpayer sovereignty.

This question is one connected to 'systems' that transcend the act of buying things—in other words, to 'politics,' and that 'politics' imposes a unidirectional effect upon every corner of everyday life. In spite of that, people do not have political parties or politicians who will represent them. Rather, they are disenchanted, thinking: 'It's all the same whoever gets to be an assembly member. Things are not likely to change,' and be conscious of self-responsibility for having chosen politicians and voting for them in the same manner as they would choose products in their favourite brand, or else having abstained from voting. The aforementioned housewife's words were imbued with the awareness of responsibility towards having settled for a 'citizen's life.'

When people seeking subjectivity in individual consumption behaviour promoted joint purchasing, it was taxpayer sovereignty that emerged as an extension of this. Moreover, the argument that said: 'that being the case, let us vote in assembly members so we can follow up how taxes are being used,' triggered development into the deputy movement. That process could be described as an evolution from 'joint purchasing of consumer goods with reliable origins' to 'joint purchasing of assembly members with reliable origins.'

Doubts over the representation system

The deputy movement formally began with a proposal in the March 1977 issue of the club bulletin, *Seikatsu to jichi* (Life and autonomy) (Iwane 1977). This proposal, dubbed 'the '77 Proposal,' was one which called for Seikatsu Club itself—as a 'group acting to protect the living environment, reform local society, and expand culture' in a political situation where 'existing political parties were unable to gain the support of citizens'—to send deputies to assemblies so as to have their activities 'reflected in local government.' This was an argument for '*seikatsusha*-participatory-type politics' which aimed at establishing citizens' autonomy through the deputy movement. *Seikatsusha* here refers to people who quit being 'citizens (*kokumin*)' reliant upon the dispensation of favours and benefit-sharing from the authorities (the government), and who broadly make the various social contradictions that come to light through daily life into the central theme of 'politics.'

Nonetheless, the word 'deputy (*dairinin*)' is one unfamiliar to the ear. What is important about this deputy movement is that it did not aim solely to send 'representatives (*daihyō*)' of the Seikatsu Club Cooperatives into local assemblies as assembly members. Under democracy, it must be guaranteed that anyone is able to become an assembly member (direct democracy), yet in actual practice, not all people can become assembly members, so they have somebody become an assembly member in their place. That constitutes the representation system (indirect democracy), but in reality the connection between 'those who represent' and 'those who are represented' has been severed. Inherent in the word 'representative' is the strong nuance that once a person has sent someone to be an assembly member, that will mark 'the end' of the matter. When one dares to employ the term 'deputy,' it is charged with the meaning that we have sent someone to take our place as an assembly member, and 'we govern the community.' In other words, a deputy is none other than a life-tool that should be used fully for living as citizens in a local community.

For voters, the mechanism of the representation system—in which having chosen a person is linked originally to having chosen a political party, and further to having supported changes in that party's policy position and even its breach of campaign pledges—is something that gives them the idea that they have been 'given the runaround.' This gives rise to the suspicion that indirect democracy has become dysfunctional. Seikatsu Club's deputy movement started from the recognition that the representation system that forms the core of democratic government is in a critical situation.

The politicisation of life, and the 'lifisation' of politics

In order that 'we' substantially 'govern the community' through a deputy, Collective members, using their critical faculties and mistrust of the kind of politics that lacks citizen sovereignty as a springboard, must individually draw out the 'politics' hidden behind daily life, and strive for the politicisation of that life. In contrast, so as to acquire substance as deputies, the assigned deputies must more deeply project 'life' onto every one of the problems discussed in assembly meetings, and work towards the 'lifisation' of politics. The deputy movement could be called a magnificent experiment that aimed for the establishment of citizen autonomy, incorporating elements of direct democracy into indirect democracy by means of attempting the simultaneous advance of two movements with differing vectors, namely such 'politicisation of life and lifisation of politics' (Nakamura 1990). In that sense, an alternative expression for the deputy movement could be *seikatsusha*' politics.

The setting of deputies' term of office at three terms, totalling twelve years (in the case of Tokyo and Kanagawa, two terms, making eight years) is nothing but an effort to avoid the industrialisation or professionalisation of deputies on the one hand, and to prevent the side that turns out the deputies from leaving everything up to those deputies, on the other.

In order that Seikatsu Club's mission for its activities be reflected in local assemblies, there is the necessity for the Club repeatedly to conduct survey and study activities on a daily basis about environmental problems such as water, greenery, and rubbish, welfare issues in an ageing society, and so on; to try concrete policy proposals from among these; and, by such means, to support their deputies and endorse their acts of 'deputation' on an ongoing basis. And what is formed at the level of local government, as a political organisation for that purpose, is the '*seikatsusha* network' (also called the 'local net').

At present, this movement is still limited to large cities, but it is gradually spreading also to other consumers' cooperative societies in regional areas, mobilising a broad spectrum of inhabitants with common values. It is yet to be seen whether the individuality of being a Seikatsu Club deputy could expand to the universality of being a deputy for the citizenry—because perhaps the answer could be said to hang upon how deeply the politicisation of life and the lifisation of politics could be extended.

Workers' collectives

Seikatsu Club spawned not only the deputy movement, but also a new type of activity called the workers' collective.

A workers' collective is a kind of cooperative organisation based not on an employer/employee relationship, but where working people jointly buy shares in an enterprise and each works as a business owner on an equal footing with everyone else. Workers' collectives, which originally developed in the West, arose amid the industrial revolution of the nineteenth century, and steadily gained franchise. What motivated them was workers' 'resolution of unemployment problems' and 'desire for freedom from managed labour,' and, furthermore, a search for 'another way' for people to interconnect in the workplace.

'Workers' collective' is the American nomenclature, while in Europe 'workers' co-operative' is often used. In Japanese, it is sometimes translated as '*rōdōsha seisan kyōdō kumiai* (workers' production co-operative union),' or called a '*shimin jigyō* (citizens' enterprise),' in the sense that though it does not deny the acquisition of profit, it does not make that its primary objective.

In contrast to the West, where workers' collectives steadily increased in number and attracted attention in their relation to the debate on a society characterised by de-employment, their existence has been all but ignored in Japan, even though they have a history of ninety years since the establishment in 1910 of Sokkisha, the first full-blown workers' production co-operative union (Ishimi 1986). Their actual number is extremely small. Why that is so is a most intriguing question, but the reason is not clear. It was not until the 1980s that the new way of working that the workers' collective comprises came to be the focus of attention.

The first workers' collective to be set up by Seikatsu Club was 'Ninjin,' launched in 1982. Its undertakings included Seikatsu Club business contracts and provision of snacks and boxed meals. Its name did not refer to 'carrot,' as the word '*ninjin*' usually means in Japanese, but was an idiosyncratic reading of the characters meaning 'people,' usually pronounced '*hitobito*.' Starting with 'Ninjin,' Seikatsu Club's workers' collectives expanded into a diverse range of fields, including those related to: 1 food (restaurant operation; food processing); 2 recycling and lifestyle (recycling and leasing; rental outlet operation); 3 information and communications (editing, publication; translation); 4 culture (academic coaching schools; marriage brokering); and 5 welfare (housekeeping-help services). As of July 1995, it had 194 workers' collectives (involving 5819 people) conducting activities in Tokyo, Hokkaido and five prefectures.

The majority of those workers' collectives are private associations that do not have corporate status. Some have been incorporated as business unions under the Small and Medium-sized Enterprise Co-operatives Act, but this does not mean that they necessarily fit the organisational form stipulated for business unions. Now, there is call for legislation specifically for workers' collectives.

These workers' collective activities are of a fundamentally different nature from conventional Seikatsu Club activities, which were characterised by their 'free-of-charge' co-operative behaviour. In that they provide goods or services 'for a fee', they have commonality with for-profit activities in the market economy. At the same time, though, they are not primarily profit-seeking enterprises. Their aim, above all, is a certain 'assertion.' In an interview, one woman employed at a food-related workers' collective describes her response to working there:

> Food is a fundamental thing in daily life, and so in that sense I have a real feeling of being connected. It's not mass production, so I recall each customer's face, thinking things like, 'How has their rheumatism been lately?' or 'Put a little less salt in their *bentō* (boxed meal).' The work itself is tough, being a wear on the nerves, but the worthwhile thing might be that I can envision where the *bentō* I have made are going to end up, as in who is going to eat them, and where. If [the motto of] Seikatsusha Club's joint purchasing is 'not to buy and use things when you don't know who made them,' then I understand a workers' collective in terms of 'not to get paid for making things that I don't know who is going to use (Oral transcript).

She interprets the activities of a workers' collective as being an expansion of 'not buying and using things when one doesn't know who made them' (joint purchasing activities) to 'not getting paid for making things that one doesn't know who is going to use.' In other words, she accepts this as being a development from being a 'user' of goods and services to a 'maker who stands in the position of a user,' that is, a process of evolution from '*seikatsusha*' to 'working as a *seikatsusha*.'

What the housewives who led the Seikatsusha Club experienced through joint-purchasing activities was that they were not merely beings that consumed, but beings with hidden ability to produce. One member who had been involved in locally-grown vegetables says, 'The desire of my family and me to eat vegetables that are as near as possible to how vegetables should be exactly overlaps a farmer's desire to cherish the soil, sow the seeds, and raise them in a satisfying way.' This comment suggests that only 'good consumers' (*seikatsusha*) qualify as 'good producers' (*seikatsusha* who produce): in other words, it means that people who can put themselves thoroughly in the position of 'users' who emphasise 'usefulness' for living have the potential to be 'those who produce while being in the position of users.'

Joint-purchasing activities were voluntary activities basically for the sake of the livelihood of the participants themselves and their families, and not for anybody else's. They were unpaid activities without commercial value, and their non-compensatory nature had important significance. By contrast, workers' collective activities were ones that did not lock away people's ability as hidden productive capacity merely as shadow work in the home, but developed it into paid activity deemed necessary by the 'local community' and made it flourish. Without decoupling 'users' from 'producers,' it has the aim of visibly creating a relationship of exchange and co-existence between the two, thereby trying to transcend simple exchange of goods or services for money.

In other words, while tying formal activity (paid labour) incorporated as an institution of economic society with informal activity (unpaid social activity) which is not so incorporated, the activities of workers' collectives are an experiment in trying to create a way of working (semi-formal) in opposition to the former, while basing themselves on the latter.

From a 'way of being made to work' to a 'way of working'

One more real basis for the birth of workers' collectives was the advent of the age of working housewives. It was in 1983 that an article headlined: 'Working housewives top 50%' occupied lead position on the front page of national newspapers. Seikatsu Club members could not be unconnected with such a tendency, either. From around 1980, in their in-house bulletin, *Seikatsu to jichi* (Life and autonomy), there began to appear all kinds of discussion over members' switch to paid employment. This included criticism of the 'current situation of [members] going out to work even if it were meaningless,' which was akin to jumping in a flurry onto a bus passing their door without any indication of its destination, and, in some branches with 'forty percent of members working,' anxiety over what to do about present conditions where the *han* activities that formed the basis of the Seikatsu Club movement were falling into crisis.

Moreover, though the majority of Seikatsu Club members were full-time housewives, there was no small number that took issue with the fact that they themselves were not 'wage-earners.' It was also into the 1980s that the bulletin began to carry such opinions as: 'When I was engaged in a direct petitioning campaign about soap, I was criticised by a man who said, "Who do you think is feeding you?" Also, when it comes to spending not only valuable time on campaigning, but money, too, I fear troubling my husband. If we truly strive to have an influential voice, we will need economic power, won't we?' Here, there is the paradoxical rhetorical question of whether the 'freedom' to do activities that change one from a consumer to a *seikatsusha* is something that will only be gained once one has the power to generate money oneself.

The issue lies in the 'way of being made to work' rather than the 'way of working.' When a housewife once confined to the home tries to re-enter formal employment, her choice is virtually limited to part-time work. In fact, part-timers account for two-thirds of housewives of the type that have re-entered employment in their post-child-rearing period. The way that these housewives are made to work is organised to be advantageous to businesses, in exchange for income that could not be called generous, and is a far cry from self-actualisation through work. If one were to describe what was in such women's mind's eye, it would probably be: 'under current social conditions, we are made to act so that we can only exist in a dilemma, whether we work or not.'

Still harbouring feelings of awkwardness and guilt towards campaigning while being financially dependent, amid their daily repetition of domestic labour that was deemed worthless because it had no exchange value in monetary terms, women turned a doubting eye respectively upon men's way of working and the state of monetary income which hitherto had been considered self-evident. What became visible in that process was the direction of mutually contributing their own funds and labour, and going on to create their own style of working.

In order for women to live independently, they had had to enter the formal sector, and assimilate and adapt to men's culture and lifestyle rhythms: in other words, the image of independence that had hitherto existed meant that women had had to secure monetary income by becoming 'men.' To borrow a phrase from Scott Burns, this was the market ideology that said: 'I was paid for, therefore I am' (1975: 62). Workers' collective activities marked this kind of conventional image of independence itself as the target they should overcome.

1. How to create conditions which enable a way of working that harmonises with everyday life, wherein each participant is a business-owner rather than being hired (the humanising of work);
2. How to create a route leading to a professional career by emphasising abilities nurtured amid domestic labour, which only exist in shadow form (the resuscitation of shadow work);
3. How to reproduce within the community a new form of exchange of goods and services based not on 'competition' in the market economy, but on 'co-operation,' and the life culture it generates (the new creation of community);
4. How to change the landscape in which people work and their way of working by casting doubt on the presently money-oriented way of working in the formal sector, and attempting to restore work that is 'useful' to people (the questioning of the socially dominant way of working).

In workers' collective activities were invested the hope of realisation of capabilities such as these four. The idea of 'a new way of working' finally had seized a clue to its embodiment at the end of a long quest to become '*seikatsusha*' through joint-purchasing activities.

The roundabout route to financial independence

The biggest problem for workers' collectives more than a decade after their launch was that in few cases had they succeeded in raising their profitability to a point where their members were financially independent. In the sense of the contribution that an 'alternative way of working' brings to society, workers' collectives have 'shining aspirations.' On the other hand, in order for them to gain social recognition as another way of working, there have to be conditions where a certain level of success is achieved within the market economy, and the people participating in the collective can feed themselves by their labour. How can one strike a balance between the two different measures of value that constitute 'aspirations' and business performance? And the fact that the actors are all 'housewives' further complicates the matter.

According to a 1994 survey of 292 members spread over 100 workers' collectives, in respect to monthly average working hours, eighty-eight percent of respondents worked less than 120 hours; while in terms of average annual income, eighty-five percent earned less than 1 million yen, six percent earned between one and 1.29 million, and a further six percent earned 1.3 million or more. The average hourly wage was about 850 yen, a level lower than part-time work in general (Tōkyō wākāzu korekutibu kyōdō kumiai 1995).

Members' expectations towards and appraisal of their income differed according to where they sought the significance of working in a workers' collective, as the following remarks reveal: 'I am enjoying doing it according to what I want, so I do not much mind the pay being low,' 'I am growing myself as I am working, so it is impossible to expect high compensation,' 'In comparison to the density of the work, the pay is just too little,' 'Even given that making money is not my primary objective, I could not refute the accusation that it is just a way for housewives to kill time.'

In the case of workers' collectives, the work process itself is basically set up in a way that makes the pursuit of efficiency impossible. 'Bon,' a food-processing collective in Machida City, for example, strives to promote its store's individuality by using additive-free ingredients. They begin by using locally-grown vegetables and fruit that are still fresh as much as possible, washing off the dirt themselves; and they use stock without artificial additives in their simmered dishes. Time-consuming processes that go the opposite way to efficient work-practices prevail. Even in terms of how a 'reasonable price' is attached to the goods and services they produce, unlike the market principle that deems value to lie in saleability, the utility value is pursued above all, and the production cost necessary to generate goods meeting that value is calculated. Just as in the case of Seikatsu Club's joint purchasing, safe goods and services are certainly not cheap to produce.

This means that the only people who can buy safety are affluent residents. That is not what the collective's women want. The expectations of people in the community tend to be towards goods and services that are both 'safe' and 'cheap,' with main emphasis evidently on the latter. What is important for the collective is to have the community know about the time-consuming process involved in the goods and services they produce, and to be convinced as to the appropriateness of their prices. That necessitates both a long personal association and the fullness of time.

That being said, the women have not given up on economic independence. To work is to have social responsibility, and if it were to end in a 'half-baked' independence, they would be unable to parry external criticism that it was a pastime for housewives with husbands. There are numerous workers' collectives whose members strive to equip themselves with specialist technology and management capability and raise labour productivity in a form that does not discard the *seikatsusha* perspective. Again according to the aforementioned survey, in response to the 'one million yen barrier' to qualify for a spousal tax deduction, and the '1.3 million yen barrier' to qualify for the special spousal tax deduction, seventeen percent replied that they 'want to exceed these at some point,' twenty-six percent said they 'want to exceed them but cannot increase their income to that extent,' nine percent said they had 'already exceeded them,' and thirty-nine percent replied that 'in future, too, they wanted to operate within the deduction limits.' As a future direction, to 'exceed' the barriers, that is, to escape from being their husbands' dependents, is the wish of the majority.

The words of one member perhaps directly speak for the emotional realm of a great proportion of members:

> Now is a time when our family itself is need of income, financially, and since the ship has already set sail with me on it, so to speak, I cannot abandon the low-paid workers' [collective], and somehow pinning my hopes on the future, on next year or the year after, I am still engaged with the collective, which is not just about earning money. Even with the same hourly wage of 850 yen, I have realised that while there are ways of working that are mentally and physically exhausting, there are also those where there is a broadening of carefree interpersonal relationships. In the end, it boils down to what abundance means to people (Oral transcript).

In this way, these women avoid advancing directly along a route to operating profit and the economic independence connected with it, taking a detour that involves deepening their social interconnectedness and empathy through dialogue with people in their community, and devoting time within their cycle of living in an effort to bring their work-space into reality.

The full-time-activist/housewife

Viewed in this manner, the way of living as '*seikatsusha*' that Seikatsu Club has pursued in its joint-purchasing activities, deputy movement and workers' collectives might appear to have been smoothly materialised. That is not the case, however. It would be closer to the truth to say that, for Seikatsu Club members, the *seikatsusha* still remains an ideal that ought to be attained.

Now, if we take deputy movement members (local Net members) as an example and try to sketch their average profile, it will come out as something like: 'women with a husband earning eight million or more per annum (seventy-seven percent); who have a high educational background (two or more years at tertiary level: sixty-three percent); and in their third life-stage, that is, their post-child-rearing period' (Waseda daigaku bungakubu shakaigaku kenkyūshitsu 1993).

These are women called 'housewives' who have both economic and temporal 'leeway'—in other words, those who belong to the 'middle-middle' or above in terms of social stratification. Such attributes are also shared by the working members of workers' collectives.

Expressed in positive terms, in counter to what Habermas terms 'the colonization of the lifeworld' by 'the system,' the *seikatsusha* belongs to the category of what Mioko Shiba has named '*katsudō-sengyō shufu* (full-time-activist/housewife),' in contrast to '*katsudō/sengyō shufu* (activist/full-time housewife).' She, as a *seikatsusha*, has a sense of crisis, daring to reject the path of employment out of irritation at the situation in which not only her husband but she herself would be drawn up into the logic of enterprise = capital. Just as Seikatsu Club's joint purchasing activities started off as a movement that 'housewives could do for the very reason that they were full-time residents,' the negative prescription of housewives' existence, in which they were seen only as half-citizens, has worked conversely as a factor in pushing them towards the deputy movement for creating citizen-driven politics. It is also true, however, that no work has been done defiantly to objectivise why the practice in that case of aiming for a *seikatsusha*-participatory type of politics is something involving women only, and housewives only, at that. The deputy movement, with housewives as its actors, seems to have come this far by venturing to avoid stepping into this 'sacred domain.'

Discommunication with husbands

For a member who is a housewife to be responsible and work continuously, whether in the local Net which supports deputies or in a workers' collective, her relationship with her family, and especially her husband, becomes involved. Though the data is somewhat old (1986), I will take my survey of a Tokyo workers' collective in Satō 1988 as an example.

As for their relationship with their husband in regard to working in the workers' collective, about four-tenths (thirty-seven percent) said that their husband agreed, but another four-tenths (forty percent) said that they had begun to work amid their husband's 'opposition' or 'indifference.' Moreover, of the husbands who had initially been 'opposed' or 'indifferent,' seventy-two percent did not subsequently change their attitude. One member writes as follows in the free response column:

> My understanding husband says, 'Now that you have begun, keep going at the workers' you-know-what. Because what you are doing has social significance. But only as long as it isn't detrimental to your family, okay?' But if I become really enthusiastic and start throwing myself bodily into this work, rather than just doing it in my spare time between household chores, my husband will instantly stop being tolerant, I'm sure. With that premonition, I blunt my emotional attachment to the workers' collective.

In response to the question: 'Whose job is the housework?' the percentage that answered: 'I think it has to be me' was low (eight percent), while the proportion that said: 'It would not matter if it were not me' was high (forty-six percent). To that extent, these women are relatively liberated from a consciousness friendly to the traditional sexual division of labour. Nonetheless, with nine-tenths of the members being housewives in nuclear families, the responses: 'I do nearly all the housework' and 'I do most of it, with the family helping a little' amounted to ninety-four percent, giving a glimpse of the figure of these women struggling hard as they shouldered the dual burden of domestic labour and their role in the workers' collective. The fluidity in the sexual division of labour in their minds was betrayed by their actual behaviour.

The weight of their responsibility in their home lives depends largely upon their husbands' way of working in their companies and the latter's awareness. In contrast to those wives who endeavour radically to re-question the way to gain income and the way of working, and the way of life that depends on that income, there are still only a few husbands who doubt the very livelihood at their feet, and have the will to change it. Many a housewife points out the discommunication with her husband, saying: 'I think we have different yardsticks for measuring how we live. We do not have a common language that is mutually understood.'

Simultaneously, however, the structure of the consciousness typical of middle-class women in large cities, which emphasises cordial relations and harmony in home life, is also important. If they try to change their social relationship with their husband and reorganise a new relationship, there is a risk that this will cause disturbance to their daily life. This mixture of communication and discommunication has a deep-rooted nature that could even be called fundamental to micro-level family relationships. The choice to take personal responsibility for the household and assume its burden, with the desire to be a 'decent' married couple, rather than making waves between husband and wife by drawing the husband into the domain of everyday life and strongly advocating changing him into a '*seikatsusha*,' is the 'present' choice of workers' collective members. The 'new type' of housewives who have an unfettered way of thinking and boundless energy in the local community also strongly adhere to a pro-'good wife and wise mother (*ryōsai kenbo*)' sentiment in the home.

There are also some members who, having tried once to change their husbands, are conversely made to realise just how hard it is to change them for the reason that the men are 'so understanding,' and, as a result, become completely absorbed in workers' collective activities:

> Curiously enough, I sometimes think that it would be better if he were stubborn and self-righteous, because it would be easy to maintain a fighting stance. When I am shown understanding that is nothing more than lip-service, with statements like: 'It's better than going out to a

part-time job. Do your best, with that housewife's power of yours!' it makes things all the more difficult (Oral transcript).

External criticism suggested that workers' collective members who chose a way of working at their own expense that involved little contribution to 'capital' actually were giving firm internal support to their husband's mode of work, which was incorporated into the logic of capital. This, one could say, had pinpointed the most fundamental husband–wife relationship and the reality of the family with unerring accuracy.

The limitations of an absence of men

When looking back at such a history of the Seikatsu Club, one suspects that one of the limitations of the Seikatsu Club movement lies in it not having positively incorporated men as movement leaders, nor having opened up the possibility of making them into *seikatsusha*. '*Seikatsusha*' is essentially a concept that takes a neutral stance vis-à-vis gender—whether one is a man or woman in social terms. Ironically, the limitations on Seikatsu Club's activism up till now might be intrinsic to the notion of the '*seikatsusha*' itself.

Seikatsu Club's *seikatsusha* concept is something which, above all, has brought the activity and way of living of 'me' as a 'human being' to the forefront, but has that not concealed the most basic male–female relationship in the day-to-day world, and caused the loss of opportunities to topicalise the disparities in roles and power relations due to gender?

> The strong 'intention' of the people who have always continued to assume leadership in our activities has been *to live first as human beings, before being wives and mothers*. I regard as ideal the figure that appears, for example, in…the practice of a way of living as seen in a campaign to banish synthetic detergent, which started simply from a feeling of wanting to avoid being the victim of skin problems, but then went further to the resolution not to become a perpetrator who flushed away contaminated water, sullied the environment and even impacted upon our descendents (Seikatsu kurabu seikyō Kanagawa 1988: 3; emphasis added).

By co-operative members emphasising their activities as 'human beings,' their gaze turns to the possibility of joint battle lines that transcend locality, nationality and ethnicity to fight against the things that easily jeopardise 'human' survival. Seikatsu Club's setting into the central axis of their campaigns the issues of Minamata and the accident at the Chernobyl nuclear power station as their own problems was an expression of this. That was effective in centrifugally broadening their activities, but it simultaneously cunningly concealed the fact that the housewives who were the subjects of activity were not 'regular' humans, but existed within a socially and culturally constructed relationship called gender, did it not? There, the supposedly gender-neutral '*seikatsusha*' came to be surrounded by one gender, namely *seikatsusha* = housewife = woman, and the importance of the logic of actively involving men in the process of practices for becoming a *seikatsusha* was overlooked, was it not?

As symbolised by Seikatsu Club's having made 'we can do it because we are housewives' the starting-point of their movement, it cannot be denied that the Club's activities hitherto have been supported and propelled by society's system of the sexual division of labour which is premised on the existence of housewives. It is not only from without, but also from within the ranks of Club members that problems have begun to be pointed out, such as doubts as to whether it is possible for members to grow from consumers into independent *seikatsusha* while still depending on the income of their corporate-warrior husbands; the 'allergy' towards politics of housewives who hesitate even to be in the position of sending deputies, let alone become deputies themselves as 'housewife councillors' in the public domain of the political world; and, in their political topicalisation of lifestyle issues, their bias towards and fixation of realms that have been seen as 'housewives' monopoly,' including rubbish and school lunches (though these are given credit as transition periods).

If one understands 'from consumers to *seikatsusha*' to refer only to the side that uses goods and services, as consumers, then this will be nothing more than a passive standpoint. In order to bring the user's vantage point into the production space and transform the things that are made, it is deemed necessary for men, also, to enter the 'private' space which aims for the reproduction of life, namely the family and community; and for women, too, to go out into the 'public' space, whether it be a workplace or the political arena.

Moreover, when one says 'the politics of lifestyle issues,' it is not simply a question on the dimension of 'transferring the housewife's kitchen sensibilities to politics.' More than anything, it must be something that includes modification to the very institution of the sexual division of labour, which has separated the 'public' from the 'private,' and enclosed the world inhabited by women within a 'private' domain. The very situation that work for the sake of the reproduction of life is separated from unpaid domestic labour and paid employment, and that each is fixed by a specific gender, must be politically topicalised.

The future of the 'Ji-ya-o Club'

The aim which Seikatsu Club's housewife members have pursued is the alternative of becoming *seikatsusha*. How could they reconfigure a home realm that had become a site of passive consumption from the dimension of utility value? How could they approach ways of production and circulation from the aspect of utility value? And how, in a climate of advancing privatisation of lifestyles and growth of the service economy, could they revive fragmented local communities into 'collective' spaces by means of the value called 'co-operativeness?' Their objective was to grapple with tasks related to 'lifestyle' in its entirety.

In order for the alternative of becoming a *seikatsusha* to establish a steady independence, there needs to be theory and practice for proactively incorporating men in the process of practices for rebuilding daily life afresh, and making them, as life-companions, into 'men who change their way of living.'

The emergence in 1991 of the 'Ji-ya-o Club' (whose name derives from reversing the order of the syllables spelling '*oyaji* (Dad/old man),' and whose membership consists of men mainly in current employment in companies), was a ground-breaking 'event' for the Seikatsu Club with its hitherto 'male-less' membership. Men at last started to change their way of living, with the ultimate goal of building a livelihood-sphere network 'for living vibrantly in the local community.' There probably had been wives' day-to-day encouragement to their husbands behind this. For human beings, life in the home and community is a universal domain for the very reason that it is indispensable for people's continuing survival. Hidden there is a wealth of meaning that cannot be apprehended in terms of monetary value. Ji-ya-o Club members were men with the spirit to query whether it was right only to allow women to monopolise its abundance and enjoy it.

As one attempt in creating work that is 'of use' to life in the local community, they took on as a personal challenge the experience of caring for the elderly and the disabled, which until then had been the province of women, and they began moves to establish this in the community, with the building of relationships of mutual aid as a lifestyle norm. Of course, such an attempt is still modest, and is only in a trial stage. There are numerous hurdles to overcome before they can establish care of the elderly as a daily job rather than a once-a-month event. One member says: 'When I am confronted by someone who cannot live their everyday life without support, I yearn to do something for them. In all honesty, I am relieved to find that I still have some appropriately human feeling, and I'm not so bad after all. I keenly realise that the presence of people I support is supporting me.'

Hidden within such down-to-earth practices by male co-operative members (or members' husbands) of trying to change their way of living is a germ of potential which will determine whether Seikatsu Club starts striding ever more boldly towards the formation of a *seikatsusha* movement. In that sense, one might say that the curtain has only just risen on Seikatsu Club's fully-fledged *seikatsusha* activism.

5 In lieu of an epilogue: an overview of the *seikatsusha* discourse and its prospects

Introduction: the effectiveness of ambiguous terminology

The '*seikatsusha*,' born in Japan

Who is meant by *seikatsusha*? *Seikatsusha* is a strange word. If we take *seikatsusha* to be a notion that encompasses all 'people living their everyday lives,' then all human beings will be *seikatsusha*. As non-*seikatsusha* do not exist, there is no positive reason to go out of our way to use the term *seikatsusha*.

Nonetheless, for the eighty-something years since *seikatsusha* was first used by the playwright Hyakuzō Kurata, it has been recalled and employed countless times within tense relationships with the times and social conditions. And even now, a decade into the new century, it is still being used.

It was not until the 1980s that the word *seikatsusha* began to be consumed in great quantities. While it had not been widely used in Japan's post-war period of high economic growth, *seikatsusha* came into frequent use without any clear-cut definition, and in the early 1990s, it had become completely entrenched. The Japanese version of this book, *Seikatsusha to wa dare ka* (1996), was also a work written with such a historical background.

The term made its appearance as a politician's statement ('*seikatsusha*-driven politics'), a political party's catch-phrase at election time ('We will protect the *seikatsusha*'), a company's advertising slogan ('An enterprise that is kind to *seikatsusha*'), and a consumer-strategy term in market research ('*seikatsusha* marketing'), and it began to take root in people's everyday lives as a keyword of the times. It would not make much difference even to reread *seikatsusha* as 'nationals (*kokumin*) = the people living their lives in this country.' For those who use it, this term *seikatsusha*, so pleasant to the ear, is probably a convenient and invaluable word that needs no definition.

In 1992, the government publication, 'Lifestyle superpower 5-year plan: aiming for the coexistence of global society,' adopted the expression: 'placing importance on the perspective of the *seikatsusha* and consumer (*shōhisha*),' and so *seikatsusha* finally won endorsement as an official term. Even in this public document, however, there is no definition of *seikatsusha*. In the Foreign Ministry's translation, '*seikatsusha* [and] *shōhisha*' are lumped together as 'consumer.'

This is probably proof that *seikatsusha* is a 'home-grown' term spawned by the life-culture of Japanese society, unlike such foreign-born words as 'citizen (*shimin*),' 'public (*kōshū*),' 'mass (*taishū*),' 'people (*jinmin* or *minshū*),' and 'consumer (*shōhisha*).' Incidentally, there are similar, foreign-born concepts close to *seikatsusha*, namely 'common man,' 'well-informed citizen,' and 'prosumer,' but, as I shall later elaborate, these either indicate a certain aspect of 'citizen' or 'consumer,' or are used as notions situated as extensions of these. Furthermore, *seikatsusha* is still not a mature, established term, and is yet to be recorded in any Japanese-language dictionaries. Even *Kōjien* (sixth edition: Iwanami shoten), deemed to be Japan's representative reference dictionary, for example, is no exception.

The background to achieving keyword status

Two reasons can be considered as having been behind the growing frequency of use of *seikatsusha* from the late 1980s through to the early 1990s.

Firstly, after the crumbling of fantasies of ideologically-centred great situationism due to the collapse at the end of the 1980s of the socialist economic bloc and the subsequent termination of the Cold War between East and West, *seikatsusha* came to be chosen as a 'verbal talisman' for the new age. The philosopher Shunsuke Tsurumi coined the term 'verbal talisman (*o-mamori kotoba*)' to mean an expression that requires no definition, is easy on the ear and can be used to fend off criticism from others, and one may truly call *seikatsusha* a typical example (Tsurumi 1946 [1976]: 12–25). That is why each political party and every administration have started to use words such as '*seikatsusha*,' 'lifestyle logic (*seikatsu no ronri*),' plus 'quality of life' and 'lifestyle superpower' in their slogans, policies and manifestos every time there is an election. In its ambiguity, the word *seikatsusha* is an advantageous expression for administrators, or, in other words, 'persons with power.' By contrast, the decline of the word 'worker (*rōdōsha*),' which had already begun around 1960, was further accelerated in this period, ending in the total downfall of its authority.

Secondly, if we take it in a positive light, the term *seikatsusha* is imbued with criticism and remorse for the current situation of Japanese society, which has been too biased towards prioritising producers. In that sense, *seikatsusha* has appeared as a term that assumes the role of reinterpreting sophisticated industrial society itself as 'self-reflexive' (Giddens 1990). Japan's GNP increased to a level just short of overtaking Western societies, but far from this meaning some leeway in its lifestyle, there was anxiety towards a reality which saw an accumulation of challenges like the environment, welfare, safety and security, and resources. As well, there was the added premonition that the 'self-evident nature of affluence' in Japanese society had begun to come apart at the seams. *Seikatsusha* could be seen as a word expressing the desire for a new type of human image, one bred by reflection and doubts about such current circumstances, and which sought an alternative way of living within a 'matter-of-course' lifestyle.

Towards the age of a twofold demise

Now that the new century, too, is a decade old, the word *seikatsusha*, far from shrinking in value, is being recalled into use as a term with even greater worth. The grounds for its recall, however, have a different aspect from that of the late 1980s to early 1990s. This is because the closed nature of Japanese society has advanced a step further.

What rapidly emerged throughout the 1990s was the perspective of globalisation. The various domains of politics, economics, society, culture, information, military affairs and the like lost the ability to be self-contained within one country, and Japanese society came to take on any move in globalising world society as an internal event. What became clear in that process was its 'demise,' in two senses of the word—the first being the total collapse of the bubble economy which had prided itself on its prosperity in the 1980s; and the second being the institutional fatigue of the existing political/economic/labour/

social system that had taken off from the poverty-stricken post-war society and supported high economic growth. The set of values to do with work and enterprise, also, underwent huge changes from the times when the residuum of Japanese-style management pivoting around the system of lifetime employment was still functioning.

In the 'lost two decades' following the collapse of the bubble economy, employment uncertainty in a situation of prolonged recession cooled people's consumer confidence, and things began to advance in a chain reaction: price-slashing → deflation → employment crisis → lifestyle crisis. As if to add insult to injury, along came the age of worldwide financial crisis, starting with the breakdown of sub-prime loans. Under crisis conditions in which casualisation of the workforce marched in parallel with growing income disparity, even taking labour legislation as an example, it is now obvious that it is almost powerless as a brake upon reality. In that sense, the grounds for the recall of *seikatsusha* have become far stricter than hitherto.

In such circumstances, people's new expectations have been invested in the word *seikatsusha*. If we make this assumption, then it would not be a wasted effort to question anew the essence of the term *seikatsusha*, which is highly evocative due to its being an ambiguous 'verbal talisman.' This perhaps is because concealed within it is the potential to reverse-expose the challenges endemic in contemporary society, and the direction in which society should be heading.

Seikatsusha negotiates the wartime regime

Japanese scholarship, minus 'lifestyle'

This chapter, entitled: 'In lieu of an epilogue: an overview of the *seikatsusha* discourse and its prospects,' is an attempt to backtrack afresh to the emergence of the word *seikatsusha*, and, with that as a starting-point, to review the changes it has undergone since the dawn of the new century 'till now.'

The word *seikatsusha* has a long history. If one traces it back through (1) life-culture discourses (Kiyoshi Miki, Itaru Nii, Wajirō Kon, Shunsuke Tsurumi, Yasuji Hanamori, Yasuko Mizoue, and so on) in the period extending from the wartime regime during World War Two to the post-war time of deprivation; to (2) consumer-society discourses (Nobuyuki Ōkuma, Seiichi Tsutsumi, Yoshiharu

Fukuhara, and the like) from the period of rapid economic growth to post-collapse of the bubble economy; and further, to (3) from civic activism (Beheiren) and the *seikatsusha* movement (Seikatsu Club Co-operatives) to a twenty-first-century-style image of society (Yoshinori Hiroi) and the *seikatsusha* discourse of 'one's own way' (Takashi Uchiyama) as new social movements, it can be seen to be a term with a long history, one that has always been used to counter changes in times and circumstances.

Under what kinds of temporal circumstances has *seikatsusha* made its appearance? And with what sort of people of what manner of social stratum as its subjects; and as something counterposed to what other categories of people; and, furthermore, carrying what sort of issues and concerns, has it done so? In order to clarify the contemporary meaning of *seikatsusha*, let me first begin by reinterpreting the word *seikatsusha* within the social context of its genesis.

The first user of *seikatsusha* as a term was the playwright Hyakuzō Kurata (1891–1943), founder of the magazine, *Seikatsusha*, in 1926. The *seikatsusha* there was something that indicated religious seekers who disciplined themselves with a stoic logic in resistance to the mundane world. It was a decade or so later that *seikatsusha* was freed of its religious connotation, and made its entrance as a bearer of actual life-culture.

Through the modernisation process since the Meiji era, it has been considered impossible for the private spheres of 'lifestyle (*seikatsu*)' and 'livelihood (*kurashi*)' to become the object of serious contemplation. There are two reasons for this. The first is that the very mode of existence of Japanese-style scholarship, which emphasises the introduction and acceptance of Western thought, has prevented the people who live the concrete reality of Japan from making everyday life into a main theme. In the academe, Japanese thought has become a 'branch office' for Western thought, detached from people's lives, and with 'thought's proper sphere' even being considered to lie in detachment. Another reason lies in the fact that responsibility for lifestyles and day-to-day life was shouldered by women. Making the private sphere where females take charge into an object of speculation has been regarded as having low value. The private sphere has been devalued for the reason that it is one where women are instrumental, and because it was thought less of, it has continued to be monopolised by women.

The inspiring force for '*seikatsu*': Kiyoshi Miki

The philosopher Kiyoshi Miki (1897–1945) is a rare philosopher who selected not 'the state' but '*seikatsu* (life)' as his principal subject, and developed a theory of life-culture and the *seikatsusha* discourse that was its instrument. In his 1941 critique, 'Seikatsu bunka to seikatsu gijutsu (Life culture and living techniques),' he gave the name '*seikatsu bunka* (life-culture)' to culture born from an emphasis on quotidian-ness itself and a positive transformation of people's own lives, in counter to the '*kokumin bunka* (national culture)' framed and standardised as state policy under the wartime regime; and he called people who create life-culture '*seikatsusha*' (Miki 1941b [1967]: 384–401).

Miki especially sought the prototype for *seikatsusha* in the figure of 'farmers' who, based on their own experiential knowledge and skills, worked on the soil and nature, brought forth products by their own hands, and designed their own livelihoods. They ploughed the land, sowed the seed, watched its growth, harvested it, and returned things that withered and died once more to the soil. He thought that farmers were the very people with the ability to read, in the process of the growth of agricultural crops, the cycle of life or life-stages as a circle—birth, ageing, death, and rebirth. They were required to wage a fierce battle with nature, and were situated within a 'landlord–tenant-farmer' relationship in village society. However, Miki found in the 'farmer' the figure of a lifestyle-creator who could not be reduced merely to those elements.

Neither 'workers,' whose 'struggle' aspect was the sole one emphasised by Marxists, nor 'nationals' who were half-spontaneously incorporated into the state's general mobilisation structure, were what Miki called *seikatsusha*. In that sense, the farmer = *seikatsusha* that appeared in Miki's life-culture discourse was particularly conspicuous at a time when the image of the masses, lumped together under the names of 'workers' or 'nationals,' was dominant.

The common people's 'techniques for living': Itaru Nii

Another who explicitly employed the word *seikatsusha* in the same times as Miki, and who attached importance to life-culture in its connection to the former, was the writer Itaru Nii (1888–1951).

Depicted in his 1940 work, *Machi no tetsugaku* (The philosophy of the streets), are the nameless people who live with the streets as their field (rice-merchants, fishmongers, greengrocers and the like), and the '*seikatsusha* of the streets' who lives through his connection with them, namely Itaru Nii himself. Unlike Miki, Nii did not discuss the *seikatsusha* ideologically, aiming for a philosophical elucidation of a 'new human type.' Placing himself outside literary and critical circles and making his living just with his pen, he endeavoured to live the life of a *seikatsusha* carrying through with his own desire for freedom of livelihood.

The *seikatsusha* in that context refers to 'common people' with roots in everydayness, and not to '*kizokujin* = those who belong,' members of organisations such as government offices, big firms, banks and the like (Nii 1940: 406). The former are not elite salaried workers who make their living under the protection of 'the authorities' or large organisations, but 'the self-employed' who maintain their livelihoods by their own efforts. Arguably, for Nii, who had also undertaken translations of American poetry and novels by Henry Wadsworth Longfellow and others, it was 'common people'—who, though nameless, had since America's founding had 'spontaneity and originality'—that represented the original form of the *seikatsusha* image, as did 'farmers.'

According to Nii, life-culture meant the 'life-skills' of the common people. Mutually-supportive relationships with others living side-by-side with them are deemed necessary for common people who are never protected by organisations as members of the latter. Common people cannot pursue only their selfish desires. Nii, therefore, says that it is easy for them to develop ways of constructing interpersonal relationships that differ from the state-led '*tonarigumi* (neighbourhood association)' system, and to obtain the wisdom and ingenuity for living. The idea of *seikatsusha* as common people (*shiseijin*) went on to be taken over by the term '*hitobito* (the people),' in the banner of '*hitobito no tetsugaku* (the people's philosophy)' that Shisō no kagaku kenkyūkai hoisted post-war.

One more characteristic of Nii's life-culture theory lies in its anti-centric orientation, with its emphasis on subregions such as villages and urban wards. Localities as sites for people's lives do not have their *raison d'être* in their connection with the 'centre.' The space called the locality has concreteness and identity from people's lives, as the site where they eat, work, sleep, rest, work, socialise, play and learn, and it has distinctive nature and a past history. In that sense, every locality is equal, and for that very reason is open towards the world.

Having stood as a mayoral candidate in Tokyo's Suginami Ward elections in 1947 and becoming Japan's first democratically-elected ward mayor, Nii made public his design specifications for turning Suginami Ward into a world cultural mecca like the German city of Weimar, where Goethe was Chief Minister of State (Nii 1975: 110). Upon Nii's death, the local utopia that he had desired lost its gloss for a time, but the philosophy of restructuring lifestyles from subregional sites was later drawn up into the *seikatsusha* movement which placed emphasis on 'locality' as interpreted by Seikatsu Club Cooperatives, and on the 'cooperation' there.

Seikatsusha negotiate post-war society

A perspective towards the macrocosm of lifestyles: Wajirō Kon

The ten or so years from Japan's defeat in the war until the mid-1950s were times when the Japanese had no choice but to face their livelihood head-on, whether they liked it or not. There has never been a period when people had a greater struggle to eke out a livelihood, or were made more keenly aware of the importance of the management of living, as that age of post-war deprivation and confusion. In the process of Japan's regaining its footing after defeat, along with the advancement of economic recovery and social ordering, the image of the *seikatsusha* of that period made its appearance in a more varied and complex form.

Wajirō Kon (1888–1973), who established the foundations of modernology and lifeology (*seikatsugaku*), understood '*seikatsu*' to mean an aggregate of activity that did not stop at the reproductive activities of the workforce, but included recreation and entertainment, and even cultural accomplishments; and he coined the term 'life culture (*seikatsu bunka*)' for that which, through workers' lifestyles and the ways they enjoy their lives, shapes the individuality of day-to-day life. Moreover, with an awareness of the intention to make life as a whole into 'something better,' he tried to discover the image of the *seikatsusha* within workers who questioned their quality of life.

A comprehensive understanding of the concept called 'life' is taken for granted nowadays. In Kon's age, however, life-studies approached living from the limited viewpoint of issues of reproduction of the workforce, the central concern being mostly the 'problematising' of such things as working hours and overwork. In counter to that, the contemporary perspective, which has an all-inclusive interpretation of life, encompassing aspects external to the labour domain such as recreation, entertainment and cultivation, is one that brought about a Copernican transformation in life-research.

That is not all. In his 1949 paper, 'Seikatsu no bunkateki dankai (The cultural stages of living),' Kon pointed out that, having passed through the first stage of working day in and day out, the primary cultural need, namely 'entertainment,' would appear for the first time in the second stage where work and rest were guaranteed, and that the secondary cultural need, for 'cultivation,' would appear in the third stage in which work, rest and entertainment were guaranteed, and he deemed the third stage, to which 'cultivation' had been added, to be 'an ideal life' (Kon 1971: 23–27). This argument can be seen as something that anticipates A.H. Maslow's hierarchy of needs, in which only after the satisfaction of lower-order needs (hunger, thirst, safety) can higher needs (esteem and self-actualisation) appear (Maslow 1954: 97–104).

Kon's viewpoint is an extremely important one, he having dared, amid circumstances of bare survival at that time, to make the spiritual 'luxuries' of entertainment and cultivation, or, in other words, a shift towards the quality of life—not 'to live,' but rather 'how to live'—into basic elements of workers' lives.

Towards a philosophy spawned from lifestyle: *The science of thought*

The same period as Wajirō Kon saw the beginning of research into 'people's philosophy' which endeavoured to mine a hidden seam of ideological ore in the lives of nameless people who were not experts in philosophising. This was one of the themes pursued consistently by the journal, *Shisō no kagaku* (Science of thought), launched in the spring of 1946, not long after Japan's defeat, by a coterie of seven: Mitsuo Taketani, Kiyoko Takeda, Shigeto Tsuru, Kazuko Tsurumi, Shunsuke Tsurumi, Masao Maruyama, and Satoshi Watanabe. 'The people' referred in the study of 'the people's philosophy' that was unfolded on the pages of *Shisō no kagaku* were, it goes without saying, *seikatsusha*, and 'the people's philosophy' constituted nothing other than '*seikatsusha*'s philosophy.'

While Miki, Nii and Kon elucidated the characteristics of the *seikatsusha*'s attributes and behavioural principles from the *seikatsusha*'s connection with the life-culture discourse in which the latter was the actor, *Shisō no kagaku* was distinctive in that it focused upon the *seikatsusha*'s 'thought,' conducting repeated methodological experiments in order to discover it.

The scholarship of professional philosophers, and Japanese philosophy which had developed as an imported discipline, were unable to resist the war. In order to create measures to prevent being caught up again in war, there was no alternative but to rely upon the power of thought that was rooted in the daily lives of ordinary people who did not make contemplation their profession. Herein lay the first objective for *Shisō no kagaku*, which began its journey bearing the burden of wartime experience on its back.

The source of 'the people's philosophy' which *Shisō no kagaku* had in mind can be traced back via pragmatism, which is also a byword for American philosophy, to the 'philosophy of the common man' expounded by Ralph Waldo Emerson (1803–82), a nineteenth-century American poet and philosopher (Tsurumi 1984: 21–25). It was in 1837 that Emerson asserted that Americans, who had come to lead their lives in a natural and social environment different from that of their British motherland, ought to weave themselves a unique ideology independent from Britain's. What is important is that his assertion advocates a 'philosophy of the common man' which would constitute the matrix for America's new life-culture, a 'philosophy of the ordinary person,' irrespective of status or title.

Emerson said that new culture and thought would not be born from culture transplanted from Britain as a kind of 'cultural accomplishment,' but were things that would be created in the process of the practice of living and daily pursuits of people raised in the New World who had no connection with Old-World culture. Thought only comes alive and begins to work by being returned to the site called daily life. In the same way as this 'philosophy of the common man' was a cultural declaration of independence from Britain, *Shisō no kagaku*'s 'people's philosophy' was none other than an ideological declaration of independence from professional philosophers.

Who, then, are 'the people,' or, in other words, the *seikatsusha*? These are people who have severally been called *shomin* (ordinary people), *minshū* (common people), *taishū* (masses), *heimin* (commoners), *jinmin* ('people' in the socialist sense) and *kokumin* (nationals), but they are not people to be lumped together by a collective noun. They are the masses who, 'one by one' have come face-to-face with such cataclysmic historical changes as military defeat and the post-war. At the same time, philosophy and thought did not mean a 'system' or 'universality,' but the view that they comprised 'all of the things which those various people think about in order to lead their own life'—in other words, that subject and object were tied together, without disjunction. In people's experience, there are issues that lifestyle needs breed for everyone, problems of the 'here-and-now' kind that cannot be left up to experts. Such emphasis on the individual thereafter was carried on as an important viewpoint in *seikatsusha* discourse.

As 'people' centred on the first-person singular 'I,' it also signified powerless 'weak individuals' who were sensitive to their own interest, and excelled in the skills for making their way in the world, occasionally being influenced by circumstances. The important point is that being obsessed with oneself is not always apprehended as having negative momentum. While stubborn adherence to the self appears at first glance to narrow one's field of vision and make one selfish, the subjectivity and active nature thus restored not only in themselves nurture one's 'power to think,' but also expand one's range of imagination vis-à-vis other people's positions. Without the gaining of activity by *seikatsusha* through the action of 'thinking,' no potential for subjective participation in philosophy is likely to develop. Therein is a directivity that strives to gain a real grasp of the *seikatsusha*'s 'cunning' and 'antiquity' and turn it into positive momentum.

In contrast to the way that Emerson's 'common man' was based on the people who made America what it is, on the image of the citizen as an active, cultural subject that had been deemed ideal since America's founding as a nation, what characterised *Shisō no kagaku* was its methodology that brought out 'in their entirety' the 'cunning' and closed nature of 'the people,' including their frailty and weakness, as the typically human energy that supports the way they lived. We can probably find later reports of such 'weak individuals' in the *seikatsusha* movements of Beheiren and Seikatsu Club.

Consumers challenging enterprises: Yasuji Hanamori

It was in the autumn of 1948, two and a half years after the inaugural issue of the journal, *Shisō no kagaku*, that *Kurashi no techō* (Lifestyle notebook) was launched. The title of the magazine at first was *Utsukushii kurashi no techō* (Notebook for beautiful life). 'Beautiful' was added because during the preparation stage, a magazine distributor said that the word '*kurashi*' had too gloomy an image. This episode gives a telling account of Japanese people's feelings and awareness about everyday life in those days, or rather, from the pre-war period.

The chief editor, Yasuji Hanamori (1911–1978) says: 'The livingroom and kitchen where families spend their lives every day usually have been stuck in a damp, dimly-lit, north-east-facing spot, just as if there were "no choice" —in other words, that was how much 'daily life' was scorned and looked down upon' (Hanamori 1971: 66). Dragging that 'living room and kitchen' which had been despised as symbols of quotidian life out into bright sunshine and setting them at the very centre of life—that was the concrete expression of Hanamori's way of thinking about living, oriented towards the age of democracy, and was what *Kurashi no techō* (hereafter, *Techō*) advocated. Incidentally, the word 'beautiful' which had been attached to the title of the magazine remained for five years, but vanished as of December 1953. It was in the same decade that books with titles beginning with the word '*kurashi*' or '*seikatsu*' (signifying life/living/livelihood/lifestyle), which hitherto had seldom appeared, started to proliferate. As such, in the post-war, *Techō* played a definite role in the notion of '*kurashi*' or '*seikatsu*' gaining acceptance (Horiba 1984).

Hanamori's experiences during World War Two were deeply involved in the first issue of *Techō*. His primary intent in the inaugural issue was to express deep 'remorse' towards his own actions in wartime when he was with the propaganda division of the Imperial Rule Assistance Association (Taisei yokusankai) and had waved the flag to encourage fighting spirit; and his sole inspiration was his wartime experiences which told him that Japan had rushed into a war because its people, including himself, had not each built a lifestyle of their own that they wanted to 'risk their lives' to defend.

Who, then, constituted the *seikatsusha* in Hanamori's mind? This is expressed in the passage—perhaps better called a manifesto—

which has been printed on the inside cover of *Techō* ever since its first issue.

This is your notebook/All kinds of things are written in it/One or two from among them will be of use straight away today in your everyday lifestyle/At least one or two of them/even if they appear not to be immediately useful/later on will sink deep into the depths of your mind/and someday will change your way of living/That is the kind of [notebook it is]/This is your notebook.

The 'you' here, whose wish is expressed as: 'I will become conscious of my lifestyle, and change "my" way of living by changing myself,' is the *seikatsusha*. The unostentatious *Techō*, which had no women's faces on the cover and promoted itself as a comprehensive lifestyle magazine, brazenly smashed the stereotype of conventional women's magazines which always depicted beautiful women on their covers, loaded themselves up with practical articles, and incorporated numerous supplements on handling the family budget, dressmaking patterns and the like. But while their practical articles were 'immediately useful,' no dreams or visions of quotidian life were conveyed from their pages. Hanamori's aim was to nurture subjects—namely, *seikatsusha*—who, as the 'you' to whom the magazine was addressed, would change their lives through the medium of *Techō*, which combined the practicality of 'the immediately useful' with the non-practicality of 'the not immediately useful,' that being the reformation and future vision of everyday living.

Seikatsusha also indicated people who were able to distinguish between the 'beautiful' and the 'non-beautiful' things in their life-sites. Nobody was as obsessive about 'beautiful' things in the living site as Hanamori, who was also an aesthete. In his article about making one's own accessories, he declares: 'Beautiful things have no connection to money and leisure, in any age' (Hanamori 1948: 18). He claims that refined sensibilities, a steady eye on one's everyday livelihood and hands that make unceasing effort will create beautiful things. By contrast, the non-beautiful includes the culture of uniforms, from military uniforms to the salaryman's suit; post-war fashions that regard everything American as beautiful; and surrendering oneself to the notion that locks gender and clothing into the 'women = skirts/men = trousers' dichotomy.

Techō seized a great opportunity in its attempt at subjectification of the *seikatsusha* in its product testing that began in 1954. Product testing meant examining the quality of manufactured goods and publishing the results, along with manufacturers' names, and that constituted a written challenge to companies which frankly indicated *Techō*'s basic stance towards living.

From a present-day perspective, where consumer rights are acknowledged, albeit imperfectly, such product testing is matter-of-course, yet *Techō*'s policy to carry no advertising whatsoever in order to guarantee the reliability of its product testing was such a risky wager that the magazine could have been forced out of business, had it made one slip. For Hanamori, the product testing, which took enormous time and human resources, was neither for the sake of protecting powerless consumers from a capital offensive that had begun to wield power along with post-war economic recovery, nor was it for cultivating 'canny consumers' who would go on sorting appropriate products from inappropriate ones.

Hanamori's greatest aim lay in bringing the position of the users of goods (consumers) to that of their makers (producers), and to nurture 'independent consumers' equipped with the capacity to change the quality of the goods produced—in other words, *seikatsusha*. Hanamori was the first to bring the concept of 'producer and consumer' boldly to the conventional notion of *seikatsusha*.

Towards the prosumer

It was in 1980, about twenty years later than Hanamori, that Alvin Toffler presented the 'prosumer,' a new consumer image combining the character of both a producer and a user, in his book entitled *The Third Wave*. When the 'First Wave' (agrarian society), where production and consumption were undivided and 'production for use' was conducted, shifted to the 'Second Wave' (industrialised society), production and consumption became separate, and the former went on to become 'production for exchange.' With the approach of the new age of the Third Wave (post-consumer society), production and consumption have again been integrated, heralding the rise of the 'producing and consuming' prosumer (Toffler 1980: 282–305). Examples of this include built-to-order manufacturing done in response to consumers' concrete needs and ideas, and product development driven by consumer initiative.

In the sense that consumers—hitherto situated outside the goods produced—change from being outsiders to being insiders, Hanamori's independent consumer = *seikatsusha* and Toffler's prosumer are in harmony with each other. If, however, we consider the *seikatsusha* that Hanamori advocates to be a subject who doubts the quality of goods offered by companies, sometimes thrusting a written challenge at firms, seeking product recall, then the *seikatsusha* can be said to have been a far more radical concept than the prosumer, who is merely a consumer involved in production.

Techō's readership, from the time of its launch through to the 1970s when its circulation was at its peak, consisted of full-time housewives who, in terms of social class, were metropolitan residents with white-collar husbands, who had a higher educational background than average females, but could not be satisfied with the women's magazines that made bulky supplements their 'selling-point.' Male readers were not few, either, and accounted for around thirty percent of the total. From the 1970s into the 80s, when industrial pollution and food safety concerns began to threaten, housewives' local activism by the likes of Seikatsu Club Cooperatives gained momentum, and it appears as if the legacy of *Techō*, and, by extension, of Hanamori himself, lives on among them.

From the countryside, from the margins: Yasuko Mizoue

Though the majority of post-war *seikatsusha* theory, as exemplified by *Shisō no kagaku* and *Kurashi no techō*, was a *seikatsusha* discourse from middle-class, urban society, what Yasuko Mizoue (1903–90), who taught philosophy and pedagogy at Shimane University, advocated by contrast was simply a *seikatsusha* discourse that sprang from the region called San'in. Her books, *Nihon no teihen* (Japan's margins) (1958), and *Seikatsusha no shisō* (*Seikatsusha* thought) (1961), which arose from her process of walking through rural villages in Shimane Prefecture and interacting with their women, accurately delineate the figure of the women as '*seikatsusha* on the margins' who live the reality of agrarian villages in the San'in region.

For Mizoue, people 'on the margins (*teihen*)' differ both from the 'lower classes' of society that were left behind in the shadow of Japan's modern development, and from 'all the rest' who support the handful of elite at the pinnacle. In the midst of economic poverty, what can one do to improve one's livelihood? How can one make one's life even a little bit better than it is now? The 'margins' meant a mother-body of 'primordial energy' where such questions and practices aimed at change are generated.

The point on which Mizoue's *seikatsusha* theory stands out is that it focuses upon the potential to transform the hardships of 'being a woman' as a social existence into an opportunity for 'awakening awareness' towards human rights. In 1950s rural society, where stagnation and feudalism held sway, more than anyone else it was the women who had no choice but to face up to the pressing questions in their livelihood. Mizoue encouraged the women to 'write about their lives,' and advocated the importance of pushing themselves out of the picture and taking an objective viewpoint through writing. The women would express themselves, and come face-to-face with the root of their hardship. Mizoue endeavoured to divine the *seikatsusha* within the process by which the 'undifferentiated self' was segregated out from the collective entities of the traditional household (*ie*) and the village (*mura*).

Mizoue's discourse of *seikatsusha* on the margins grew to become a 'humankind *seikatsusha*' declaration, which held that it is precisely the history created by *seikatsusha* living the regional 'margins' in a subjective manner that carries an all-humankind sort of universality. In an age when there was not yet even a hint of the notion of globalisation, the audacious 'humankind *seikatsusha*' declaration was in close-enough range to foresee the age that is 'now.'

Seikatsusha, navigating consumer society

From consumer to *seikatsusha*: Nobuyuki Ōkuma

If we take the *seikatsusha* theory examined heretofore to be something from an age when the frame of 'post-war' in a broad sense was still extant, then who did the *seikatsusha* become from the 1960s into the 1970s, when Japanese society took off in a full-fledged sense from the post-war, via its period of rapid economic growth?

Wajirō Kon, *Shisō no kagaku* and Yasuko Mizoue have emphasised 'daily life (*seikatsu*)' as a wellspring from which thought is generated, or else as a matrix, and the transformative power rooted in 'daily life.' As Japanese society increased in affluence, however, the word '*seikatsu*' began to take on the negative connotations of 'prioritisation of personal life,' the 'family-first' principle, 'devotion to the private at the expense of the public,' and so on. People's desires and concerns were consistently oriented towards 'private life,' and 'private life' changed into something tinged with self-reclusivity, passivity and self-protectiveness.

While on the one hand inheriting the potential inherent in '*seikatsu*,' the *seikatsusha* discourse in this period started to be expanded with the support of the dual nature of problem-consciousness that attempted to reinterpret '*seikatsu*' in a critical manner. This was because people's everydayness was undergoing a change into something constructed by the state and business. '*Seikatsusha*' came to be called back anew as a new key concept to requestion such a situation and to reclaim life's richness.

At the beginning of the 1960s, the start of Japan's takeoff towards a mass consumer society, it was the economist Nobuyuki Ōkuma (1893–1977) who was the first to employ the '*seikatsusha*' concept in place of 'consumer' in the field of economics. The word 'consumer,' which is contraposed to 'producer,' is one spawned by modern economics, which takes a commodity-oriented perspective. Ōkuma advocated that 'we' (the salaryman demographic generated in large quantities at that time) become '*seikatsusha*' from the people-oriented viewpoint of the maintenance and continuance of life (1963 [1974a]: 191).

Like *Shisō no kagaku* and Yasuji Hanamori, Ōkuma's *seikatsusha* theory was also born from deep remorse at himself for having been half-spontaneously implanted with the nationalistic tone prevailing during the Second World War, and for having become a spokesperson for the state's all-out war. With his gaze fixed on his own wartime errors , Ōkuma published his book, *Kokka-aku* (State evil) in 1957 and wrote *Katei-ron* (On the home) (1963) in a quest to find in the idea of the home the instrument of an opposing principle for interrogating state evil. In economic terms, that meant reconstructing the theory of market-centred reproduction of commodities as a reproductive theory of human life as the essence of the family.

Ōkuma was also strongly influenced by the art critiques of John Ruskin (1819–1900), the British economist and aesthete whose works Ōkuma had read and reread since his youth. In particular, a quotation from Ruskin's *Unto this Last* (1888), 'There is no wealth but life,' is what forms the key concept of Ōkuma's economics, and

Ōkuma was never to depart from this epithet until the end of his life at eighty-four.

The *seikatsusha* in that context signified, firstly, subjects living out the cycle of production and consumption as a total livelihood process of maintenance and continuance of life; secondly, as people who placed importance not upon exchange value in terms of money, but upon life value and utility value as their behavioural principles; and, thirdly, subjects who distinguished the wants created by the hand of enterprises from their own livelihood needs.

Wajirō Kon held that in the midst of living in post-war poverty, people's suitably-human lives began from a spiritual 'luxury' that transcended livelihood 'needs.' In the very thick of the period of rapid economic growth, Ōkuma considered people's suitably-human lives to start from having the power to determine what constituted 'needs' in their own existence. Both of these can be said to be notions of 'needs' that touch upon the essence of life in their respective times.

Ōkuma's *seikatsusha* theory—which had started off from a criticism of modern economics that had purged 'living' (the undertaking of human life-support), from 'production,' and had confined it within 'consumption'—did not gain many supporters in Japanese society at the time, where the values of economic prioritisation had begun to take deep root in people's consciousness. The times did not favour Ōkuma, and no genuine attempt to accept his proposals, pass them on or develop them manifested itself.

'*Seikatsusha* marketing'

From the late 1970s into the 80s, amid transformation of the 'masses' in consumer society, with the appearance of the 'segmented masses (*bunshū*)' who sought diversification, in place of the uniform and undifferentiated 'masses (*taishū*)' on the one hand, and with a risk-awareness brought about by transfiguration of the mass market in the high-growth period through saturation of demand on the other, companies began to realise that it was not sufficient merely to take consumers to be simple buyers of goods (customers).

For one to achieve an accurate grasp of a consumer's needs, it is not enough merely for the latter to appear in a shop. One cannot respond adequately without knowing about the diversity of lifestyles and the individuality of wants. It was in this period that '*seikatsusha*,' rather than 'consumer,' went on to become a fixed keyword among marketers who set up consumer society. This constituted so-called *'seikatsusha* marketing.'

From the marketing perspective, a consumer is a person who purchases and consumes goods and services, and a *seikatsusha* is one who carries out individual living activities with a diverse set of values. It was the Austrian-born Peter F. Drucker (1909–2005) that provided the theoretical driving force for this kind of Japanese *'seikatsusha* marketing.' Though he does not use the term *'seikatsusha' per se* when he says that marketing is 'the creation of a customer' (Drucker 1977: 57), that customer is a *seikatsusha* who lives through a diverse life-process while possessing a variety of wants and values. In contrast to businesses that start with the question of 'What should we do to ensure that our products sell?' true marketing, Drucker says, must start with asking: 'What does the customer want to buy?' The *'seikatsusha* marketing' of this period was something that followed the example of Drucker's argument, but at least as long as the insatiable pursuit of profit by the market economy is the basic strategy, its *seikatsusha* will ever remain the target of sales promotion, and will be nothing more than the *seikatsusha* caught in the gaze of enterprises.

If, however, one changes perspective, then one can also position *seikatsusha* marketing as a criticism of the uniformity of the conventional notion of the consumer, and it has elements that overlap both Ōkuma's *seikatsusha* discourse and Alfred Schutz's 'well-informed citizen.'

The 'well-informed citizen'

For Ōkuma, the value of goods lay not in the exchange value that the goods themselves possessed, but in the values and abilities of the people who appraised, accepted and made use of them in their own ways. People's living processes in that vein were likely to be individual, not uniform.

It was in the 1960s that the builder of the foundations of phenomenological sociology, Alfred Schutz (1899–1959), expounded his theory of multiple realities. According to Schutz, people are not living a 'single reality' such as is generally understood to be 'reality.' Rather, they are living 'several, probably an infinite number of various orders of reality' (1964: 135). The existence of a plurality of everyday worlds points to the idea that we have limitless choices as a daily occurrence. For Schutz, however, a consumer society that offered an abundance of goods was no more than a society where people's living processes were standardised and averaged-out by the mass media and fashions.

With the idea that 'reality' changes according to the quality of knowledge possessed by the people who apprehend it, Schutz presents three human types on the basis of the social distribution of knowledge: 1 the 'man on the street'; 2 the 'expert'; and 3 the 'well-informed citizen' (Schutz 1970: 239). The one upon which Schutz focused was the 'well-informed citizen,' standing between the 'man on the street' and the 'expert,' and though such a man is not equipped with specialist knowledge, this does not mean that he is satisfied with a 'mere recipe knowledge' (1970: 240), that is, simple everyday common sense. His is a way of knowing that reinterprets the 'taken-for-granted-ness' of everyday life and the obviousness of common sense, and is a new way of knowing distinct from both immersion in general knowledge and reliance upon lucidness; and it can be translated also as something like 'enlightened citizen' or 'discerning citizen.' It could be seen as an expression corresponding to 'the public,' used in counterpoint to 'the masses' in a work by the American sociologist, C. Wright Mills, *The Sociological Imagination* (1959).

For the record, it was Schutz's life circumstances of being both a banker (practical business) and a scholar (research) that led his quest for new knowledge. That duality of living in the everyday world made him confront the dangers arising from the divergence of his scholarship from his livelihood, and made him seek a path for breaking away from there in a way of living as a 'well-informed citizen' (Nishihara 1991: 17).

Schutz's 'well-informed citizen' overlaps Ōkuma's theory on the *seikatsusha* in the sense that both are able, by means of the quality of their own knowledge, individualistically to give full play to the lifestyle goods they have purchased in the market, in resistance to the encoding and standardisation of goods and human beings. Nonetheless, let us note that, in contrast to Ōkuma's establishment of the *seikatsusha* as an extension of quite ordinary people, Schutz's 'well-informed citizen' bears the marked hue of the ideal type of citizen as a rational and active subject. *Seikatsusha* in Japanese society are rather closer to Schutz's 'man on the street.' The emphasis is on a dynamic daily practice that gradually pulls away from the triviality of common sense by people's making conscious their everyday lives.

Seikatsusha movements that change ways of living

Disputes over freedom of lifestyle

From the 1970s into the 1980s, there was a surge in movements by people groping for a *seikatsusha*'s way of living as an everyday practice, in a form that marked a departure from *seikatsusha* theory in terms of the above discourses. This constituted the entrance of Beheiren (Betonamu ni heiwa o! Shimin rengō) (Citizens' federation for peace in Vietnam) and the Seikatsu kurabu seikyō (Seikatsu Club Consumers' Co-operative Union) (one of the regional cooperatives based on the Consumer Co-operatives Act, and hereafter abbreviated as 'Seikatsu Club' or SSCU).

Both Beheiren and Seikatsu Club are positioned as 'new social movements' spawned in the late 1960s and becoming firmly established in the '70s. The grounds for the 'newness' in 'new social movements,' so named by the French sociologist Alain Touraine, lay not in their being disputes over the institutionalised distribution of wealth, but in their resistance for the sake of guaranteeing the value and freedom of individual lifestyles. Beheiren was a movement that demanded the post-materialist value of peace and the right of self-determination for the Vietnamese; and Seikatsu Club was one aimed at reclaiming a quality of life based on post-industrialist values.

What prepared the way for the emergence of these two movements was a huge transfiguration of people's 'life-world.' The 'life-world' here means the pluralistic, empirical world where quite ordinary people carry on their quotidian lives. In the process of Japanese society's fluctuations during the period of high economic growth, the goods and services which companies and the government offered penetrated into all processes in the human life course ('from cradle to grave'), and the degree of social dependence in people's lives continued to escalate.

The never-ending permeation of goods and services as products for the life-world suggests that people's everyday life-world is commodified and reified to that extent. To borrow words from J. Habermas, it is none other than a 'colonised life-world' caught up in the politico-economic complex he calls the 'system' (Habermas

1987: 307–8). The Beheiren and Seikatsu Club movements were an expression of 'contestation' against such a trend.

Between citizens and *seikatsusha*: Beheiren

Beheiren, which disbanded along with the 1974 conclusion of the Vietnam War, played a huge role in making people change their conventional way of thinking about 'public versus private.' As written, 'public' and 'private' in this expression are parallel, but it has signified that their relationship is not equal, 'private' being subordinate to 'public.' 'Public' in fact means 'officialdom' (administrative organs), while 'private' is 'the people' (members of the nation).

By simultaneously calling themselves '*seikatsusha*' and 'citizens' within the movement, Beheiren members aimed on the one hand to overcome their internal consciousness of 'the authorities (*okami*),' dependent upon 'the bureaucracy.' On the other hand, freed for a time from being 'weak individuals' who prioritised their own convenience over the logic of the movement, they endeavoured to question the meaning of the Vietnam War from their own life-sites.

'Citizens' here meant none other than the posing of a viewpoint for looking back at the state as single 'private individuals,' while *seikatsusha* meant non-professional activists who had a site where they carried on their day-to-day livelihood, and participated in the movement at the tempo of daily life.

In this manner, Beheiren demolished the orthodox pre-image of the Japanese as not attempting to emerge from the cycle of daily life, being the most distant from the world of politics, and never defying 'the authorities' unless for some extraordinary reason.

The alternative/glocal/relational individual: Seikatsu Club

The leaders in the 'contestation' movement of Seikatsu Club, which was founded in the same year as Beheiren (1965), were full-time housewives belonging to the urban new middle-class. Its salient feature was that it was expanded into a 'movement' in which these members changed their own way of living in the direction of de-housewifisation, and, further, towards becoming post-consumers = *seikatsusha* in the course of their involvement in Seikatsu Club's activities. The movement began with the joint purchasing of foodstuffs, 'from production, through distribution, and finally to disposal,' and extended yet further to the whole sphere of living to do with politics ('deputy' activities that sent representatives to local government assemblies) and labour (workers' collective activities that created locally-based, self-managed citizens' enterprises).

Seikatsusha in that context can be understood as beings who take on the following three definitions: firstly, that of *'seikatsusha'* as people who, while reflecting upon their individual lifestyles, go on choosing 'alternative' ways of living that differ from a 'matter-of-course' way of life. Secondly, the 'locality' is where their movement is unfolded; and this movement is a 'glocal' one which aims for solutions to global problems such as the environment, resources, welfare and peace as issues inherent in their local lifestyle. The 'locality' as a 'shared' domain which, while making private interest its basis, is created in a manner that transcends 'the personal,' constituted a new perspective which had not been seriously expanded within conventional *seikatsusha* theory.

Thirdly, the movement, which strove to mobilise people and increase the number of like-minded participants, was a process of trial-and-error in which people with diverse values would meet, clash and search for common ground through mutual dialogue, and was based not on the simple 'individual,' but on the 'individual within a relationship.' This 'relational individual' was carried over into the *seikatsusha* discourse of the new century.

The greatest problem that Seikatsu Club currently faces is that of '*seikatsusha* and gender.' Why are the daily practices for becoming a *seikatsusha* the sole province of women, and housewives, at that? An overhaul of the *seikatsusha* concept has been partially indicated by Yasuko Mizoue and Nobuyuki Ōkuma, but it is a new issue that has not been properly examined. What kind of logic for the movement will its members create for incorporating men actively in the process of praxis for becoming *seikatsusha*, so that they will themselves become *seikatsusha*? There is a need for construction of that type of new logic.

Seikatsusha, traversing the new century

The political sloganising of *'seikatsusha'*

As previously observed, from the 1990s through into the beginning of the new century, *'seikatsusha'* was recalled from two directions and triggered a type of boom phenomenon. One was the policy of 'emphasis on the *seikatsusha*' advocated by politicians and political parties, and the other the '*seikatsusha*' mentioned by business operators, a usage which had hitherto seldom appeared in *seikatsusha* discourse.

There had never been a time when politicians and parties had so vied to hammer out a basic principle for policy management with the banners of 'emphasis on the *seikatsusha*' and '*seikatsusha* sovereignty.' As voter de-alignment progressed even further, the word *seikatsusha* came to be consumed in yet greater quantities among parties and politicians who sought to gain reassurance by attaching it as a label for non-partisan voters. But who on earth are these '*seikatsusha*' that have turned completely into political slogans?

The slogan of the 1960 Hayato Ikeda Cabinet was the 'national income-doubling plan.' After the subsequent three decades of precipitous economic fluctuation, the slogans of the 'Lifestyle Superpower 5-year Plan' instigated by the Kiichi Miyazawa Cabinet established in December 1992 (a reshuffled Cabinet lasting until August 1993), when the Bubble economy started to teeter, were 'lifestyle superpower' and a 'pro-*seikatsusha*/consumer perspective.'

As I have previously mentioned, there was no definition of who the *seikatsusha* was, but the point worth noting is that the government came out with 'respect for the individual' as a basic line of policy for the first time. There, having defined a 'lifestyle superpower (*seikatsu taikoku*)' as a society where each and every member of the nation could have a real sense of abundance and latitude within their daily life, the example was cited of a shift towards a policy enabling people to get a solid sense on an 'individual level' not only of income as a flow, but also of enhancement of their living environment in terms of spare time and stock aspects.

The problem is that 'respect for the individual' has been inherited by cabinets since those of Miyazawa. 1993 saw the start of a non-Liberal-Democratic Party (LDP) coalition, the Morihiro Hosokawa Cabinet (August 1993–April 1994). In his book, *Nihon Shintō: sekinin aru henkaku* (Japan New Party: responsible reform), Prime Minister Hosokawa declared: 'There are aspects of the producer-oriented economic and social system up to now that have brought about today's prosperity from the post-war ruins. Now that Japan has become a superpower in economic terms, we must change the system into one which prioritises *seikatsusha*, and establish *seikatsusha* sovereignty' (1993: 110).

The assertion of the 'establishment of *seikatsusha* sovereignty' appears to have gone a step further than a 'pro-*seikatsusha*/consumer perspective.' This, however, is not the case, because when the basic principle for establishing '*seikatsusha* sovereignty' was 'relaxation and abolition of regulation,' *seikatsusha* sovereignty then was none other than accentuation of self-responsibility in the name of greater freedom, and preferential treatment for 'strong individuals,' which stands in the logic of the strong. The baton for this policy of preferential treatment for 'strong individuals' was handed down from the LDP's Jun'ichirō Koizumi Cabinet (April 2001–October 2005) to the Shinzō Abe Cabinet (September 2006–September 2007)'s relaxation/abolition of regulation in accordance with the neo-liberal line. The Koizumi Cabinet's 'structural reform for the sake of the *seikatsusha*,' especially, is actually connected with the easing of public regulation and the promotion of privatisation, and it is common knowledge that it made a great 'contribution' to the emergence of the current unequal society and large numbers of 'the weak.'

The government of Yukio Hatoyama (Democratic Party of Japan), having broken the long reign of the LDP and effecting a change of regime in the summer of 2009 with the catch-phrase: 'from concrete to people,' came out with a 'budget to protect life and livelihoods' and an 'economy for human beings' as its basic policy, deciding in its budget allocation to make broad cuts to its public works spending and to concentrate funding upon 'people-nurturing,' namely in areas such as children, employment, social welfare and the environment. These various 'pro-*seikatsusha*' policies made people anticipate a transformation in the style of government/administration and finance which had continued over sixty years since the end of the war, but that cabinet was short-lived, ending after a mere eight months while still lacking a long-term social vision.

There has never been an age in which 'pro-*seikatsusha*' has become as fixed a political term as now, at the turn of the century. One thing that historic cabinets have had in common is that '*seikatsusha*' has continued to be used as an image strategy to justify the cabinets' own policies, and as a keyword for gaining popular support. Another is that in spite of the above, most cabinets— barring the Koizumi regime—have been short-lived.

Perhaps the greatest achievement of the over-inflation of '*seikatsusha*' as a political term is its having robbed the word of its magical power and, by extension, its utility as a 'verbal talisman.' Alternatively, it might be that people have begun to equip themselves with the linguistic ability to see that '*seikatsusha*' is nothing more than a mere 'verbal talisman,' with the words: 'Every darn cabinet claims it is "pro-*seikatsusha*," but the cupboard is bare.'

The 'social logic' of business operators

The above applies not only to politicians and political parties. After the collapse of the Japanese Bubble economy, as the formation/consolidation of business organisations oriented towards 'growth' and 'expansion' almost ceased to function as centripetal objectives, the owners and top management of large firms began to enter the '*seikatsusha*' debate from the late 1990s. It is possible to read into this their 'restlessness,' to the tune that unless they adopted not only a conventional type of enterprise logic, but also a way of business management that took the perspective of the *seikatsusha*, then post-Bubble Japanese enterprises would have no future.

The book *Bunka shihon no keiei* (The management of cultural capital), published at the end of the 1990s by Yoshiharu Fukuhara, Chief Executive Officer of a major cosmetics company (Shiseido), is a new life-culture argument—a theory on *seikatsusha*—as captured in the corporate gaze. According to Fukuhara, life-culture means something born from 'society' which is sandwiched between the companies that produce goods and a lifestyle of consuming the goods. Now, on the consumption side, the passive consumer has vanished, and instead there exists the *seikatsusha* who has begun to present and express their living space according to their own lifestyle vision. One example of this is the building of their own home, taking account of the streetscape and urban scenery. The question, in Fukuhara's words, is how companies can continue to respond to *seikatsusha* needs, and with what kind of social vision, and he says that a social logic to replace company logic (the pursuit of economy and efficiency) is being put to the test (1999: 145–7).

It was in the 1980s, the age of the 'segmentation of the masses,' that 'culture' as a lifestyle made its appearance as the life-culture strategy of enterprises. In that context, it was companies that actively proposed life-culture, while consumers were mostly positioned on the side of passively choosing. The biggest difference between the '80s and now, Fukuhara asserts, is that (1) what must change is company logic; and (2) in order to give full play to the creative power of *seikatsusha*, companies must clearly display their social vision. There is no subsequent mention of social vision, however, Fukuhara going no further than to indicate that the overriding necessity is to reinterpret the relationship between consumption and production from the *seikatsusha*'s perspective.

Shōhi shakai hihan (A critique of consumer society) (1996), a book by Seiji Tsutsumi, the actual owner of a huge distribution corporation, published in 1999 in English translation as *Japan's Consumer Society: a critical introduction*, is of great interest as one answer from top management to this question. If one employs the word 'consume' according to its etymology, it means 'use up,' or 'exploit to the fullest.' Fundamentally, it is 'consumer society' that subordinated such 'consumption' (which is a 'human individual life-process') to 'production,' and drove it towards codification and non-individualisation. Tsutsumi proposes that companies should, above all, carry out a paradigm shift in their recognition of 'consumption,' going back to that of an 'individual life-process' in its original sense (1996: 24–5).

Though he does not specifically use the term '*seikatsusha*,' when Tsutsumi refers to 'original consumption,' or, in other words, to the individuals who seek an 'individual life-process,' this has the same meaning as the '*seikatsusha*' discussed by Nobuyuki Ōkuma and Yoshiharu Fukuhara. Tsutsumi regards the most vital challenge for companies in an age of the emergence of a hyper-consumption society as being the problem of what manner of management principles to construct in order to respond to such a *seikatsusha* image. Here, too, however, there is no further explanation about 'hyper-consumption society' or management principles for responding to the 'individual life-process' of *seikatsusha*.

The social image of the twenty-first-century: the sustainable-welfare society

A decade into the new century, politicians have still not ceased depending upon the magical power of the term 'pro-*seikatsusha*.' Business operators have yet to come out with a concrete direction in their endeavour to review the connection between consumption and production, and to find a base for their vision of twenty-first-century economic society in responding to the *seikatsusha*'s 'individual life-process.' Where, then, will those of us who are probing for a path to the *seikatsusha* seek a base for our respective visions?

Currently, a real sense of the lifestyle that surrounds us can be found both in the loss of a bright future promising that yesterday will be better than today, and in the absence of a social objective that spurs us on, positively and dynamically. What is being sought instead is a way of living in which we will feel a modest satisfaction in our daily lives. If we are to seek such a 'real sense of lifestyle' for ourselves, then one answer would probably be what the economist Yoshinori Hiroi has dubbed a 'sustainable-welfare society (*teijōgata shakai*).'

In plain terms, a sustainable-welfare society is a society which takes 'zero growth' as its constant state, having neither 'economic growth' nor 'expansion of material wealth' as its major premise. It is also a perspective which cements a mature society—namely, one that has a shrinking birth-rate and ageing population—together with an environmentally-friendly society which finds value in the conservation of limited resources. If the question is whether this is a depressed society in which dreams and hopes are small, as it understands zero growth to be the usual situation, then the answer is no. Rather, it is a thrilling sort of society in which people, freed from the constraints of the major premise that 'growth must continue,' will recognise a sense of fulfilment in their day-to-day livelihood and lifestyle.

Hiroi's 'sustainable-welfare society' is characterised by its projection on the one hand of a total societal image of a 'society where individuals' livelihoods are firmly guaranteed, and this can endure over the long-term in coexistence with resource- and environmental constraints,' and by its depiction as a societal image attractive even to individuals, on the other (Hiroi 2001: 1–2).

Towards *seikatsusha* who go their respective ways

With the understanding that the static situation will be a constant, experimentation by *seikatsusha* has already begun, with people variously exploring alternative values, modes of behaviour and lifestyles as substitutes for 'growth.' Rather than being conducted by 'movement' participants in organisations like Seikatsu Club, these are people's experiments, more fittingly described as more personalised, more the practice of a way of living embodying their own style.

Takashi Uchiyama, a private philosopher who commands a unique theory of labour and ontology, says that one of the things he has reclaimed since beginning to live in Ueno Village in Gunma Prefecture, which he had visited as a fisherman, is a sense that he has his own definite 'life.' Having begun to cultivate a tiny field with the encouragement of the village residents, Uchiyama was astonished to find that there was a world in which he could realise with such clarity the connection between his own labour, an awareness of the seasons, and the villagers. He writes:

> It is mysterious how, when in the village, I, too, start to get the feeling that it is very wrong not to turn the soil once spring comes. This is probably because my life in the village is seated within a relationship with the changes of nature, and my connection with the villagers who till the fields. If I were to sever this relationship, my very life in the village would not be viable (Uchiyama 2006: 198).

In Uchiyama's vicinity, since about the turn of the century, there have been increasing numbers of youths who aim to become farmers. These young people want to make a living by raising crops by their own hand and delivering them directly to consumers. By breaking away from 'the self as a consumer who has no choice but to continue single-mindedly to consume,' they seek to forge solid connections— firstly between nature and humans; secondly between producers and consumers, within the sphere of producers; and thirdly between one human and another as distinct entities.

By contrast, cities have also seen the emergence of men searching for a way of living that shift from being that of a company man towards one of a lifestyle-oriented man, with the ultimate goal of building communities designed to share illness, old age and disability. Men who have taken on as their own issue the care of the elderly and disabled, which until now has been 'monopolised' by women, and have begun activities in their local area in a quest to create mutually-supportive relationships—these are people who are striving to replace the schema of *seikatsusha* = housewives = women with one that says *seikatsusha* = househusbands = men.

In lieu of an epilogue

The various experiments now being put into practice by people seeking a path to becoming *seikatsusha* are, in essence, attempts to take back a solid life as an individual amid relationships with others, or to build connections with others that support the fulfilment of a life as an individual. These could be called experiments aimed at individual ways of living that take account of relationships, and at the forging of relationships which are conscious of the individual.

These differ from the individualistic direction aspired to by Western modernity, which takes the individual to be a self-evident unit, and always starts from the individual and returns to the individual. Attempts to create, within the 'recombination of relationships' with others with whom one lives side-by-side, a lifestyle that is autonomous of, or, in other words, antagonistic to, the dominant values of the respective times—when these thicken, then the potential of the '*seikatsusha*' who inhabit the twenty-first century is likely to deepen.

Moreover, a summary of the attributes, behavioural principles and similar concepts arising in other countries that have been elucidated in the process of tracing the formation of the *seikatsusha* image in modern times is to be found in Table 5.1.

Table 5.1: Genealogy of the seikatsusha concept

	Period	Social stratum	Contrasting concepts	Action (movement) principle	Similar concepts spawned in other countries
Kiyoshi Miki (1897–1945)	Under wartime regime (1935–1945)	• Farmers	• Passive 'cultural seikatsusha' • Culturati • Nationals	• Lifestyle creators aiming for an autonomous lifestyle departing from the lifestyle demanded by the state • Actors in productive culture • Subjects of the times and history	• People of middle class and below • Common people
Itaru Nii (1888–1951)	Under wartime regime (1935–1945)	• People of middle class and below • Common people (shiseijin)	• People of middle-class and above • Intelligentsia • Kizokujin (= those belonging to institutions)	• People who 'organise and run their own lives themselves' • Emphasis on freedom and mutual solidarity • Micro-regionalist/anti-centrist orientation	• The 'common people' (pioneers in the New World)
Wajirō Kon (1888–1973)	Post-war chaos period (1945–1955)	• Workers		• Lifestyle subjects as the 'entirety' of activity • Lifestyle reformers	
Shisō no kagaku (1946–)	Post-war chaos period (1945–1955)	• Workers	• 'Autonomous individuals' in the masses • Professional philosophers • The people's masses	• 'Individuals' who create their own words and ideas • Decision-makers in micro-situations	• Ralph Waldo Emerson's 'philosophy of the common man' = citizens as active, cultural subjects with a philosophy of their own within their lifestyles
Kurashi no techō (1948–)	Post-war chaos period (1945–1955)	• Urban middle-class	• Passive consumers • Cunning consumers • Producers solely pursuing profitability	• People who distinguish 'the beautiful' from 'the non-beautiful' • Challengers who bring the seikatsusha's standpoint to the producers' side, and continually change the quality of goods	• Alvin Toffler's 'prosumer' = a new image of the consumer combining the character of both producer and consumer (The Third Wave, 1980)
Yasuko Mizoue 1903–1990	Pre-high economic growth period (Late 1950s)	• Female agrarian workers • Seikatsusha on the margins		• 'Individuals' who generate questions within their own lifestyles • Subjects of responsibility for livelihood • Challenge towards the root of discrimination	
Nobuyuki Ōkuma (1893–1977)	High economic growth period (1960s)	Unspecified	• Consumers	• 'Lifestyle' subjects who merge production and consumption • Discerning 'needs' from 'wants' in lifestyle	• Alfred Schutz's 'well-informed citizen' = a rational citizen who reflexively

			• Emphasis on the reproductive value/utility value of life	reinterprets the self-explanatory nature of the quotidian world's 'matter-of-course' and common sense • C. Wright Mills' 'the public'

Movement	Period	Subject	Characteristics
Beheiren (Citizens League for Peace in Vietnam) (1965–1974)	Post-period of high economic growth (Late 1960s–1970s)	Unspecified	• Career politicians • Peace-movement specialists • Workers • Consumers • Nationals	• Statements from own 'life-site' • Movement based solely in individual initiative and responsibility • Emphasis on 'empathy,' taking as one's own responsibility the pain of the embodiment of suffering
Seikatsu Club (1965–)	Post-period of high economic growth (Late 1960s–1970s)	• Urban middle-class	• Consumers • Nationals	• Confrontational perspective towards existing order and values • Emphasis on local region as a 'common' space • Emphasis not on competition but on cooperative values • Realisation that the self is an environmental presence • Free horizontal discussion and horizontal ties as relationships
Political parties' manifesto	Post-bubble economy (Late 1980s–1990s)	• 'Strong individuals' in urban middle-class and above	• 'The weak' in a competitive society	• Pursuers of self-determination and self-responsibility through relaxation of regulations • Successors to behavioural norms centring on healthy adult males
Enterprise owners	Post-bubble economy (Late 1980s–1990s)	Unspecified	• Passive consumers	• Consumers who design their own lifestyle based on their own lifestyle vision • People who seek an individualistic lifestyle suited to themselves
Seikatsusha in a sustainable-welfare society	Currently, in 21st century	Unspecified	• Western-type individuals	• People liberated from 'pro-growth' ideology who create a lifestyle based on their own values • Relational individuals who create individual lifestyles amid connections with nature and others • People who change the gender relation that equates 'seikatsusha' with 'female'

Afterword

It was in 1996 that the Japanese version of this book, entitled *'Seikatsusha' to wa dare ka?* (Who is meant by *'seikatsusha'*?), was published. Even now, fifteen years later, the ambiguous term *'seikatsusha,'* far from being obsolete, has been recalled time and again, and enjoys circulation in the world of politics, administration, management and marketing, and in people's social lives, as well.

In Western society, the words 'citizen' and 'the public' have a long history as notions equipped with substance, not merely conceptual meaning. This is not the case, however, in Japanese society. The concept of *'seikatsusha'* is a 'home-grown' concept spawned by Japanese society and its life-culture.

Under what kind of temporal circumstances did the word *seikatsusha* make its appearance in Japan, and bearing what manner of issues and concerns? And what sort of questions has it posed to the times and to society? It is an unanticipated pleasure that the English version of this volume, which traced the historical and contemporary significance of this concept as an alternative discourse on Japanese culture or Japanese society, is to be published.

Before my interest in the concept of *'seikatsusha'* became a book, I enjoyed the support and encouragement of many. In the Nettowāku kenkyūkai (Network study group) at Waseda University, centred around (now Professor Emeritus) Yoshiyuki Satō, I was able to conduct repeated surveys of people seeking a revolution in their lifestyles, with *'seikatsusha'* as the keyword. Even earlier, the starting-point for my idea of understanding issues in society and history in terms of their connection with humans' 'Life,' comprised of 'survival, livelihood, and lifetime,' can be traced back to the teachings of Professors Takashi Nakano, Kiyomi Morioka and the late Hiroshi Hazama during my graduate-school years. I express my deep gratitude to them.

Above all, I would like to express my sincere gratitude to Professor Wolfgang Seifert of the Institute of Japanese Studies,

University of Heidelberg, for writing a preface that has given the book both weight and depth from the independent perspective of Japanese Studies.

Finally, for giving me the opportunity to bring this book to life once more and gain a new readership outside Japan, I wish to express my heartfelt thanks to Emeritus Professor Yoshio Sugimoto of Trans Pacific Press, and the translator, Dr Leonie Stickland.

The publication of this book was supported by a 2010–2011 Grant-in-Aid for Publication of Scientific Research Results provided by the Japan Society for the Promotion of Science.

Masako Amano
July 2011

Bibliography

Adachi, Jun, 2001, 'Seikatsusha saikō (Rethinking *seikatsusha*), *CEL*, vol. 58, September.
Akamatsu, Tsunehiro, 1994, *Miki Kiyoshi: tetsugaku-teki shisaku no kiseki* (Kiyoshi Miki: a locus of philosophical speculation), Minerva shobō.
Akasaka, Norio, 1995, 'Miyamoto Tsuneichi, mata wa sekenshi (Tsuneichi Miyamoto, or a man of the world),' *Shisō no kagaku* (Science of thought), September.
Akiyama, Kiyoshi, 1974, *Kochū no uta: watashi no gunsho gunzō* (Songs in the pot: my many writings and sculptural groups), Kamensha.
Amano, Masako, 1988, 'Wākāzu korekutibu ni okeru "ju"-dō kara "nō"-dō e no jikken (An experiment in workers' collectives [moving] from "pass"-ive to "act"-ive),' in Yoshiyuki Satō (ed.), *Joseitachi no seikatsu nettowāku: Seikatsu kurabu ni tsudou hitobito* (The women's lifestyle network: people who gather at the Seikatsu Club), Bunshindō, pp. 387–438.
Asahi shinbun, 1993, Senryū (Poems), 'Readers' Column,' 26 August.
————, 1994, 'Seikatsusha wa kazarimono na no ka? (Is *seikatsusha* just a decoration?)' Editorial, 10 January.
————, 1995, 'Naze, Nihon e no ryūgakusei ga heru no ka? (Why a decrease in overseas students to Japan?),' 26 September.
————, 1996a, 'Hito kikō (A traveller's journal of people),' Sunday edition, 28 January.
————, 1996b, 'Daishinsai borantia tenkeizō wa? ([What is] the typical image of the Great [Hanshin–Awaji] Earthquake Disaster volunteer?),' evening edition, 11 January.
Bellah, R.N. (ed.), 1985, *Habits of the Heart: Individualism and Commitment in American Life*, with Richard Madsen, William M. Sullivan, Ann Swidler, and Steven M. Tipton, Berkeley: University of California Press.
Baudrillard, Jean, 1970 [1998], *La societe de consommation: ses mythes, ses structures*, Editions Planete. *The Consumer Society: Myths and Structures*, London: Sage Publications Ltd.
————, 1972 [1981], *Pour une critique de l'economie politique du signe* (For a critique of the political economy of the sign), trans. with an introduction by Charles Levin, St. Louis, Mo: Telos Press.
Burns, Scott, 1975, *Home, Inc.: The Hidden Wealth and Power of the American Household*, New York, NY: Doubleday.
Dag Hammarskjöld Foundation, 1975, 'The 1975 Dag Hammarskjöld Report on Development and International Co-operation "What Now,"' *Development Dialogue*, special issue 1/2.
Dentsū sōken (ed.), 1990, *Senryaku-teki seikatsusha: kore kara no shijō o*

tsukuru shin shūdan pawā (Strategic *seikatsusha*: a new group power to build future markets), Purejidentosha.

Drucker, Peter Ferdinand (ed.), 1977, *Management*, Abridged and revised, London: Pan Books.

Ebisaka, Takeshi, 1994, 'Mienai dassōhei to atarashii shiminzō (Invisible deserters and the new image of the citizen)' in Shunsuke Tsurumi et al. (eds), *Kaette kita dassōhei: Betonamu no senjō kara nijūgonen* (The deserter who came back: twenty-five years after the Vietnam battlefields), Dai-san shokan, pp. 61–67.

Friedrich, Carl, 1942, *The New Belief in the Common Man*, Boston: Little, Brown and Co.

Fujita, Shōzō, 1975, *Tenkō no shisōshi-teki kenkyū* (Studies in the ideological history of turnaround), Iwanami shoten.

Fukuhara, Yoshiharu, 1999, *Bunka shihon no keiei* (The management of cultural capital), Daiyamondosha.

Giddens, Anthony, 1990, *The Consequences of Modernity*, Cambridge: Polity Press.

Gonda, Yasunosuke, 1921, *Minshū goraku mondai* (Problems of popular entertainment), Dōjinsha shoten.

———, 1931, *Minshū goraku ron* (Theory of entertainment for the masses), Iwamatsudo shoten.

———, 1935, 'Minshū goraku no hōkai to kokumin goraku e no junbi (The collapse of popular entertainment and preparations for national entertainment), *Chūō kōron* (Central review), May.

Habermas, Jürgen, 1981 [1987], *Theorie des kommunikativen Handelns*, Frankfurt am Main: Suhrkamp Verlag. *Komyunikēshon-teki kōi no riron* (Theory of communicative action), vol. 2, trans. Takashi Maruyama et al., Miraisha.

———, 1990 [1994], *Strukturwandel der Öffentlichkeit: Untersuchungen zu einer Kategorie der burgerlichen Gesellschaft*, Frankfurt am Main: Suhrkamp Verlag. *Kokyōsei no kōzō tenkan* (The structural transformation of the public sphere), trans. Sadao Hosotani and Masayuki Yamada, 2nd edition, Miraisha.

Hakuhōdō seikatsu sōgō kenkyūjo (ed.), 1985, *'Bunshū' no tanjō* (The birth of the 'segmented masses'), Nihon keizai shinbunsha.

Hanamori, Yasuji, 1948, 'Jibun de tsukureru akusesari (Accessories one can make oneself),' *Kurashi no techō* (Lifestyle notebook), January.

———, 1971, *Issen gorin no hata* (A one-and-a-half *sen* flag), Kurashi-no-techō sha.

Hanazaki, Kōhei, 1981, *Ikiru ba no tetsugaku: kyōkan kara no shuppatsu* (Philosophy of the living-site: starting from empathy), Iwanami shinsho 147, Iwanami shoten.

Hidaka, Rokurō, 1968 [1974a], 'Chokusetsu minshu-shugi to rokugatsu kōdō (Direct democracy and June action), in *Shiryō: 'Beheiren' undō* (Materials: the Beheiren movement),' vol. 1.

Hiroi, Yoshinori, 2001, *Teijōgata shakai: atarashii 'yutakasa' no kōsō* (A sustainable-welfare society: conceptions of new 'abundance'), Iwanami shinsho.

Horiba, Kiyoko, 1984, 'Kurashi no techō,' in Asahi jānaru (ed.), *Onna no* sengoshi 1: Shōwa nijūnendai (Women's post-war history 1: the second decade of Showa), Asahi shinbunsha.

Hosokawa, Morihiro, 1993, *Nihon Shintō: sekinin aru henkaku* (Japan New Party: responsible reform), Tōyō keizai shinpōsha.

Illich, Ivan, 1981, *Shadow Work*, Boston; London: Marion Boyars.

Inglehart, Ronald, 1977, *The Silent Revolution: changing values and political styles among Western publics*, Princeton University Press.

Irokawa, Daikichi, 1975, *Aru Shōwa-shi: jibun-shi no kokoromi* (A particular history of Showa: an attempt at self-history), Chūō kōronsha.

Ishigaki, Ayako, 1955 [1982], 'Shufu to iu dai-ni shokugyō ron (On the second job of [being a] housewife),' *Fujin kōron* (Women's review), February: 48–53, in Chizuko Ueno (ed.), *Shufu ronsō o yomu: zen kiroku* (Reading the housewife debate: the entire record), vol. 1, Keisō shobō, pp. 2–14.

Ishimi, Hisashi, 1986, *Nihon no wākāzu korekutibu* (Japan's workers' collectives), Gakuyō shobō.

Iwane, Kunio, 1974, 'Kyōran bukka ni furimawasareta shōhisha (Consumers shaken around by crazy price spiral),' *Ekonomisuto* (Economist), 25 March.

———, 1977, 'Ima koso seiji e no hatsugen o (Now is the time to make statements towards politics),' *Seikatsu to jichi* (Life and autonomy), 1 March.

———, 1993, *Atarashii shakai undō no yonhanseiki* (A quarter-century of new social movements), Kyōdō tosho sābisu.

Ji-ya-o Club (ed.), 1995, *Tsuma no pinchi da. Otto no deban!* (Wives are in a jam—time for husbands to make an entrance!), Shinjidaisha.

Kamei, Katsuichirō, 1956, 'Gendai rekishika e no gimon (Doubts towards modern historians),' *Bungei shunjū*, March: 63.

Kamisaka, Fuyuko, 1959, 'Shokuba no gunzō (Workplace groups),' *Shisō no kagaku* (Science of thought), January–May.

———, 1986, 'Kyōto no kai (The Kyoto group),' *Shisō no kagaku* (Science of thought), January–May: 96.

Kan, Takayuki, 1980, *Tsurumi Shunsuke ron* (On Shunsuke Tsurumi), Daisanbunmei-sha.

Kanamori, Toshie, Masako Amano, Fusako Fujiwara and Yoshiko Kuba, 1989, *Josei no nyū wāku ron* (Discourse on women's 'new work'), Yūhikaku.

Kano, Masanao, 1988, *'Torishima' wa haitte iru ka?* (Is 'Torishima' included?), Iwanami shoten.

Karaki, Junzō, 1966, *Miki Kiyoshi* (Kiyoshi Miki), Chikuma sōsho 73, Chikuma shobō.

Kataoka, Teppei, Yasunari Kawabata and Susumu Ueda (sup. eds), Shinano Mainichi Shinbunsha (ed.), 1940–41, *Nōson seinen hōkoku* (Agrarian youth reports), Takemura shobō.

Katō, Hidetoshi, 1953, 'Minoue sōdan no naiyō bunseki (Content analysis of personal consultation),' *Me* (Shoots), September: 49.

Kawashima, Takeyoshi, 1946, 'Nihon shakai no kazoku-teki kōsei (The family-like composition of Japanese society),' *Chūō kōron* (Central review), June.

Kawazoe, Noboru (ed.), 1982, *Seikatsugaku no teishō* (Advocating lifeology), Domesu shuppan.

———, 1984, *Seikatsugaku e no apurōchi* (Approaches to lifeology), Domesu shuppan.

Keizai Shingikai (Economic Council), 1992, 'Seikatsu taikoku go-ka-nen keikaku: chikyū shakai to no kyōzon o mezashite (Lifestyle superpower five-year plan: aiming for coexistence with global society).'

Kenkyūbu (Research division), 1948a, 'Hitobito no tetsugaku ni tsuite no chūkan hōkoku (Interim report about the people's philosophy) (1),' *Shisō no kagaku* (Science of thought), February: 1.

———, 1948b, 'Hitobito no tetsugaku ni tsuite no chūkan hōkoku (Interim report about the people's philosophy) (2),' *Shisō no kagaku* (Science of thought), March: 43.

Kinoshita, Junji and Kazuko Tsurumi (eds), 1954, *Haha no rekishi: Nihon no haha no isshō* (A history of the mother: the life of Japanese mothers), Kawade shinsho.

Kishida, Rie, 1995, 'Naze, Nihon e no ryūgakusei ga heru no ka? (Why is there a decrease in overseas students to Japan?),' *Asahi shinbun*, 26 September.

Komatsu, Ryūji, 1982, 'Machi no seikatsusha: Nii Itaru no sekai (The urban *seikatsusha*: the world of Itaru Nii),' in Seikatsu kenkyū dōjinkai (ed.), *Kindai Nihon no seikatsu kenkyū* (Studies of modern Japanese life), Kōseikan.

Konaka, Yōtarō, 1968 [1974a], 'Hansen no rinen (The idea of anti-war),' in *Shiryō: 'Beheiren' undō* (Materials: the Beheiren movement),' vol. 1, Kawade shobō shinsha, p. 484.

Kon, Wajirō, 1945 [1971], 'Jū seikatsu (Dwelling life),' in *Kon Wajirō shū* (Collected works of Wajirō Kon), vol. 5, Domesu shuppan.

Kon, Wajirō, 1946 [1971], 'Hito no sumu jūkyo (Houses where people live),' in *Kon Wajirō shū* (Collected works of Wajirō Kon), vol. 5, Domesu shuppan.

———, 1947a [1971], 'Seikatsu no kakumei (A lifestyle revolution),' in *Kon Wajirō shū* (Collected works of Wajirō Kon), vol. 6, Domesu shuppan.

———, 1947b [1971], 'Seikatsu no kōzō (The structure of lifestyles),' in *Kon Wajirō shū* (Collected works of Wajirō Kon), vol. 5, Domesu shuppan.

———, 1949a [1971], 'Danshi to kasei (Boys and household economy),' in *Kon Wajirō shū* (Collected works of Wajirō Kon), vol. 5, Domesu Shuppan.

———, 1949b [1971], 'Seikatsu no bunkateki dankai (The cultural stages of living),' in *Kon Wajirō shū* (Collected works of Wajirō Kon), vol. 5, Domesu shuppan.

———, 1951 [1971], 'Seikatsugaku e no kūsō (Musings on lifeology), in *Kon Wajirō shū*, vol. 5, Domesu shuppan.

———, 1956 [1971], 'Seikatsu ni okeru kokoro to mono (The heart and goods in lifestyles),' in *Kon Wajirō shū* (Collected works of Wajirō Kon), vol. 6, Domesu shuppan, pp. 64–74.

———, 1963 [1971], 'Seikatsu kaizen ni tsuite (On improvement of living conditions),' in *Kon Wajirō shū* (Collected works of Wajirō Kon), vol. 6, Domesu shuppan, p. 492.

Kōno, Eiji, 1985, *Seikatsu kurabu no hōshin to kongo no tenbō* (Seikatsu Club's objectives and future outlook), Seikatsu kurabu seikyō.

Kuno, Osamu, 1967, 'Miki Kiyoshi kaisetsu (Kiyoshi Miki explained),' in

Miki Kiyoshi zenshū (The complete collected works of Kiyoshi Miki), vol. 14, pp. 585–595.
Kurata, Hyakuzō, 1917, *Shukke to sono deshi* (Monks and their disciples), Iwanami shoten.
———, 1926, 'Seikatsusha to bundanjin (*Seikatsusha* and literati),' *Tōkyō asahi shinbun* (Tokyo asahi newspaper), 27, 28 and 29 April.
Kurihara, Akira, 1994, *Jinsei no doramaturugī* (The dramaturgy of life), Iwanami shoten.
Maslow, A.H., 1954, *Motivation and Personality*, New York: Harper and Row.
Matsumoto, Sannosuke, 1994, 'Ōkuma Nobuyuki ni okeru kokka no mondai (The issue of the state in Nobuyuki Ōkuma),' *Shisō* (Thought), March, pp. 4–39.
Miki, Kiyoshi, 1926 [1966], 'Pasukaru ni okeru ningen no kenkyū (The study of humans in Pascal),' in *Miki Kiyoshi zenshū* (The complete collected works of Kiyoshi Miki), vol. 1, Iwanami shoten, pp. 1–191.
Miki, Kiyoshi, 1938a [1967], 'Gendai Nippon ni okeru sekaishi no igi (The significance of world history in contemporary Japan),' in *Miki Kiyoshi zenshū* (The complete collected works of Kiyoshi Miki), vol. 14, Iwanami shoten, p. 143.
———, 1938b [1968], 'Nikki (Diary),' in *Miki Kiyoshi zenshū* (The complete collected works of Kiyoshi Miki), vol. 19, Iwanami shoten, pp. 180–181.
———, 1940a [1967], 'Bunka seisaku ron (On cultural policy),' in *Miki Kiyoshi zenshū* (The complete collected works of Kiyoshi Miki), vol. 14, Iwanami shoten, pp. 356–375.
———, 1940b [1967], 'Kokumin-teki seikaku no keisei (The formation of a nation-like character),' in *Miki Kiyoshi zenshū* (The complete collected works of Kiyoshi Miki), vol. 14, Iwanami shoten, p. 349.
———, 1940c [1967], *Tetsugaku nyūmon* (Introduction to philosophy), Iwanami shinsho, in *Miki Kiyoshi zenshū* (The complete collected works of Kiyoshi Miki), vol. 7, Iwanami shoten, pp. 3–194.
———, 1941a [1966], 'Dokusho henreki (A record of reading),' in *Miki Kiyoshi zenshū* (The complete collected works of Kiyoshi Miki), vol. 1, Iwanami shoten, p. 370.
———, 1941b [1967], 'Seikatsu bunka to seikatsu gijutsu (Life culture and living techniques),' in *Miki Kiyoshi zenshū* (The complete collected works of Kiyoshi Miki), vol. 14, Iwanami shoten, pp. 384–401.
———, 1941c [1968] 'Tetsugaku nōto, jo (Philosophy notes, introduction),' in *Miki Kiyoshi zenshū* (Complete collected works of Kiyoshi Miki), vol. 17, Iwanami shoten, pp. 338–339.
Mills, C. Wright, 1959, *The Sociological Imagination*, New York: Oxford University Press.
Misawa, Ken'ichi, 1993, *Gendai seikatsu to ningen* (Modern life and people), Kōyō shobō.
Mita, Munesuke, 1965, *Gendai Nihon no seishin kōzō* (The spiritual structure of contemporary Japan), Kōbundō.
Miyakawa, Tōru, 2007, *Miki Kiyoshi* (Kiyoshi Miki), Kindai Nihon no shisōka (Thinkers of modern Japan), 9, Tōkyō daigaku shuppan kai, p. 124.
Miyamoto, Tsuneichi, 1971, 'Wasurerareta Nihonjin (The forgotten Japanese),' in *Miyamoto Tsuneichi chosakushū* (Collected works of Tsuneichi Miyamoto), vol. 10, Miraisha, p. 215.

Mizoue, Yasuko, 1958, *Nihon no teihen: San'in nōson fujin no seikatsu* (Japan's margins: the lives of women in San'in rural villages), Miraisha.

———, 1959, *Junan-jima no hitobito: Nihon no shukuzu, Okinawa* (The people of the suffering isles: Okinawa, a microcosm of Japan), Miraisha.

———, 1961, *Seikatsusha no shisō: zoku Nihon no teihen* (*Seikatsusha* thought: Japan's margins, continued), Miraisha.

———, 1980, *Watashi no rekishi* (My history), Horupu.

———, 1992, *Watashi no jinsei kōkyōgaku* (My life symphony), Kage shobō.

Morioka, Kiyomi, 1983, 'Nichijō seikatsu ni okeru shihitsu-ka (Privatisation in everyday life),' *Shakaigaku hyōron* (Japanese sociological review), 34(2): 12–19.

Morisaki, Kazue, 1991, 'Jibun no senryō ga owatta hi (The day my occupation ended),' in Tsuneo Yasuda and Masako Amano (eds), *Sengo taiken no hakkutsu: jūgonin ga kataru senryōka no seishun* (Unearthing postwar experiences: fifteen people tell of youth under the occupation), Sanseidō, p. 105.

Murakami, Yasusuke, 1984, *Shin chūkan taishū no jidai* (The age of the new middle mass), Chūō kōronsha.

———, 1985, 'Yuragi no naka no taishū shakai (Mass society in fluctuation),' *Chūō kōron* (Central review), May.

Muramatsu, Takeshi, 1963, 'Joseiteki jidai o haisu (Rejecting a womanish age),' *Bungei shunjū*, August.

Nagano, Junzō, 1939, *Kokumin seikatsu no bunseki* (Analysis of national life), Jichōsha.

Nakamura, Tatsuya, 1992, *Yutakasa no kodoku* (The loneliness of abundance), Iwanami shoten.

Nakamura, Yōichi, 1990, 'Chiiki no josei to seiji (Women and politics in local areas),' in *Onna no jidai o tabi suru* (Journeying through the age of women), Yukkusha.

Nakamura, Yōko, 1995, 'Watashi to Seikatsu Kurabu (The Seikatsu Club and I),' in Yoshiyuki Satō, Masako Amano and Hisashi Nasu (eds), *Joseitachi no seikatsusha undō* (The women's *seikatsusha* movement), Marujusha, pp. 135–136.

Nakamura, Yukihide, 1989, *Tetsugaku nyūmon: seikatsu no naka no firosofī* (Introduction to philosophy: philosophy in [daily] life), Aoki shoten.

Nii, Itaru, 1921, *Sakei shichō* (Leftist thought), Bunsendō.

———, 1940, *Machi no tetsugaku* (The philosophy of the streets), Seinen shobō.

———, 1941, *Nosuzume wa kataru* (Wild sparrows speak), Seinen shobō.

———, 1943, *Kokoro no nichiyōbi* (Sundays of the heart), Daikyōdō shoten.

———, 1975, *Ikō: Nii Itaru Suginami kuchō nikki* (Posthumous manuscript: Itaru Nii's Suginami Ward Mayoral Diary), Nami shobō.

Nishi, Sadako, 1987, 'Seikatsu no jichi ryōiki o hirogeru undō (Movements to expand the domain of lifestyle autonomy),' *Gendai no riron* (Modern theories), 9, Gendai no riron sha.

Nishihara, Kazuhisa, 1991, *Genshōgakuteki shakaigaku no tenbō* (The development of phenomenological sociology), Seidosha.

Nōrinsuisanshō (Ministry of Agriculture, Forestry and Fisheries), 1994, 'Nōgyō kōzō dōtai chōsa (Survey of agricultural structure dynamics).'

Oda, Makoto (ed.), 1969, *Beheiren* (Citizens' league for peace in Vietnam), San'ichi shobō.

Oda, Makoto, 1970 [1974a], '"Mi ni shimiru koto" ni "mizeni o kiru" koto ("Paying out of one's own pocket" for "piercing issues"),' in *Shiryō: 'Beheiren' undō* (Materials: the Beheiren movement),' vol. 2, Kawade shobō shinsha, p. 356.

——, 1971 [1974b], 'Koto wa hajimatta bakari da (Things have only just begun,' in *Shiryō: 'Beheiren' undō* (Materials: the Beheiren movement),' vol. 3, Kawade shobō shinsha, p. 518.

Oketani, Hideaki, 1994, *Itō Sei* (Sei Itō), Shinchōsha.

Ōkuma Nobuyuki kenkyū kai (ed.), 1990, *Ōkuma Nobuyuki kenkyū* (Studies on Nobuyuki Ōkuma), no. 8.

Ōkuma, Nobuyuki, 1957, *Kokka-aku* (State evil), Chūō kōronsha.

——, 1963 [1974a], 'Shōhisha kara seikatsusha e (From consumers to *seikatsusha*),' in *Seimei saiseisan no riron: ningen chūshin no shisō* (A theory of life reproduction: human-centred thought), vol. 1, Tōyō keizai shinpōsha.

——, 1963, *Katei-ron* (On the home), Shinjusha.

——, 1974, 'Ningen seimei no saiseisan riron (Theory on the reproduction of human life)' in *Seimei saiseisan no riron: ningen chūshin no shisō* (A theory of life reproduction: human-centred thought), vol. 1, Tōyō keizai shinpōsha.

——, 1977, *Bungakuteki kaisō* (Literary recollections), Daisan bunmeisha.

——, 1979, *Senchū sengo no seishinshi* (The spiritual history of wartime and the post-war), Ronsōsha.

——, 1993, *Aru keizaigakusha no shiseikan* (A certain economist's view of life and death), Ronsōsha.

Ōmura, Ryō, 1958, *Mono iwanu nōmin* (Taciturn farmers), Iwanami shinsho.

Orito, Nobuhiko, 1983, 'Taishū undō toshite no undō/soshiki ron (Theories on movements/organisations as mass movements)' in Shakai undō kenkyū sentā (ed.), *Kyōdō kumiai undō no atarashii nami* (New waves in cooperative movements), San'ichi shobō, p. 51.

Ruskin, John, 1888, *Unto This Last: four essays on the first principles of political economy*, London: G. Allen.

Saki, Akio, 1953, 'Minoue sōdan no kigen (The origins of personal consultation),' *Me* (Shoots), September: 2–7.

Sakurai, Tetsuo, 1994, *Kanōsei toshite no sengo* (The postwar as potential), Kōdansha.

'Saron anākisuto Nii Itaru (Itaru Nii, salon anarchist),' (author and publication details unknown). Held by Suginami Central Library, Tokyo.

Sasaki, Ken, 1987, *Miki Kiyoshi no sekai: ningen no kyūsai to shakai no henkaku* (Kiyoshi Miki: human salvation and social reform), Daisanbunmei-sha.

Satō, Tadao, 1986, '"Ninkyō ni tsuite" no koro (Around the time of "On heroism"),' *Shisō no kagaku* (Science of thought), May.

Satō, Yoshiyuki, 1996, *Josei to kyōdō kumiai no shakaigaku* (The sociology of women and co-operatives), Bunshindō.

Satō, Yoshiyuki, Masako Amano and Hisashi Nasu (eds), 1995, *Joseitachi no seikatsusha undō* (The women's *seikatsusha* movement), Marujusha.

Schutz, Alfred, 1964, 'The well-informed citizen,' in *Collected Papers, vol.*

II, Studies in social theory, Arvid Brodersen (ed.), The Hague: Martinus Nijhoff, pp. 120–34.

———, 1970, *On Phenomenology and Social Relations*, ed., with an introduction by Helmut R. Wagner, Chicago: University of Chicago Press.

Seikatsu kurabu seikyō Kanagawa (ed.), 1981, *Ikikata o kaeru onnatachi* (Women who change their way of living), Shinsensha.

Seikatsu kurabu seikyō, 1988, *Dairinin undō: sono kanōsei* (The proxy movement: its possibilities), Seikatsu Club.

Shakai-undo-ron kenkyūkai (ed.), *Shakai-undō-ron no tōgō o mezashite* (Aiming for a synthesis of social-movement theories), Seibundō.

Shimizu, Tomohisa, 1985, *Betonamu sensō no jidai* (The times of the Vietnam War), Yūhikaku.

Shinano mainichi shinbun, 1940–41, 'Nōson seinen hōkoku (Rural youth reports),' nos 1–3, Takemura shobō.

Shinohara, Hajime, 1988, *'Shimin to seiji' go-wa* (Five tales of 'citizens and politics'), Yūshindō kōbunsha.

Shiryō: 'Beheiren' undō (Materials: the Beheiren movement),' 1965 [1974a], vol. 1.

———, 1965 [1974b], vol. 2.

———, 1965 [1974c], vol. 3.

Shisō-no-kagaku kenkyū kai (ed.), 1995, *Shinpan tetsugaku/ronri yōgo jiten* (New edition dictionary of philosophy [and] logic terminology), San-ichi shobō.

Tada, Michitarō, 1962, 'Taishū geijutsu (Mass arts),' *Shisō no kagaku* (Science of thought), May: 80.

———, 1986, 'Tanin-shi o yomu koto (Reading other people's histories),' *Shisō no kagaku* (Science of thought), May: 80.

Takeda, Kiyoko, 1948, 'Futatsu no seikatsuken: Yoshikawa Eiji no sakuhin ni yoru (Two lifeworlds: according to the works of Eiji Yoshikawa),' *Shisō no kagaku* (Science of thought), February: 8–20.

Taketani, Mitsuo, 1946, 'Tetsugaku wa ika ni shite yūkōsa o torimodoshiuru ka (In what way could philosophy reclaim its validity?),' *Shisō no kagaku* (Science of thought), May: 1–9.

Tanaka, Yoshihisa, 1978, *Shakai ishiki no riron* (The theory of social consciousness), Keisō shobō.

Terade, Kōji, 1982, 'Rōdōsha bunka ron no keisei to hen'yō: Gonda Yasunosuke (The formation and transformation of workers' culture theory: Yasunosuke Gonda), in Seikatsu kenkyū dōjin kai (ed.), *Kindai Nihon no seikatsu kenkyū* (Life research in modern Japan), Kōseikan, p. 178.

———, 1994, *Seikatsu bunka ron e no shōtai* (An invitation to theories of life-culture), Kōbundō.

Toffler, Alvin, 1980, *The Third Wave*, London: Pan.

Tōkyō wākāzu korekutibu kyōdō kumiai (Tokyo workers' collective cooperative), 1995, *Wākāzu korekutibu fōramu* (Workers' collective forum), Tōkyō wākāzu korekutibu kyōdō kumiai.

Tōyama, Shigeki, Seiichi Imai and Akira Fujiwara (eds), 1955, *Shōwa shi* (A History of Shōwa), Iwanami shinsho.

Tsurumi, Kazuko, 1951, 'Puragumatizumu no rekishi riron (The historical theory of pragmatism),' *Shisō* (Thought), February.

———, 1992, 'Shuppatsu ga kasanariatta (Departures overlapped),' in

Tsuneo Yasuda and Masako Amano (eds), *Sengo 'keimō' shisō no nokoshita mono* (The legacy of postwar 'enlightenment' thought), Kyūzansha.

Tsurumi, Shunsuke, 1946 [1975], 'Kotoba no o-mamori-teki shiyōhō ni tsuite (About the usage of words in the manner of a protective charm),' in *Tsurumi Shunsuke chosaku shū* (Collected works of Shunsuke Tsurumi), vol. 3, Chikuma shobō, pp. 12–25.

———, 1954 [1968], 'Iwate no hoken (Iwate health),' in *Futeikei no shisō* (Amorphous thought), Bungeishunjū, p. 284.

———, 1955, 'Denki ni tsuite (About biographies),' in Shisō-no-kagaku kenkyū kai (ed.), *Minshū no za* (The seat of the masses), Kawade shinsho.

———, 1956 [1975], 'Setchūshugi no tetsugaku toshite no puragumatizumu no hōhō (The methodology of pragmatism as a philosophy of eclecticism),' in *Tsurumi Shunsuke chosakushū* (Collected works of Shunsuke Tsurumi), Chikuma shobō, p. 300.

———, 1961, *Nihon no hyakunen* (Japan's century), vol. 2, Chikuma shobō.

———, 1982, *Senjiki Nihon no seishinshi, 1931–1945* (A spiritual history of Japan in the war period, 1931–1945), Iwanami shoten.

———, 1984, *Jinrui no chiteki isan, 60: Dyūi* (The intellectual heritage of the human race, 60: Dewey), Kōdansha.

———, 1993, 'Kokka no nijūsei to ie no nijūsei (The duality of the state and duality of the household),' in *Ōkuma Nobuyuki kenkyū* (Nobuyuki Ōkuma studies), no. 10, Ronsōsha, p. 18.

———, 1994, 'Kenpō no yakusoku to yowai kojin no undō (Constitutional promises and weak individuals' movements),' in Shunsuke Tsurumi et al., *Kaette kita dassōhei: Betonamu no senjō kara nijūgonen* (The deserter who came back: twenty-five years after the Vietnam battlefields), Dai-san shokan, p. 142.

Tsurumi, Shunsuke, Sadako Yokoyama, Yoshiyuki Tsurumi, Hiroyuki Gotō and Hiroshi Hanzawa, 1956, *Minoue sōdan* (Personal consultation), Kawade shobō.

Tsurumi, Shunsuke, Yūichi Yoshikawa and Shinobu Yoshioka (eds), 1994, *Kaette kita dassōhei: Betonamu no senjō kara nijūgonen* (The deserter who came back: twenty-five years after the Vietnam battlefields), Dai-san shokan.

Tsutsumi, Kiyoshi, 1940, editor's postscript, in Teppei Kataoka et al., *Nōson seinen hōkoku* (Agrarian youth reports), Takemura shobō, vol. 1, p. 329.

Tsutsumi, Seiji, 1996, *Shōhi shakai hihan* (A critique of consumer society), Iwanami shoten.

Tsutsumi, Seiji, 1999, *Japan's Consumer Society: A Critical Introduction*, trans. Frederick M. Uleman, Tokyo: ARC Publishing Inc.

Tsūshōsangyōshō (Ministry of International Trade and Industry) (ed.), 1990, *Yutori to yutakasa* (Leeway and abundance), Keizai sangyō chōsa kai.

Uchiyama, Takashi, 2006, *Sensō to iu shigoto* (The job called war), Shinano mainichi shinbunsha.

Ueno, Chizuko, 1982, *Shufu ronsō o yomu* (Reading the housewife debate), vol. 1, Keisō shobō.

———, 1987, *'Watashi'-sagashi gēmu* (The search-for-'me' game), Chikuma shobō.

Umesao, Tadao, 1988, *Onna to bunmei* (Women and civilisation), Chūkō sōsho.

——, 1959 [1982], 'Tsuma muyō ron (The theory that a wife is unnecessary),' *Fujin kōron* (Women's review), June, in Chizuko Ueno (ed.), *Shufu ronsō o yomu* (Reading the housewife debate), vol. 1, Keisō shobō, pp. 191–206.
Usui, Yoshimi, 1964, 'Sengo chisei no kōzu (The composition of the post-war mentality),' *Tenbō* (Outlook), October, Chikuma shobō: 130–131.
Wachtel, P.L., 1983, *The Poverty of Affluence: A Psychological Portrait of the American Way of Life*, The Free Press.
Wamaki, Kōsuke, 1991, *Hyōden: Nii Itaru* (A critical biography: Itaru Nii), Bunchidō shoten.
Waseda daigaku bungakubu shakaigaku kenkyūshitsu (ed.), 1993, *Seikatsusha nettowāku ni kansuru chōsa to kōsatsu* (Surveys and inquiries relating to *seikatsusha* networks), Waseda University Faculty of Letters.
Watanabe, Katsumi, 1954, 'Tankōfu (Coalminer),' *Me* (Sprouts), May: 2–8.
Watanabe, Kazuyasu, 1988, 'Miki Kiyoshi (Kiyoshi Miki),' in *Nihon daihyakka zensho* (Great encyclopaedia [of] Japan), Shōgakukan, p. 275.
Watanabe, Noboru, 1991, 'Chihō seiji ni okeru "seikatsusha seiji" no kanōsei: "dairinin" undō no bunseki o tōshite (Potential for "*seikatsushai* politics" in regional politics: through analysis of the "proxy" movement),' *Toshi mondai* (Journal of municipal problems), 82(10), 71–87.
Yasuda, Tsuneo, 1987, *Kurashi no shakai shisō* (Social thought on life), Keisō shobō.
——, 1992, 'Hajime ni (Introduction),' in Tsuneo Yasuda and Masako Amano (eds), *Sengo 'keimō' shisō no nokoshita mono* (The legacy of post-war 'enlightenment' thought), Kyūzansha, pp. 7–8.
Yamazaki, Masakazu, 1984, *Yawarakai kojinshugi no jidai* (The age of soft individualism), Chūō kōronsha.
Yamazaki, Tetsuya, 1988, 'Daidokoro kara sekai ga mieru (From the kitchen one can see the world),' in Yoshiyuki Satō (ed.), *Onnatachi no seikatsu nettowāku* (The women's lifestyle network), Bunshindō, p. 220.
——, 1993, 'Seikatsusha e no ikikata no hen'yō o megutte (Concerning changes in ways of living towards [becoming] *seikatsusha*),' in Ken'ichi Misawa (ed.), *Gendai seikatsu to ningen* (Contemporary life and people), Kōyō shobō, p. 233.
Yoshikawa, Yūichi, 1994, *Shimin undō no shukudai: Betonamu hansen kara mirai e* (Citizens' movements' homework: from anti-Vietnam War to the future), Shisō no kagaku sha.
Yoshino, Shōji, 1986, 'Seikatsu bunka to nijūisseiki (Life-culture and the twenty-first century),' in Nada Kōbe Seikatsu Kyōdō Kumiai Seikatsu Bunka Sentā (ed.), *Seikatsu bunka o kangaeru* (Thinking about life-culture), p. 77.
Yoshizaki, Shūichi, 1970 [1974b], 'Ichi/ni hibōryoku chokusetsu kōdō no hōkoku (Report on the first and second non-violent direct action), *Shiryō: 'Beheiren' undō* (Materials: the Beheiren movement),' vol. 2, Kawade shobō shinsha, p. 241.

Index

activists 30, 123, 127, 133–4, 159, 187
age of a twofold demise 168
age of high mass consumption 89
age of the new middle mass 109
aid for deserters from the American military 132
Akasaka, Norio 44
All-together-ism 83
alternative culture 125
Ampo (US–Japan Security Treaty) struggle 133
analysis of personal consultations 60
anarchism 31–2
anti-centrist orientation 35

Baudrillard, Jean 116–17
Beheiren 11, 122–33, 142, 144–5, 170, 176, 186–7
Bellah, R. N. 113–4
Berlin Wall 5
biographical description method 64
Burns, Scott 156

changing men to be like women 99–102
clarification of meaning 54
coded consumer society 116
common man 29, 36, 32, 57–8, 167, 175–6, 186, *see also* common people

common people 10, 16, 23–30, 32–4, 38, 53, 59, 60–3, 65–6, 73–5, 121, 127–8, 171–2, 176, *see also* common man
community 2, 22, 36, 82–3, 86, 96, 101, 122–6, 133–4, 138, 144–7, 150, 154, 156–7, 159, 161, 164–5
cultural 36
local 82, 96, 101, 122, 133–4, 138, 144–6, 150, 154, 161, 164–5
full-time residents of the local community 134
micro-community emphasis 145
company logic 191–2
consumer 1–4, 7, 9–11, 30, 32, 89–91, 93, 95, 99, 102, 108, 109–10, 113–14, 116–123, 135, 137, 139, 143–4, 149, 151, 154–5, 163, 166–7, 169, 177, 179–87, 189, 191–2, 194, 196–7, *see also* prosumer
comparison with Seikatsusha
Consumer Co-operative *see* Seikatsu Club
cunning 121, 196
passive 139, 191, 196–7
post- 187
rights 179
sovereignty 121

210

Index

consumer society 9–10, 89, 109, 116, 179, 181–5, 192
  coded 116
  post- 179
consumption-type culture 14
conversion, see Tenkō
cultural capital 191
cultural revolution 34, 36–8
cultural stages of living 49, 174
culture that has a body 15

Dag Hammarskjöld Foundation 135
Das Kapital 94
domestic labour 23, 69, 95, 97, 155–6, 161, 164
Drucker, Peter F. 184

Ebisaka, Takeshi 124, 132
Emerson, Ralph Waldo 57–8, 175–6
empirical knowledge 107
environmentally-friendly society 193
essence of consumption 139
expert 14, 185

forgotten Japanese, the 44
Fujita, Shōzō 22
Fukuhara, Yoshiharu 170, 191–2
full-time-activist/housewife 159

Gonda, Yasunosuke 23, 73
Gotō, Hiroyuki 71

Habermas, J. 146, 159, 186
Hanamori, Yasuji 24–5, 169, 177–80, 182

Hanzawa, Hiroshi 71
hard death 129
Hashimoto, Shōko 82
Hidaka, Rokurō 127
Hiroi, Yoshinori 170, 193
historical recording methods 64
housewife 1, 7, 46, 66, 69, 77, 82, 94–100, 133–7, 147–9, 153–64, 180, 187–8, 194
  housewife debate (*shufu ronsō*) 97, 99–100
  full-time 96–7, 159
  working 97, 154
human beings' self-production 140

Illich, Ivan 95
Imperial Rescript on Education 72
individual historicity 70–1
individual within a relationship 188
individualism 109, 111–14
  biblical 113
  expressive 114
  hard 111
  modern 111
  soft 109, 111–14, *see also* Yamazaki
interest politics and lively politics 48
Irokawa, Daikichi 68
Ishigaki, Ayako 97, 100
Ishikawa, Sanshirō 31, 103
Ishimoda, Tadashi 63

Japan's Consumer Society 192
Ji-ya-o Club 164

Kagawa, Toyohiko 30

Kamisaka, Fuyuko 62
Katō, Hidetoshi 70
Kawai, Eijirō 30
Kawashima, Takeyoshi 42
Kobayashi, Takiji 104
Koizumi Cabinet's structural reform 190
Konaka, Yōtarō 128, 145
Konoe, Fumimaro 22, 23
Kon, Wajirō 10, 40–53, 92, 169, 173–5, 181, 183
Kurashi no techō 25, 177–80
Kurata, Hyakuzō 12, 166, 170

life culture 5, 10, 12–16, 18–19, 21, 23–30, 32, 34–5, 38, 40–1, 45, 48–52, 119–121, 145, 156, 161, 169, 170–3, 175, 191–2, *see also* Kon, Miki, Nii, and Yanagida
and living techniques 14, 18, 23, 171
discourse 14, 40, 52, 121, 169, 171, 175
life-culture renaissance 120
strategy 119
theory 10, 12–14, 23–5, 27, 34–5, 53, 172
lifeology 10, 40, 46–8, 50–1, 173
life-recording movement 60, 66–7
life research in Japan 47
lifestyle ideology 71–2
lifestyle revolution 42
lifestyle superpower 5, 168, 189
5-year Plan 3, 189
lifestyle vision 191
lifeworld 57, 74–5, 146, 159

colonised 146, 186, *see also* Habermas
common people's 74–5
warrior's 74–5
local utopia 39, 173
logic of consumption 112
logic of production 112–13
loss of identity 96
lost two decades 169

man on the street 185
Maruyama, Masao 53, 55, 174
Maslow 50, 174
mass society 110, 119
materialist values 123, *see also* post-materialist values
Matsumoto, Sannosuke 13, 106
me in the third person 142
micro-community, *see* community
middle class 32–3, 38, 52, 86, 90, 109–10, 114, 161, 180, 187, 196
Western 109
upper- 78
whole-populace-has-turned-middle-class 109
women 161
Miki, Kiyoshi 10, 12, 14–19, 21–28, 30, 34, 38, 53, 69, 121, 169, 171–2, 175
Mills, C. Wright 185
Ministry of International Trade and Industry (MITI) 120
Miyamoto, Tsunekazu 43–4, 73
Mizoue, Yasuko 10, 77, 80–7, 145, 169, 180–1

modernology 10, 40, 45–6, 173
Morisaki, Kazue 59
Murakami, Yasusuke 109–10, 119
my-home-ism 96, 101, 114

Nakayama, Miki 69
national culture 23, 24, 171
national entertainment 23–4
national income-doubling plan 189
national spiritual mobilisation campaign 32
neighbourhood associations 30, 33, 172
new human typology 7, 19, 21, 25, 28
new middle mass theory 110, 119
new social movements 11, 123–4, 127, 170, 186
Nihon no teihen (Japan's margins) 80, 180
Nii, Itaru 10, 12, 27–38, 53, 66, 76, 121, 127, 145, 169, 171–3, 175
Nishida, Kitarō 16, 18
nonaligned citizens 127
not to live as we have up till now 135

obviousness of abundance 6
Oda, Makoto 129, 130–2
Ōkuma, Nobuyuki 10, 12, 89–94, 97, 98–108, 119, 121–2, 140, 145, 169, 181–5, 188, 192
Ōmura, Ryō 78–9
organisational pluralism 54
otaku-fication 115

part-timisation of housewifery 95, *see also* housewife
Peirce, C.S. 56
people on the margins (*teihen*) 180
people's philosophy 10, 52–3, 57–8, 60–1, 63, 67–8, 72, 76, 79, 85, 172, 174–5
personal consultation 60, 68–72, 76–7
origins of 68
phenomenological sociology 184
philosophy for living 78
politics of lifestyle issues 164
philosophy of the common man 57, 175 *see also* common man
philosophy of the streets 27, 172
pluralistic perspective 59
political sloganising of seikatsusha 188–9
politicisation of life and lifisation of politics 151
politico-economic system 146
popular arts 60, 72–6
post-materialist values 123, *see also* materialist values
pragmatism as a method 56
privatisation of the family 96
producer's supremacy 6
product-oriented (material-oriented) perspective 90
product testing 179
professional housewife (*sengyō shufu*) 95, *see also* housewife
prospective dimension 64
prosumer 167, 179–80

public sacrifice for the private good 100–2

quality of life 5, 16, 51–2, 124, 168, 174, 186

recombination of relationships 195
reinterpretations (*yomikae*) 138
reproduction 90, 117, 137, 146
  of communities 187
  of human life 90–1, 93–4, 98, 104, 106, 108, 140, 163–4
  of the workforce 47, 49, 174
retrospective dimension 64
Ruskin's *Unto This Last* 103

Saki, Akio 68, 70
Satō, Tadao 75–6, 78, 160
Schutz, Alfred 184–5
Second Housewife Debate 97
second occupation of being a housewife 97, 100
segmented masses 109, 115, 117–18
Seikatsu Club 7–8, 11, 39, 122–4, 133–7, 139–45, 147–55, 157, 159, 162–5, 170, 173, 180, 186–8, 193
  Consumers' Co-operative Union 7, 186
seikatsusha and gender 188
seikatsusha = househusbands = men 194
seikatsusha = housewives = women 163, 194
seikatsusha marketing 166, 184
seikatsusha on the margins 80–1

self-reflective 168
shadow work 95, 154–6
Shisō no kagaku 10, 52, 62, 76, 78, 133, 172, 174–7, 180–2
Shisō no kagaku kenkyūkai 52, 56, 133, 172
Showa research association 22
small locally-autonomous society 145
social historicity 70
social logic 191
social vision 190–2
soft individualism *see* individualism
state evil 106, 107, 182
sustainable-welfare society (*teijōgata shakai*) 193

taciturn farmers 79
Tada, Michitarō 62
Takeda, Kiyoko 53–5, 73–5, 174
Taketani, Mitsuo 53–5, 174
taxpayer sovereignty 149
Tenkō (Conversion) 64
Terade, Kōji 45–7
Toffler, Alvin 179–80
transforming men into seikatsusha 102
Tsurumi, Kazuko 53–4, 59, 66, 69–70, 174
Tsurumi, Shunsuke 4, 30, 33, 36, 43–4, 53, 55–6, 58–9, 61, 65–7, 71, 78, 104, 133, 167, 169, 174–5
Tsurumi, Yoshiyuki 71
Tsuru, Shigeto 53–4, 174
Tsutsumi, Kiyoshi 19
Tsutsumi, Seiichi 169
Tsutsumi, Seiji 192

Uchiyama, Takashi 170, 194
Ueno, Chizuko 99–100
unconscious dependency with conscious co-operation 141
unhappiness 68, 71–2
  genealogy of 68, 72
unpaid domestic labour and paid employment 164
Usui, Yoshimi 63

verbal talisman (*o-mamori kotoba*) 4, 167, *see also* Tsurumi, Shunsuke

Wachtel, P.L. 146
Watanabe, Satoshi 17, 53, 55, 63, 174
way of being made to work 154–5
way of working 11, 135, 152, 154–6, 158, 161–2
weak individual 130–1, 133, 144
well-informed citizen 167, 184–5
White Paper on the Economy 89
Women's Lib movement 99
women and politics 147
workers' collectives 11, 135, 145, 151–4, 156–60, 160–2, 188
workers' co-operative 152

Yokoyama, Sadako 71
Yamazaki, Masakazu 109–15, 118–19, 138, 144
Yanagida, Kunio 43–5
Yoshikawa, Eiji 73–5, 125
Yoshino, Shōji 24